Pam's book is an emotional journey that clearly shows her resilience and strength in coping with that dreadful train crash. What I can associate with is how important the 'team' around Pam were in supporting her through difficult times.

Since then Pam has found time to help others, and my charity, the DKH Legacy Trust, benefited hugely from her involvement in Reading. Thank you, Pam, for inspiring others.

– Dame Kelly Holmes, Double Gold Olympic Champion and Chair of the Dame Kelly Holmes Legacy Trust

I, like many others, vividly remember the news reports and pictures from the site of the Ladbroke Grove rail crash and the later front-page images of Pam Warren wearing her mask. Who could forget?

But in between and since those headlines there is another story which, until I picked up this book, I knew nothing of.

Pam's amazingly brave journey back to health via scores of operations and months of therapy is inspiring enough in itself, but the fact that she never sought to point the finger of blame nor seek revenge, preferring to concentrate on ensuring it never happened again, is truly humbling.

All of us who travel by train owe Pam and her fellow survivors a debt of gratitude for their tenacity and dedication to improving rail safety.

– Sir Roger Moore KBE

With candour about her own strengths and limitations, Pam guides readers through the rollercoaster of pain, disfigurement, depression, the relentless pressure of being in the public eye and the inevitable tensions between the various parties seeking compensation and improvements to rail safety.

Many years ago, when first hearing the words 'indomitable spirit', I wondered if I would ever have cause to use them. This book has provided me with the perfect opportunity. In this vivid, candid and very personal account, Pam Warren illustrates how her indomitable spirit has won through.

– Professor Nichola Rumsey, Co-Director, Centre for Appearance Research, Department of Psychology, UWE Bristol

FROM BEHIND THE MASK

PAM WARREN

WITH GARETH OWEN

Biteback Publishing

First published in Great Britain in 2014 by
Biteback Publishing Ltd
Westminster Tower
3 Albert Embankment
London SE1 7SP
Copyright © Pam Warren and Gareth Owen 2014

ISBN 978-1-84954-666-9

A CIP catalogue record for this book is available from the British Library.

Set in Caslon and Bodoni

Printed and bound in Great Britain by
CPI Group (UK) Ltd, Croydon CR0 4YY

MIX
Paper from
responsible sources
FSC® C020471

CONTENTS

PREFACE BY SIMON WESTON

Pam's book, *From Behind the Mask*, for me, is not so much about the person Pam was before, even though that is important to understand. This is about the person Pam has become.

On the face of it (no pun intended), Pam and I have little in common. What we obviously share is that we have both been involved in dramatic, life-threatening events. We have both been very badly burnt and we have both survived. In fact, we have more than survived – we have thrived.

Being badly burnt is devastating. Getting through the immediate aftermath and the endless rounds of surgery is one thing. Dealing with the psychological damage it leaves afterwards is something entirely different. You've got an altered body image, and when Pam got injured, being a young woman, it caused the biggest part of her angst; we live in a society where women are judged on their looks.

We met in 2002, via the Healing Foundation, where both Pam and I were (and still are) ambassadors. It was at a time in Pam's recovery when, to the outside world, things were going well, but Pam knew she was getting caught up in a web of drinking and it was complicating all of her thinking and decision processes. She asked to come and see me privately as I think she realised she needed help and wanted to open up with someone she knew had been through a similar experience and a person she could trust. She was reticent to talk at first, but being a forthright, chatty kind of guy – who knew all about recovering from burns – I decided to be bold, and asked her some pretty penetrating questions. I soon discovered that drink was causing her biggest problems. As someone who had 'been there and done that', I could really empathise with what Pam was going through and I wanted to help and support her if I could. I was glad that she let me and we have been firm friends ever since.

So, for me, this book is the story of a woman whose terrible ordeal, which would have put paid to a lot of other people, has taken her on an incredible journey and made her an incredible person.

Pam told me, not long after the tenth anniversary of the crash, that she had been asked to write a book about her experiences. When I encouraged her to do so she told me, 'I want to be completely honest with any reader and how can I do that until *I* am certain I have definitely come out the other side?' Well, she must be certain now as here is the book which, knowing Pam, will have had a lot of care, love and effort put into it.

The Paddington rail crash dramatically altered Pam's life, but she has triumphed over terrible adversity and come through. By reading this book you will see what I mean: you get to see the real Pam, 'warts and all'. She is searingly forthright about her negative attributes as well as her positives. That is what I love about Pam – her willingness to stand up to her fears and face the future, rather than be bowed by the weight and pressure of the past, as well as having a relentless optimism and zest for life.

Pam's story is a story of success, courage, bravery and fortitude and I am proud, as someone who has lived through something similar, to call her my friend.

FOREWORD BY SIR TREVOR McDONALD

One of the things I've always thought of as a journalist is how quickly we move from one subject to another in our work, from one major story to another. Yesterday's incidents, yesterday's disasters are soon relegated to the file of things past, always recalled when the occasion demands, but in the main gone from the active mind.

Pam Warren's book about the Paddington rail crash and how it dramatically changed her life is a reminder to us all that there are some things we should never forget. She will never be afforded the luxury of consigning the accident entirely to the past. Warren recalls with touching detail the first anxious moments when it was obvious that something had gone terribly wrong. Approaching Paddington station with only the thought of having a last cigarette before leaving the train, the carriage she was sitting in 'jerked violently. Extremely violently. The jerking immediately gave way to shuddering and the sound of screeching metal-on-metal brakes.' That was only the beginning of the nightmare. Pam Warren suffered terrible burns to her body and to her face and on recovery was given a plastic mask to make up for what had been a beautiful face. That mask was never able to hide the person Pam Warren is.

With great warmth and enormous dignity, Pam Warren writes about her early life, which was not without its family dysfunctions and complications, relationships that didn't always work out the way she intended and then, boldest of all, how doctors and surgeons helped to restore her traumatised body and how she bravely and with exemplary courage sought to rebuild her life. This is an unforgettable account of an unforgettable crash. Pam Warren brings humanity to a bitter, life-changing experience.

Shortly after 8 a.m. on the morning of 5 October 1999, two trains collided on a stretch of track just outside Ladbroke Grove, near Paddington station in London. Thirty-one people died that day:

CHARLOTTE ANDERSEN, DEREK ANTONOWITZ, ANTHONY BEETON, OLA BRATLIE, ROGER BROWN, JENNIFER CARMICHAEL, BRIAN COOPER, ROBERT COTTON, SAM DI LIETO, SHAUN DONOGHUE, NEIL DOWSE, CYRIL ELLIOTT, FIONA GREY, JULIET GROVES, SUN YOON HAH, MICHAEL HODDER, ELAINE KELLOW, MARTIN KING, ANTONIO LACOVARA, RASAK LADIPO, MATTHEW MACAULAY, DELROY MANNING, JOHN NORTHCOTT, JOHN RAISIN, DAVID ROBERTS, ALLAN STEWART, KHAWAR TAUHEED, MUTHULINGAM THAYAPARAN, ANDREW THOMPSON, BRYAN TOMPSON, SIMON WOOD.

INTRODUCTION

I was asked some years ago to write a book about what happened to me in and after the Paddington rail crash, but I couldn't find the enthusiasm to sit down and do it, perhaps also realising my journey of recovery was not yet complete.

In (finally) putting pen to paper now, I feel it is important to be totally honest with myself and any readers, and I am pleased to say that though I have written with my heart on my sleeve, these words come from a position of personal strength and contentment which has taken me many long years to achieve.

I have written this book very much from my perspective, and I can only share with you my own point of view, memories and how I saw things at that particular time; some of these views have changed as I have matured and I am not saying I am always right. I'm sure others will have different views about the same events, and remember them differently. It is not my wish to hurt or upset anyone by telling my story; this is simply my version of events and how they impacted on my life.

I have changed many of the names of people in the book to respect their true identities and so as not to cause embarrassment – that is, except for those people who I know won't mind, whom I have not named fully or who have already spoken and written about me in the public domain, as their identities are already known.

There are so, so many people without whom I would not be the person I am today, or still be alive, for that matter. I have mentioned a few in the pages ahead but there are many more to whom I send my heartfelt thanks and love – you know who you are and I cannot thank you enough; I send you all a hug and hope you are as happy and as well as I am. That simply leaves me to say that I hope you find my story of interest, and thank you for choosing to pick it up to read. To borrow an old Scottish saying: 'Lang May Yer Lum Reek.'

Pam Warren, 2013

CHAPTER 1

THE CRASH

The train sped through the beautiful Berkshire countryside. The contrast between the lush green of the grass and trees and the bright blue of the cloudless sky was wonderful, especially given it was an October morning. As this gave way to the more closed-in urban scene of buildings – the environs of London – I looked down at the train's table where my gloves, newspaper and cigarettes were lying.

Have I got enough time to have a last cigarette? I wondered as we approached London's Paddington mainline rail station.

It would be the last one I'd be able to have for quite a few hours and just as I reached forward for the pack, the train carriage I was sitting in jerked violently. Extremely violently.

The jerking immediately gave way to shuddering and the sound of screeching metal-on-metal brakes. The noise was both painful and intense and seared right through my head like a knife. All that happened next was over in a few minutes, seconds even, but there and then time seemed to slow down infinitely and each second felt like an eternity, and every detail of the horror which unfolded is etched into my memory – and will be for the rest of my life. Of course, my first thought was that someone had pulled the emergency handle and the train was stopping, but no sooner had that scenario briefly crossed my mind than my eyebrows rose in puzzlement as I looked at the man who sat opposite me. I realised something wasn't right as I was much higher than him, but was still in my seat. It was as though we were on opposing sides of a see-saw. We looked at each other with open mouths before expressions of horror crossed our faces as the realisation dawned that something was very, very wrong.

Then bedlam broke out.

Briefcases, handbags, coats and other personal possessions within the carriage began flying all around us as the carriage tilted, twisted, turned, left the tracks and took on the feeling of the most extremely sickening roller-coaster. The morning light, so bright a moment before, was extinguished and total darkness replaced it.

Through the noise of screeching and twisting metal, I became aware of people screaming, shouting and crying. It took me a fraction of a second to realise why the screaming worried me so much – because it was men I could hear, men screaming in appalling pain and terror. It was far and away the most disturbing and frightening thing I'd ever experienced in my life.

With no time to think, I instinctively pushed myself as far back into my seat as I could. *Make yourself small, Pam. Curl up.* As I pulled my legs up to get into a foetal position within the chair I turned my head over my right shoulder, and just then caught sight of something coming down the carriage towards me. It was a huge ball of fire – orange, yellow, red and black – swirling and roaring down the aisle. It was just like a fireball from a huge explosion you see in the movies. But this one was very real, and was making one hell of a noise – part roar, part whoomph. I clamped my hands to my face, sure that I was going to die and convinced there was simply nothing I could do.

They say when your life is about to end everything flashes in front of your eyes. To be honest, the only thought flashing around my mind was: *It hasn't been worth it, my life has not been worth it.* I was considered a successful businesswoman, and, yes, I had money in the bank and the trappings of some wealth, but right then they weren't worth a damn to me.

I felt I had wasted the privilege and potential life had given me; that my life had taken a wrong turn and I was not the person

I could or should have been. It was the most unselfish thought I'd probably ever had, but it appeared to have come all too late.

The fireball had engulfed the whole carriage behind me and now was upon and over me, and my whole body felt the indescribable heat at its heart. My body must have gone into some form of shock, but I knew I was alive as I could still hear the roaring sound all around me, disorientating me like a gale-force wind. Then I became aware of a new sound, a crackling, and realised it was my hair, skin and the material all around me on the train frazzling to a crisp. I must have been screaming as the flames and smoke tore down my throat and deep into my lungs. The fireball passed just as quickly as it had arrived in the carriage, and moments later the roar of the 'wind' had gone. I was too terrified to take my hands away from my face, and the acrid smell of burning and the horrific sound of men still screaming did nothing to alleviate my terror. I was so frightened that it simply extends beyond anything I can adequately describe. I was not certain if the fire had passed for good or even if the train had come to a complete halt; in fact, I was beginning to doubt that I was even alive – I knew I should be in enormous pain but I didn't feel it. I later discovered my brain had shut it out.

When I did eventually summon up the courage to open my fingers and peer through the cracks I could see very little: the carriage was dark and dense black smoke was all around. I was still in my seat, though it was twisted out of position so my back was now to the window and I was facing into the carriage. My left leg was trapped underneath the deformed train table and my right leg hung over the right armrest of the seat.

I struggled to focus on what had happened before, suddenly noticing my right leg was still on fire. Without stopping to think, I reached out with my hands and patted out the flames, not realising how badly burnt my hands already were.

The noise all around me now became silenced and, apart from a low groaning, it seemed unnaturally quiet. I turned my head to where the man had been sitting opposite me.

'Are you OK?' I asked quietly.

'Yes, thank you,' he replied politely, equally quietly.

It was bizarre that even on the verge of death we were being so polite. It all seemed unreal and so surreal. Suddenly I had a horrible thought that the fireball might come back again.

'I have got to get out of here. We have got to get out of here,' I said to anyone and everyone who might be in earshot.

I pulled at my left leg and the table was so charred that it broke up into tiny pieces. The window once beside me had shattered, and looking through the hole it left behind, I realised the carriage must have tilted on its side as I was staring at the grey aggregate on the track below. It didn't look too far to drop, so with all the strength I could muster I swivelled on my bottom and pulled my legs around and out of the window. I then pushed back against the seat with my hands and propelled myself out of the carriage; as I hit the track my legs gave way and I twisted my ankle badly on the uneven ground. I hadn't stopped to think that I had my high-heeled boots on, and they, believe me, are not ideal to be jumping out of things in!

I then heard a crunch behind me and realised someone else must have jumped out too. For the first time in what seemed like an eternity I felt a sense of hope, a hope heightened by the thought of other people freeing themselves and escaping the train too. Of course, none of us had stopped to think whether it was safe to jump out of the train – what if the rails had been live? Or another train was passing? In truth, none of us knew just how bad the crash really was.

I managed to haul myself back onto my feet and remember thinking how ridiculous it was that I should be struggling to walk. Hunched over, I hobbled forward slowly, all the time thinking how eerily quiet it seemed. At that moment some of the first real pain hit me: it practically disabled me. I shouted, as best I could, for help.

'Someone, please, please help me!'

My voice sounded weird and wasn't much more than a croak; I realised that my vocal cords and throat must have been damaged by the smoke. Though, mercifully, it was just strong enough to solicit help from a man I saw approaching me. I remember thinking how attractive he was – it is completely absurd what goes through your mind at the unlikeliest of times! – and his gentle voice said, 'It's all right, I'm here, I'm here to help you.'

CHAPTER 2

THE IMMEDIATE AFTERMATH

I'm here to help you are words I will remember for the rest of my life.

They were the kindest and most wonderful words, words that gave me hope, and they came from a man who ran out of a haze towards me: he became my hero.

Though barely a few minutes had passed since the impact, it seemed an eternity to me. I still didn't quite know what had happened, and that confusion, coupled with my loss of coordination, blotted out the enormity of everything that was actually just a few feet around me. I'd emerged from my carriage into the apex of the crashed trains, so was in the middle of the V they had created; my brain could not absorb what my smoke-filled eyes were recording. Of course, other senses were working overtime to compensate for my hazy sight: there was an awful smell of diesel fuel and choking smoke; I was aware of an almost total silence, although in the distance I could hear sirens drawing ever nearer. Though surrounded by wreckage and disaster, I remember thinking it was eerily quiet; that was the most frightening and confusing thing of all, until I heard that reassuring voice.

'Who are you?' I struggled to whisper.

'I'm Matt,' he replied, before putting his arms around me from behind, and holding me gently by my elbows. 'Can you walk?' he asked.

'I'm not sure … my legs are hurting.'

'Then we'd better get you to the side of the track.'

Looking around, I couldn't see anything beyond the smoking mangled mess of steel surrounding us; directly in front was an overturned carriage, its wheels grotesquely hanging in mid-air, like something you see in a disaster movie. Matt asked if I thought I could climb over the carriage to the other side of the track, but my legs were hurting so much I could barely lift them.

'OK, we will walk around to the end of it, and get round that way,' he said calmly.

I told him I didn't think I could even manage that. He stopped, thought for a moment, and said, 'Then we will have to go under the carriage.'

Common sense would say *don't walk under the wreck of a train carriage suspended a few feet in the air*, but as terrified as I was there was no way I could walk any further. So, as Matt supported me, we crept forward before bending down on all fours to move underneath. I remember as my nose moved closer to the gravel below the intensity of the diesel fumes increased dramatically and I suddenly felt sickening, gut-wrenching fear like never before. The smell terrified me then, and does to this day, over a decade on.

On the other side of the track I became conscious of people all around and the sounds of groaning, weeping, hushed talking and pleas of help became all too clear and immediate. There was no screaming, though; it was still relatively quiet – perhaps it's just a British thing that we don't react that way? I believe my survival instinct now took over as I focused all of my senses onto my own person and blocked out everything else. The pain in my legs was becoming ever greater and spreading. Slowly, we continued shuffling along to the trackside.

Once there, Matt screamed, 'I need help, NOW!'

Gone was the calm, reassuring tone that told me not to worry; I now only heard terror in his voice as he frantically scanned around, looking for assistance.

'My legs are hurting,' I said feebly; the pain was searing and fast becoming unbearable.

'Why don't you lie down?' suggested Matt with his calm voice.

'No, I just want to sit.'

'You need to lie down,' he affirmed.

'No, no, I don't want to,' I said, desperate not to slip into unconsciousness, and perhaps, too, feeling it might make me more vulnerable. Something in my brain was saying, *Stay awake at all costs and keep calm.* I asked Matt if he could prop me up from behind. He stood with his front to my back, a bit like a gentle hug, and lowered himself in unison with my body; I slumped down onto my bum, and he became a chair for me.

I could hear talking and offers of help but there was no sign of the emergency services, though their sirens were ever present. I began shaking with cold and shock, but I tried to focus on staying awake and upright – I felt if I could sit up, then it wouldn't be so bad. Funny, the things that go through your mind, isn't it?

'Does anyone know first aid?' Matt asked.

A fair-haired young woman, Evelyn Crosskey, stepped forward. 'Yes, me.'

'I feel cold,' I said to her.

With that, she draped her coat around my shoulders. I remember the expression of disbelief in her eyes: my skin and flesh were still smouldering, and smoke was rising off my whole body. A dark-haired woman standing nearby said, 'Look, she is still cooking.'

Evelyn dropped to her knees, produced a bottle of mineral water and began sprinkling it on my hands and the parts of my clothes that were smoking. The darker-haired lady asked if she could call anyone for me.

'Yes, I must call my husband.' I reeled off the phone number, and my first-aiders scribbled it down.

The dark-haired lady said, 'There is no reply.'

I realised Peter would not have made it home yet after dropping me off at the station.

'Phone his mother,' I heard myself saying, 'but be careful, she is in her eighties, don't frighten her.'

A few moments later, I heard the dark-haired lady speaking to my mother-in-law. She told her that there had been 'a train accident', but that I was OK and needed to get in touch with Peter, and she left her mobile number.

Suddenly I looked up and saw a man who identified himself as a policeman looking at me. He told me his name was Ian Pledger; I told him my name but could not manage much more. He examined me for a short while and later told me that when he first saw me, looking like a little huddled-up old woman, he thought I was wearing a lace dress. It was actually a full-length black wool outfit, or what was left of it, at least.

With my charred clothes dampened, there was a sudden thump. I looked down to see the plastic armrest from the seat I had been on lying beside me; it must have melted and stuck onto the arm of my jacket, and had then cooled down enough to have just fallen off. Everyone around me breathed an audible sigh of relief, as they had thought it was impaled in my side.

By now, the pain was stabbing me all over.

'My forehead feels funny,' I said. I raised my hand to try and touch it when, instantly, three hands pushed against me, moving my hand away from my face. Ian decided that there was not much he could do to help me immediately, so asked the people who were with me to stay while he went off to help others and to get the additional help I needed.

'Oh, for goodness' sake,' I snapped in exasperation at Ian as he left, letting some of my fear express itself. I just wanted the pain to stop, and all I had was people asking me to stay there and reassuring me I would be OK, but not actually doing anything to alleviate the gnawing, teeth-gritting, intense and all-consuming pain.

'Why don't you lie down?' Matt asked again.

'No, I must stay awake.' It was now not just the fear of becoming unconscious, which might have actually proved to help me bear the pain. I also remembered I was wearing contact lenses and had heard stories about lenses slipping behind your eyeball if you fell asleep with them in.

After a while a paramedic squatted down in front of me, with my kindly policeman, Ian, at his side.

'What's your name?' he asked.

'Pam, Pam MacKay.'

'Let's take a look at you, Pam.'

The paramedic didn't seem unduly alarmed at the white shade of my skin. He obviously assumed that was its normal colour. Perhaps I should have mentioned to him that I am Asian, as apparently if Asian skin is burnt and turns white, it is a very bad sign. He fumbled with some sort of gel pack but could not work out how to open it, until Ian read out the instructions, and the paramedic covered my hands in the jelly-like substance and wrapped them in plastic bags.

'Right, Pam,' he said, 'we've got to get you into an ambulance.' He raised his head and saw the steep embankment wall behind us.

Together with someone else, the paramedic helped me walk the few steps to the base of the high wall and an awaiting chair. With ropes tied to both sides of the chair, and me strapped into it, I was hauled up. Though the elation of being rescued was wonderful, I found myself looking at an aerial view of the carnage that lay below.

Don't take it in, my survival brain said to me. *We'll make sense of it all later.*

My attending paramedic and others pushed the chair up over their heads, helping my elevation. I said, 'I bet you're glad I'm not Ten-Ton Tessie!' I remember then saying something about it being a bit like abseiling.

Matt and the two ladies who had helped me were at the top of the embankment as I was laid onto a stretcher. How they got there I'll never know, but it felt good to have them with me. I kept insisting that I would not close my eyes because of my contact lenses; the darker-haired lady then offered to take them out for me, and threw them to the ground.

'OK then,' I said, 'I'll lie back in the stretcher and maybe I'll shut my eyes. I feel a bit tired.'

A man appeared beside me at the back of the ambulance. 'Pam, I'm a doctor. Are you in a lot of pain?'

I nodded slightly and gritted my teeth. I found myself thinking he seemed very young to be a doctor, and perhaps I ought to ask for some sort of ID. Before I could say anything, he continued, 'I'm just about to give you an injection of morphine and you should feel a lot better.'

He pressed into my left arm and a warm feeling took over; I remember seeing a kaleidoscope of bright colours, and the lamp posts above me started swaying. A feeling of total happiness swept through my body and Matt started giggling as I leaned up on my elbow and called after the doctor, 'Come back – I want to marry you!'

I lay back on the stretcher and slipped into a dream world of unconsciousness from which no one knew when, or if, I would ever wake up.

CHAPTER 3

THE MORNING COMMUTE

On 5 October 1999 I took that morning train to London in the hope of bettering my life. It certainly changed my life, that's for sure.

Over a decade earlier, and just before my eighteenth birthday in 1985, I began work as a receptionist at the Scottish Life Assurance Company in Reading. It was during my years there that I actually met both of my (now) former husbands – Scott MacKay and Peter Warren. Peter was the man I was married to that fateful day; in fact, he dropped me at the railway station.

The 1980s was the time of the yuppie, the Filofax, expense accounts and making money. Whether or not you had to tread on people or lie and cheat to get to the top, you were considered an entrepreneur, and entrepreneurs were actively encouraged and nurtured by Margaret Thatcher's Tory government. You see, back then money was power and if you had it, everyone looked up to you.

When I first started work I couldn't afford new clothes, so wore the only items vaguely respectable – my old school uniform of white shirt, grey skirt and black cardigan. I vividly remember my first day at Scottish Life – I was so nervous I could feel my knees shaking!

I gazed in amazement at my new sophisticated surroundings, while the office manager's secretary, Jane, led me the short walk to my desk in the reception area, chatting away happily, trying to put me at my ease while explaining what they wanted me to do: answer the phone – simple, really. As an impressionable young woman starting out on the career ladder, I was completely in awe of my female colleagues wearing their big hair and 'power' suits with the shoulder pads in the jackets, actually looking more like they'd left the hangers in. To my naive eyes, this epitomised all that was glamour, and I so wanted to be like the women I worked with – gorgeous, successful and living life to the full. I keenly felt my own inadequacies, and inwardly sighed *I can't wait to get older so I can have a life like theirs – it must be so much fun.* Talk about wishing my youth away!

The hub of my new world was one of those 1970s concrete creations; from the outside it resembled a squashed tower block with only five floors, with its grey construction inset with some peculiar-looking green cladding. It was hardly something from *Dallas* or *Dynasty*.

Scottish Life was on the ground floor and stretched out in an open-plan design, with a few 'formal' offices at each end and the remainder divided into work cubicles. My desk faced the front doors at the top end of the office, and from it I could observe the branch manager, who had one of the formal offices at my end of the floor. He had a set of small traffic lights outside his door and the procedure was to knock, await the red light turning amber, and then when it went green you could enter.

I found it really comical, and not unlike boss CJ in the television programme *The Fall and Rise of Reginald Perrin*. Many was the time I watched a nervous employee standing, staring and willing the amber light not to turn green.

I settled in quite comfortably to answering the telephone but was so painfully shy that the only other words I would speak in the office were 'hello' and 'goodbye'. I guess it was a combination of it being my first job in the big wide world and feeling awestruck by those around me, though they were never anything but friendly to me. I consequently kept myself to myself, until one day when Jane said to me, 'Pam, one of your other responsibilities is to shout "Post" down the whole office at 4.45 so they know the postman is here to collect our post for the day.'

It's hard to imagine how such a simple and inconsequential instruction drove sheer terror into me. I stared at Jane open-mouthed and felt the colour drain from my face. I had heard someone give this call every day, but now they wanted me to stand up and shout it?

As the time ticked by that day, I started to feel increasingly wobbly and willed the clock to stop, go backwards, do anything so I wouldn't have to stand up and shout. Just before 4.45 Jane came to my desk and nodded at me; I stood up, gripping the desk for support and, while sweating profusely, opened my mouth and bellowed 'POOOOOSSSSTTT' – though all that came out was a very squeaky, high-pitched 'Post!', rather like a little mouse might have called it. My terror intensified when every-one immediately stopped what they were doing and a silence fell over the office – that is, until the manager popped his head out of the door opposite me and, with a puzzled expression, quipped, 'What the fuck was that?' The whole floor dissolved into laughter. I was mortified, and when she saw the tears running down my face, Jane took sympathy on me and let me go home early.

I was made to shout 'Post' every day thereafter and gradually I not only became louder and more assured with that, but I began to also come out of my shell and my terrible shyness dropped away. Three months later I remember feeling so proud to be a fully functioning and important part of the team and even looked forward to going into work every day. Initially I thrived: I learnt a lot from my peers as to how the insurance industry worked and seemed to pick up tasks I was assigned easily and quickly. Soon I was given more responsibility – not just answering the phone but looking after and ordering the stationery supplies and sending out client documents to financial advisers – and along the way learnt how to administer an insurance application from start to finish. I also invested in a new wardrobe and like to think I looked the part!

The powers that be must have spotted some potential, as they decided to promote me to a sales consultant's assistant, and hired a new receptionist. I was appointed to a chap called Nick, who, although he had been there longer than I, was still fairly junior within the office hierarchy and was also considered to be the grumpiest consultant. If greeted with a cheery 'hello' in the morning, he'd just grunt. Within a few months of my working with Nick the other girls were amazed I had succeeded in getting him to respond to greetings with a 'hello' of his own, and a smile, too; he also made me cups of tea rather than the other way round.

Nick was consultant to a number of financial advisers, all of whom I regularly spoke with and wrote to on his behalf. One of them was really quite horrible to deal with: he was very dictatorial, shouted a lot, was blatantly rude and obviously thought women were second-class citizens. I couldn't stand him and dreaded having to phone him. One day Nick gave me a pile of dictations to transcribe and I noticed the first one was to this particular adviser. Now, the normal procedure was for the assistant to type up the letters, then return them to the consultant for double-checking and signing. However, as Nick had come to trust me completely by this point, I sent out the letters straight away, signed on his behalf, and he only ever browsed over copies later, before they were filed away. Well, on this particular day I couldn't resist substituting a dummy letter for Nick to browse over, one in which he told the adviser a few home truths, mixed in with some expletives and insults for good measure. The scream of 'PAM!' and the noise of files, papers and his chair falling to the floor in Nick's cubicle were priceless, and I quickly popped out to the loo, just to prolong his panic for a little while longer.

Nick and I remained friends for a long time after we'd both

left Scottish Life. He was an enormous support when I parted from my first husband, and we always made an effort to meet at least once a year – which continued all the way up to and just past my recovery after the train crash, when we unfortunately lost touch.

Scottish Life, meanwhile, soon outgrew its office and moved to a beautiful, large Georgian-style building in Kings Road, Reading, where us staff were spread over four floors; I was based on the ground floor, as was Peter Warren, the assistant manager. I didn't have much to do with Peter on a day-to-day basis and I never thought of him in any other light than as 'the boss'. However, just as with Nick, I gradually warmed to Peter over time, and we became a little more friendly, though never socially.

On Fridays a gang of us would walk the well-trodden path from the office and hit the Wynford Arms on Kings Road; there, a kitty would be set up which we all contributed to, and the drinks would start flowing – wine, spirits, beer and, on special occasions, champagne. We kept going – chatting, laughing and drinking – until we were completely drunk, we had run out of money or, as was more often the case, the landlord called closing time, which was 11 p.m. in those days. That wasn't the end of the night, though, as many of us headed off to a bistro called BJ Moon's to eat bowls of very hot chilli and pitta bread. I am sure my memories of this bistro's chilli are probably clouded by alcohol but I've always said it was the best-tasting chilli in the whole world. I relished every mouthful and always seemed to want more!

Other times, kitty withstanding, we'd head to one of the night-clubs in Reading for more drinking, dancing and partying, well in to the wee small hours of the morning. It's amazing none of us ever suffered from alcohol poisoning, though I do remember a few tumbles and broken bones being nursed. We worked hard and, boy, did we play hard.

One morning, out of the blue, Peter Warren told me he was leaving Scottish Life to set up his own financial advisory broker-age, working, initially, for Heron Homes. He asked me if I fancied joining his new firm as the administrator; my ears pricked up. It was a more opportune offer than he could have possibly realised at the time.

You see, I had become disillusioned at Scottish Life after two and a half years. No, I think it would be fairer to say I was becom-ing bored with the job. I was twenty and had quickly moved up the ladder from receptionist to Nick's personal assistant, but there I had remained, handling insurance application forms, correspondence and appointments and dealing with financial advisers' queries. At first it was varied and interesting work, but having done it day in and day out for so long, I really craved more of a challenge. I had asked the branch manager – red, amber, green and go – on several occasions if he might bear me in mind for any other roles in the company, saying that ideally I wanted to train to become a saleswoman. Why I thought I wanted to be one of the sales force I don't know, but it seemed a natural progression from being an administrator. He turned me down flat, but never gave me an answer as to why. *At least give me a try*, I thought. If nothing else, I showed enthusiasm and a desire to better myself, but it wasn't picked up on.

Youthful impatience, combined with my sense of unfairness at my lack of progression, meant that I had turned my thoughts to leaving and had started to apply for other jobs. That was precisely when Peter made his offer and it seemed to be the answer to all my problems, so I accepted immediately. Though it wasn't really a 'promotion' in the sense of me becoming a saleswoman, I did see the move as a chance of progression, and one which offered something more than the now mundane life of an office clerk at a huge conglomerate. As I've grown older I've discovered I thrive on challenge and change – both in my work and in my private life. I have quite a low boredom threshold and a keen urge to explore. This doesn't always work in my favour, of course, but I have found I prefer to be like this than someone who settles for the easier, quieter, accepting kind of life.

Initially, it was just Peter and me working from a spare bedroom in his apartment, which we turned into a functional, if only basic, office. Working in such close proximity we got to know each other better and I'd like to think became firm friends. To begin with I'd regarded him as 'a bit flash and all about the money', whereas he was actually an OK sort of guy and a very hard worker. I had a boyfriend at the time, Scott, and together with Peter and his wife we all socialised occasionally, too.

Peter and I were operating the 'financial adviser' part of the insurance chain, so stood between the client and the insurance company. My job was to handle every piece of paper that came in, whether it be related to a mortgage or insurance issue, keep everyone updated on the progress of their applications, chase money owed to us and pay the bills. At the heart of my high-tech admin department I had an old golfball electric typewriter, which I had to whack the return handle on to move down to the next line and which was precariously balanced on an old ironing board that served as my desk. I loved my ancient piece of typing machinery and it was always with a sense of achievement that I enthusiastically hit that handle.

From this inauspicious start we managed to deal with a huge volume of work from Heron Homes, and our firm very quickly started moving onwards and upwards, taking on new clients and bigger opportunities. By the time I turned twenty-two, Peter had invited me to join him and another colleague, Paul, in a full partnership: Peter was the chief, I was in charge of the internal office systems, finances and administration team, and Paul looked after our sales consultants.

Part of my expanded role within the firm was to interview and decide on the administrators we took on – and despite record unemployment I discovered finding someone was much harder than I had first thought. One interviewee had a PhD and for the life of me I could not see why she wanted a junior position, nor could she tell me; another girl stated quite aggressively, 'Well, I expect I will have your job within the year,' which didn't exactly endear her to me; and a third, when told about the filing she was expected to do, asked, 'What's alphabetical?' I did actually employ the third one – she was very sweet and I made sure she understood what alphabetical was before giving her any filing!

The 1980s in Reading was a time of boom for businesses. New companies, mainly computer and high-tech firms, were moving into the area, which would soon be dubbed 'Silicon Valley'. The area was quite literally awash with money and new opportunities; it was the perfect time for our new company to expand, and expand rapidly.

In two years we moved from being a back-room operation to one with a turnover of £1.5 million, a sales staff of seven and an administration team of six. Thankfully, our good fortune meant I could wave goodbye to my ironing board and we moved into a lovely airy office in Wokingham, complete with proper designer desks and computers. We all drove cars such as XR3s, BMWs or Mercedes and were very much part of the 'yuppies in wine bars with Filofaxes' culture. I dressed to impress, had the 'big' hair I'd so much admired at Scottish Life and bought what I thought were wonderful designer suits with huge shoulder pads. *Move over, Joan Collins.*

I watched and listened to how our sales consultants achieved their goals and thought, *Well, I'm sure I could do better than that.* Oh, the arrogance of youth!

'You have two things going against you,' Peter said when I told him of my aspirations. 'One, you are a woman, and, two, you are black.' He said, years later, that he was joking. However, at the time, it didn't sound like a joke.

To say I was furious would be an understatement. In fact, I was rendered speechless. Yes, I am a woman; yes, my skin is brown; but what on earth did my gender or colour have to do with my ability to do a job? I saw red. But, with the flipside of youth being deference, I didn't tell Peter what he could do with his job, nor did I walk away; instead, I decided to channel my anger into proving him completely wrong. I took some time out to train in the specialised area of pensions and investment advice, and set up a new division within our company. I'd like to think I made quite a success of it, too; it became my own department and I loved it. I tried to treat all my clients the way I wanted to be treated myself. They, in turn, liked me and I liked them.

We were riding the crest of a wave and nothing could stop us. It felt as though we were untouchable.

Then, in 1989, the property market crashed.

Interest rates under the Conservative government spiralled out of control, hitting 15 per cent. Repossessions were rife, mortgages became too expensive and customers began dumping their insurance policies in order to free up any spare cash to try to simply meet their outgoings. As a result, much of the financial advice sector crashed and within months our firm was on the brink of bankruptcy. In a way, we became a victim of our own success: we were a large company with large overheads and lots of staff. Suddenly, the rug was pulled out and we simply had too few clients arranging mortgages, with all the associated insurances, which cut our income severely. We were top heavy and sinking fast.

I had never experienced failure before; this was a business I had helped to build from nothing and now I could see it falling back to nothing. Worse still, I had to watch helplessly as our staff and colleagues, who had also become friends, were laid off in an effort to keep the company afloat. It sounds terribly selfish, but I couldn't bear the thought of losing my beautiful home, my nice car or the lifestyle modest success had afforded me. I didn't want to have to follow my colleagues out of the office carrying a box full of desk possessions and face the dole queue. I had worked so hard to escape the damp, unsanitary conditions of the bedsit life of my youth and the uncertainty of not knowing if I could afford the next meal. Now, because of the recession and circumstances beyond my control, I faced the possibility of this becoming a reality again.

Quickly, Peter and I set about restructuring and adapting.

'Pam, can you call our landlords and explain we're having to tighten our belts and may need to move out unless we can negotiate a reduction in our rent,' Peter said. 'Maybe they will be sympathetic to us and cut us a deal.' With many businesses going under, landlords were witnessing tenants moving out left, right and centre. Unfortunately, ours were not receptive to our plight; the office was owned by a firm who were, in all probability, the most avaricious and unsympathetic lot I have ever come across. We tried to renegotiate but they were having none of it and demanded full payment upfront. Paul, our third business partner, bailed out at this point and both Peter and I stopped drawing salaries for a while, trying to gain breathing space and trade our way out of the problem. We cut our operation back to the bare bones: the last of the staff were let go, posh furniture was sold and our flash cars were returned.

Our landlords simply wouldn't back off and give us more time to pay up, and they instructed bailiffs to knock on our door. With a little tenacity, the promise of some income soon and the realisation that we didn't really have anything left worth seizing, they eventually gave us a brief respite to sort ourselves out as best we could. We were virtually insolvent and company liquidators were poised to pounce.

Recession had well and truly gripped the UK. The pound performed very robustly at almost a $2 exchange rate, but in turn manufacturing became unviable. American investment in Britain became unaffordable and unemployment hit new highs. Against this backdrop, somehow, someway, Peter and I battled our way on, though winning new clients proved particularly tough, as just about every other surviving financial advice company tried to outbid their competitors by offering ridiculously low commission terms. Said commissions then trickled through into our cash flow much slower than we'd have liked and it really became a story of surviving from one deal to another. I stopped worrying about my image and the model of car I was driving and ran around in a second-hand one that was bought and paid for; I forgot about overseas holidays and rarely had the energy or means to think about partying. I started suffering from insomnia, and every morning woke from broken sleep with a sick, empty feeling in the pit of my stomach.

One of our steadiest-performing portfolios turned out to be 'pensions' – my area. While many other aspects of our business contracted, my clients seemed to still be thinking about their old age. There were other advantages to them keeping up their pensions too, such as added tax reliefs and benefits from piling money into personal pension pots. It made me think.

Peter and I were manacled together on a sinking ship, and while we baled out water as fast as we could, life was pretty damn miserable for us both. Consequently, in 1993, we made the decision to wind up our partnership.

Luckily, and with a little fortunate foresight, I transferred our only successful portfolio – pension clients – into a new company of which I had total control. I was determined to salvage something from the mess, while also looking after some of our longest and most loyal customers. I was almost twenty-seven, had worked solidly for nine years to build a more stable life, and thought if I could rescue something to start again with, then I should. Peter joined me in this new set-up on a consultancy basis with what he could salvage from the mortgage side of our old business.

However, with lessons learnt, I was determined to avoid the mistakes of the old partnership. I fostered working relationships with my clients whereby I catered for all their financial needs on a yearly basis, and thereby changed the way I was paid by them. I introduced 'fee-based advice', which meant I got paid for the work I did and not on commission. In return, they received genuine independent financial advice. This new strategy, not widely used in the financial sector at the time, proved to be a winning formula. The other nice thing was that I got to know my clients very well over the years; some became friends and remain so to this day.

When I was then offered the position of independent financial adviser to two large national insurance companies, I accepted with excitement. You see, one of the consequences of collapse in the financial markets was that the mis-selling of products by insurance companies became exposed to public awareness ... and criticism. The companies therefore needed independent advisers, such as me, to review their cases and give our opinion on what, if anything, had been done incorrectly. Then compensation could be offered to the policy holders.

I joined them as one of many freelance independent consultants. It was hard work, with long days and few free weekends,
and the paperwork we had to wade through was enormous; but
it was good money, too, and gave me a financial security I hadn't
had for the past few recession-filled years. The only problem
turned out to be that the insurance companies concerned didn't
seem to like the findings. We were critical of the insurance work-
force that had, in some cases, forced their products onto people
with what I would call bullying or downright deceit of clients.
The companies baulked and after a few months got rid of us all;
I suppose if you were a large corporate you would be somewhat
peeved at paying a group of people to tell you that you'd effectively 'ripped off' customers and now had to pay out even more
money to compensate.

Throughout this, my personal sense of injustice, especially for
others, remained a strong driving principle. Financial advisers did
not have a very good public image, and understandably so when
so many people had lost their homes. I tried to redress some
of that in my work, ensuring fair and sympathetic treatment.
If I found that my clients had what they needed and required
nothing new, I would tell them so. If they were considering
unnecessary products, I would tell them that too.

By forgoing even more weekends and burning the midnight
oil, I also began studying for exams to bring me up to speed
with, and enable me to offer, different types of accountancy and
tax-planning advice, under the auspices of the ever-changing
Financial Services Act. It was not acceptable to me just to be a
good financial adviser. I wanted to be the best.

I felt the exams, which culminated in recognised professional
qualifications, would instil further confidence in my abilities
amongst my clients and extend the services I could offer them,
which, from a business point of view, would mean more work for

me so I would get paid more. It was a no-brainer as far as I could see. I had passed four of the seven required and was studying for the fifth in late 1999. The actual exam date was set for late October 1999.

My courses were initially conducted via correspondence, with the odd face-to-face refresher held in Reading. However, a shortage of candidates for the October '99 exam meant the next refresher course was going to be held in Moorgate, London. It was not much of an inconvenience, really, just a bit of a nuisance having to commute and lose three days' work while I was in London.

I love autumn mornings – there is something about the freshness of the air and the clarity of the early-morning light. It was just like that on 5 October when I emerged onto platform 5 at Reading station. It was slightly chilly and crisp, so I was wearing warm woolly clothes and gloves but didn't feel the need for a coat. The sky was a cloudless blue and the sun shone so brightly it made me squint. *Should've brought my sunglasses*, I remember thinking. I stood with my face tilted upwards, eyes shut, revelling in the feeling of the sunshine, mentally hugging myself in that moment of enjoyment. It truly was a glorious day and one when it felt good to be alive.

I had bought tickets for all three days of the course in advance, so, on this second morning, I was able to hurry directly to the platform and edged past other passengers to the 'Gold Zone' at the far end of the platform, the section for first-class passengers, just in time to catch the 07.44 First Great Western express from Bristol. Commuting by train was not an everyday occurrence for me, so I ignored my fellow passengers, as I was unlikely to know anyone. Instead, I concentrated on my enjoyment of the sunny weather until the train rumbled up to the platform. *I'm in luck*, I thought as coach H drew up directly in front of me.

I had always enjoyed catching the train. Sometimes, on a rare day off, just for fun I would jump on random trains at Reading simply to see where I would end up. The thrill of an adventure, of going somewhere new, was so exciting. After the fairly recent Clapham and Southall crashes I did sometimes wonder, *Is it safe to travel by train?*, as I'm sure many people did, but as I boarded I'd reassure myself: *Things will have changed – there were inquiries. It must be much safer now.* I drew mental analogies with the aviation business, where, after any incident, everything stops while investigations are carried out and improvements made before normal service is resumed.

On this particular day, standing next to me, although I didn't know him then, was a tall gentleman named Keith Stiles. Further down the platform stood a bespectacled man, Tim Streatfield. Tim, I found out later, had missed his regular 07.30 train, having decided to treat himself to a full cooked breakfast. How weird can fate be when we change our normal routines? For us and the other passengers stepping onto that train, it was a journey that ended in carnage, and one that would change our lives forever.

Reading was the last stop before London's fourteen-platform Paddington station. Paddington is one of London's busiest main-line terminuses and perhaps one of its grandest, built by Isambard Kingdom Brunel in 1854. But like the other forty million people who pass through it each year, I never gave it much thought – it was just somewhere to hop on and off the train home as far as I was concerned.

As the doors slammed shut in Reading, the destiny of the four hundred people on board the train was sealed. Four hundred people, with four hundred reasons for boarding that train on that particular day.

At that time of the morning there is always a scramble for seats, so I quickly moved down the carriage and took one of the single window seats in the smoking area at the rear of the carriage, with my back to the direction of travel. The coach was already pretty full and, while not taking in the specific details of the other passengers' faces, I was aware that most were wearing suits and many had wallet folders out on the tables and were leafing through documents. There was a general feeling of freshness in the carriage and the sunshine was streaming in through the slightly grubby windows, highlighting the small dust particles dancing in the air. I placed my bag and briefcase at my feet and spread some revision papers along with a copy of the *Daily Telegraph* on the table in front of me. Unsurprisingly, I didn't do much revision.

Even a cursory look at my notes, I decided, was not as interesting as the crossword puzzle in my newspaper, which in turn, I decided, was not as interesting as watching the passing countryside and trains through my window as we zoomed from the Berkshire countryside to the outskirts of London.

Just over twenty minutes into the journey, at 08.06, a three-carriage Thames Turbo train driven by the newly qualified Michael Hodder pulled out of platform 9 at Paddington bound for Bedwyn in Wiltshire. It was on time and pretty full.

The train passed a green signal as it exited the station, giving the driver the all-clear to proceed on the journey. Twenty seconds later, as the train moved through Royal Oak, an audio warning sounded in Michael Hodder's cab, telling him that he was passing a 'double yellow' signal – indicating there was a red 'stop' signal showing not far ahead. He was expected to slow down and come to a halt.

For reasons we will never know, Hodder continued at a steady pace and though he cut his speed momentarily at one point before accelerating again, he continued driving the train down the track unquestioned. After another twenty seconds, as the train passed Westbourne Park, the warning horn sounded again. This time it was indicating a single yellow light ahead, which in turn warned him that the very next signal was set on red and he had to stop. Again, for reasons unknown, he ignored it.

I have never personally blamed Michael Hodder as an individual for what happened. It is my opinion that he was a small cog in an already deeply flawed, dysfunctional rail industry machine. Although I don't know what was going through his mind at this precise moment, I do know he had everything to live for – he was happily married. As a newly qualified driver I don't believe he fully appreciated what the repercussions of his simple actions might be.

He continued to drive the train around the long curved track and started accelerating. Directly ahead was signal number SN109, which was set to red. It was positioned just on the western side of Portobello Bridge. Now, just thirty-five seconds after the previous warning, the horn in his cab blared out again, this time warning him of the red signal directly ahead. Hodder silenced it and continued accelerating towards SN109. He paid no attention to the signals, the audio warnings … and no one questioned why.

I turned my head to the right for a few moments and recognised the graffiti-covered metal-bricked embankment through the opposite window. Turning the other way, I noticed the yellow and grey Eurostar trains standing waiting for action. *I must try to take a trip to Paris sometime to see what the Eurostar is like.* I then wondered if I had time for a last cigarette before we pulled into Paddington.

It was eight minutes and twenty-nine seconds past eight.

Meanwhile, an alarm sounded in the signal control centre at Slough. A red line appeared on the large screen in front of the three signalmen on duty, indicating a train had passed signal SN109, which was set on red. They waited for a moment to see if the train would slow to a halt.

It didn't.

Five seconds later a second alarm sounded, and then a couple of seconds later a third, more intense, alarm, warning two trains were approaching each other head-on. For reasons I don't fully comprehend, the two trains were on the same single piece of line and heading towards each other at speed – something that in my opinion should not have been possible. They were on a collision course.

One of the signalmen leapt forward in desperation, changing the next signal on the line to red in the hope of stopping them. There was nothing else he could do. There was no direct communication available between signal boxes and train drivers at that time, so the signalmen could only watch, hope and pray.

Not realising anything was wrong, I began to reach out for my final cigarette.

CHAPTER 4

REASSESSING LIFE

In hospital, surrounded by machines, tubes and cables, I lay flat out in an induced coma.

Despite some medics saying you do not remember anything of the time you spend in a coma, I'm here to tell you I do remember the very weird, wild and varied dreams I had. Running through many of them were threads, thoughts and memories of how my life had been in the past. If I were religious, I suppose I might say I was having one very long epiphany.

To understand the person lying comatose in the hospital, I really ought to fill you in a little more about my life. My surname used to be Tewari, after my biological father; then it changed to Simms, after my adoptive dad – my mother's second husband and the man who brought me up; it then became MacKay after I married my first husband, which is actually the surname I have always liked best. Pam MacKay had a nice ring to it, I thought. Finally, it changed again, though this time without my consent, to Pam Warren.

Just call me Pam!

I say I'm not religious – I'm probably more of a lapsed agnostic if the truth be known – but I was born into a Indo-Fijian family, and was, for some strange reason, baptised a Catholic before becoming 'Church of England'. It's all quite a mixture – no wonder I seemed confused as to how or where I fitted in. My fingers used to be long and slender with filed nails, sometimes painted, and nothing like the amputated, mesh-grafted finger-nail-less stubs that stab at my keyboard now. My skin was once soft and scar-free, my face without make-up in the mornings was pretty OK, and I moved without pain or the constant fear of debilitating flashbacks. Better still, I slept soundly and without nightmares.

Growing up was a trial for me and, at times, I felt very alone. I was a quiet, thoughtful child, quite introverted and painfully shy with strangers. My teens were not overly happy years and I increasingly felt like an outsider within my family; I didn't feel unloved, but nobody seemed to understand me or what I was going through. I had zero self-confidence and wasn't happy in myself. I know a lot of those feelings I experienced can be accounted for by the changes that take place during puberty, but despite there being some happy times, looking back, the teenage Pam found life a bit grim.

My deep-rooted insecurity probably stems from the circumstances of my birth. There are no photo albums or possessions with a backstory in my family; my mother and her family who had known my biological father didn't ever seem to want to talk about him and were happy to leave those years to obscurity. I naturally grew curious and wanted to know who I was and what was so bad about my father that no one ever spoke about him. If he was that bad, was I, too? What did he look like? Did I look like him? Had he not wanted me? Maybe the reason he was not part of my life, or talked about, was my fault in some way? These were just some of the many questions that would continually pop up in my head as a child and I don't think anyone realised how much of a void the lack of information was leaving deep down within me.

'Mum, why don't we have a photo of my father?' I once asked.

She quickly changed the subject. I would occasionally ask the same question with the same outcome, so it became obvious even to me that he was a topic that was being avoided. Unfortunately, though probably understandably, this only served to fuel my curiosity further and further, though I never pushed the issue much – I was too much of a shrinking violet to do that.

Then one day, in the heat of an argument, my mother said in frustration, 'You are just like him! You have his temper and moods.'

'Who?' I asked.

'Your father.' I could tell she meant this was a bad thing, which I presumed made me a bad person – didn't it?

She wouldn't say any more.

Years later, in my twenties, my mother did acquire and show me a picture of her and my father together. It's a beautiful black-and-white photograph taken before I was born, and they made a handsome couple. As I stared and stared at the image, it shocked me that I looked so much like him; it then started to become a little clearer why my mother had said some of the things she did when angry. At the time she probably hadn't just seen her tearaway teenage daughter in front of her, she may have been seeing echoes of her ex-husband. Far from satisfying my nagging curiosity, seeing the photograph raised more questions about who he was.

Over the years, I tentatively broached the subject with various members of my family, and Mum did tell me a little once she saw I wasn't going to let the matter drop. From her and various other sources I have managed to form a very sketchy story. What is true, and what is not, I am still unclear about, but I have come to the conclusion that I will never know the entire story, so have learnt to live with what I do know.

'You were born on 16 February 1967,' Mum told me. It was a difficult birth for both my mother and me, so it was decided that the delivery team would use the ventouse delivery method. 'Basically, you were sucked out by a Hoover,' she said. Now there's a nice image!

For a large part of my life I thought I had been born in Singapore. My birth certificate, meanwhile, of which I only have an extract rather than the full paper, states 'Registry of birth – Andover'.

Mother went into labour on 13 February and had planned to call me Valentina. No doubt that was the reason I refused to be born until 16 February – and proved a difficult birth!

I arrived in this world with thick black hair covering my entire face. In fact, I was a very hairy baby indeed! My mother would joke, 'I screamed at the sight of you and thought you were a monkey.' Unfortunately, my fragile self-confidence took this joke very much to heart and chose to believe the negative inferences from it.

Because of the difficult birth, Mother was unable to see or hold me for the first few hours of my life, despite her pleading with the medical staff. Perhaps this explains the ill-developed mother–daughter bond? Don't get me wrong, my mother has always loved me, as I do her, but there have been many, many times when we have just seemed unable to communicate or understand each other at all, which has led to fiery exchanges and long periods of silence.

I dug a little deeper and discovered that my biological father, Yogash Tewari, was also known as Peter; he was of Indian origin and a member of the British Army. It was in Fiji that he met, fell in love with and married my mother, herself of Indian ancestry but born and raised in Fiji.

I spent the first years of my life in Singapore, as my father was stationed there in the army. We lived in a large clapboard house with dark blue shutters, just off Orchard Road, which is now the embassy district of the city. I went back to Singapore in my mid-twenties to visit my mother, who had then moved back there with her work, and I managed to track down the house. I was struck by just how lovely it was; it had become a research centre for something or other.

I remember our nanny, who would scoop me up under her arm and feed me with chopsticks from a deep Chinese bowl. It was a rice and chicken 'porridge' dish which I came across again on my return trip, and I remembered the taste so vividly. (I have since learnt how to cook it and it is one of my favourite comfort foods.) I also remember having a pet monkey, a miniature long-tailed macaque called Sheila. She would sit on my shoulder, drape her tail around my neck and squash her bananas into my hair!

My trip down memory lane in Singapore was heightened by the warmth and humidity of the climate. I thought Singapore was lovely, pretty, very, very clean, but too full of shops – shopping is a national pastime there. Personally, I have always loathed browsing in stores – although if you ever need a silk suit for a bargain, I can tell you where to go.

I was also lucky enough to visit the historic Raffles Hotel, which lovingly holds onto its colonial ambience and charm; there, in the bar, you can shell and eat peanuts and throw the waste on the floor – a custom that has been going on for years, leaving the floor completely carpeted with peanut shells, all giving off a lovely smell which is enhanced as you walk and crush them all further. It was there that I developed a taste for the Singapore Sling, a local alcoholic drink which I found, after three of them, reprogrammed my legs to do strange things.

However, there was also an undertone to Singapore that I did not like so much. In a way, it was too clean, the people too well behaved, the rules and regulations too strict and too fully enforced, and the buildings and roads too manicured. I have since visited Malaysia, which is within spitting distance of Singapore, and I much prefer the more real, earthy, genuine lifestyle and atmosphere.

By the time I reached the grand old age of three, my mother and father's relationship had all but broken down. I'm not sure why, but can only surmise it might have been due in part to his family's strict religious beliefs, and to the fact that they were higher-caste Indians, so his marrying my mother was not accept-able to them. Sadder still, I have been told that my father may have developed a drug habit and there is a possibility that he tried to harm both me and my mother.

Regardless of reason, I soon found myself on a plane to London with my mother, and don't recall ever seeing or hearing from my father again. As we fled with hardly any possessions, my mother had to go straight out to work when we arrived in England – there was no welfare state or council housing for immigrants then. Life was certainly not easy for a woman with a child in tow in the early 1970s, and in order to gain work, Mum had no other choice but to lodge me with some friends, an Indian family, in north London. I have such fond memories of this period, and to this day still remember 'Auntie Jubi' and her two teenage sons taking me under their wing and treating me like a little sister – something I had never experienced before.

'Come on, Pam, we'll look after you,' they said. Though that didn't extend to when I wandered into the kitchen one night and saw a rat scuttle across the floor; it terrified me and is the first conscious event I remember which gave me the sick, cold and empty feeling in the pit of my stomach which I have come to know so well whenever I am scared, nervous or upset.

The noise, smell and senses of being in a new (and huge) city were very exciting and at the same time terrifying. I remember feeling happy to have my 'brothers' and being the centre of atten-tion for a while, though I desperately missed my mother.

Mum used to come and visit me every weekend and take me off to her digs to spend time with me, bringing little treats, but she always seemed to be very tired. I know it wasn't her fault, nor was it her ideal living arrangement, as she was working every hour possible, but it was around this time that I began to become very suspicious of the word 'love'. She said she loved me, but as a child I didn't *feel* it. It has left an insecure streak in me that I doubt I will ever lose.

One Saturday she took me to a tall, white Englishman and introduced me.

'Pam, this is Richard. Richard Simms,' she said.

I remember him being kind, gentle and warm towards me; he paid attention to me and listened as I shyly talked about my week.

Mum often brought Richard with her on her weekend visits in the ensuing weeks, and we'd all go out on exciting excursions to places like London Zoo. It began to dawn on me what it might be like to have a father figure in my life. One day Mum said, 'Pam, I have some news. You are going to come and live with me and Richard in a new house in the country. You'd like that, wouldn't you?'

I nodded enthusiastically, though wasn't quite sure what it all meant. I felt sad to leave Jubi and her family but was excited and pleased that I now had my own family to live with. We duly moved into a small end-of-terrace house at the end of an unadopted road in Cookham Dean, Berkshire. At the end of the unmade, pothole-ridden road were rolling green fields. After the bustle of north London, the sight of all this open land and the feel of fresh country air were wonderful.

Richard worked as a statistician for a firm in Slough, so the move was really for him to be close to his work – not that I was complaining. He bought me a lovely ginger tom kitten when we moved in, whom I immediately called Honey. I fell asleep cuddled up to my warm, soft, purring bundle of fur while Mum and Richard moved our few possessions into the new house.

I have great admiration for Richard's parents, my adoptive grandparents. They came from a very different era and a fairly middle-class white environment, with 'certain expectations' for their offspring – which wouldn't have included a divorced 'coloured' woman with a young child from her previous marriage turning up one day, and their son saying, 'This is the woman I want to be with, although we won't be getting married.'

Nowadays that wouldn't mean anything, but back then it must have been a hell of a shock. Marvellously, though I am sure with at least some misgivings, they rose to the news and accepted me and Mum with open arms. Later on, my adoptive grandmother told me that when I arrived on that first day to meet them I was 'a very shy, quiet young lady, who wouldn't say "boo" to a goose' – the polar opposite of my mother, who was extrovert, beautiful, gregarious and very trendy in her miniskirt and knee-length leather boots.

I developed a painfully shy nature. I found that sitting quietly and not making a fuss was the thing to do; either that, or burying my head in a book. I'm still shy today, to a certain extent, especially with people I don't know, and some have mistakenly accused me of being aloof or standoffish. This misconception of me is a problem I still struggle with when meeting people for the first time.

Richard was brilliant as my new 'dad'. He was patient, caring and a great teacher – before I went to school I knew the three Rs and was quite far ahead of my peers. Books became a very important part of my life and Dad was always on hand to take me down to the library once a week, where I would choose and subsequently devour at least four or five volumes. I am still a veritable bookworm and can easily get through an entire book a day if left to my own devices.

I began by enjoying books about myths and legends, as I loved transporting myself into different worlds, although, years later, Dad insisted I balance these with classics such as D. H. Lawrence, Austen, Kipling, Hugo and many more. However, I found I could never get on with Dickens, despite forcing myself to read a few of his stories.

In addition to being well read and intelligent, Dad is also very logical, not that keen on small talk, and, while not a tactile man, he does try to show his affection in other small ways. Mum, on the other hand, is very emotional, affectionate and generous, gets on with anyone she wants to, and is an extremely tactile person, though logic can sometimes go out of the window! Generalisations, I know, but maybe it was their differences that attracted them in the first place.

Not long before my fourth birthday my sister Jane was born. I was not pleased at the time, as I was sent to stay with neighbours the day she arrived, and was no longer alone in being the centre of attention. I was never spoilt, but having a younger sibling that everyone kept cooing over did put my nose out of joint a bit.

I was meanwhile enrolled at the nearby Holy Trinity Church of England School at the beginning of the new school year. To this small child, it was an intimidating establishment, almost gothic-looking, and it was a place where discipline and religion were firmly instilled in all of us. There also seemed to be a never-ending round of prayers, which we had no option but to take part in.

It was here I first became conscious of being a 'coloured' girl. Up until then I had been blissfully unaware of racial prejudice. I was the only coloured person in the school and was often called hurtful names – they say children can be cruel and how right 'they' are. I did make a few friends in my first year, and one of them invited me to her birthday party. It was a hugely exciting occasion, as Mum had dressed me up in a new party frock, fashioned my hair into ringlets and adorned them with ribbons. I waited excitedly at home to be picked up.

'You look so pretty,' Mum said. 'The belle of the ball.'

The minutes ticked by, and my excitement grew; but no one

arrived to collect me. The minutes became an hour and Dad went out to find out what had happened. It transpired that my young friend's parents said they refused to have me in their house 'because she is coloured'.

Dad seemed shell shocked, and in that moment I felt the true pain of racism for the first time. It was no longer just a few ignorant children in the playground saying things, it was grown adults.

I found out from Dad much later, when I was in my thirties, that my biological father had come to England and asked to meet Dad at the airport. Yogash, my father, told Dad he realised that he had no future with Mum and asked Dad to look after and care for me.

'I have never seen someone look so defeated as when he walked away,' said Dad.

On another occasion I remember an Indian lady coming to the house in Cookham dressed in a most magnificent sari of dark purple with gold edging. It turned out she was my father's sister. She visited us once a few years later, by which time we had moved to a new house in Tilehurst, and apparently came with my paternal grandmother, although it was never made clear to me who they were or what relation they were to me. Mum was trying to protect me, in her own way, but all through my first three decades I believed my biological father never wanted to see me.

Schooldays are the happiest days of your life, or so it's said. I didn't enjoy my time at Holy Trinity School one bit and this was really brought home to me when we moved to Tilehurst, near Reading. Dad was still working for the company in Slough and when my grandparents retired and moved to Milford on Sea in Hampshire, Dad bought their house – which has been in the

Simms family since it was built – and it became our new, bigger family home. We always referred to it as '197'.

197 was one of those semi-detached houses built just before the Second World War; it had a gabled front which, from roof to ground, bowed out, covering the lower front room and the top front bedroom. My great-grandparents had bought the house from new and it was situated along a long, tree-lined road in what was considered the 'posh end' of the village. My grand-parents inherited the house and my dad still lives there. Its formal 'front room', which I remember my grandmother referring to as the parlour, and the more laid-back 'family room' at the back are much the same, as is the long back garden planted with apple trees in the top half and vegetables and soft fruit in the bottom part – we were never short of home produce. This is the house I have always considered my childhood home.

I was eight years old when I left Holy Trinity behind and found myself in a much more fun and racially accepting school, Springfield Primary. There was another coloured girl in my year, Angela, and though we were for a while the only children in the school from an ethnic minority, it didn't matter one jot to the other pupils or teachers. Angela and I soon became good friends and as the years passed I developed a small circle of other close girlfriends – boys being too 'yucky' to be friends and still considered a whole other species to be ignored, in the main.

Home life, after the school bell, was pretty strict but not overbearingly. I didn't see my friends out of school apart from occasional birthday parties, nor do I remember being allowed to go to their homes for tea or sleepovers. Both Mum and Dad were working full-time, so Jane and I would return from our schools and go round to the next-door neighbour, a retired schoolteacher, whom we called Auntie Doreen. She was a lovely old lady who had a good way with children, and she was canny too. One of the 'jobs' she got us to do was to crawl along her back lawn cutting the long, thin reeds of grass that looked a bit like tiny bulrushes. For every hundred we cut she would pay us a penny – it was a large lawn and you have no idea how many of those blooming reeds there were. However, we never seemed to make many pennies despite spending hours on our stomachs!

Auntie Doreen also liked to bake and I can still smell the delicious aroma of the hot buns, brandy snaps, cookies, fairy cakes and gingerbread that she made – it makes my mouth water. Once the goodies were cool, we were sat down with a cup of strong tea and one or two of the treats. I think it was Auntie Doreen who first sparked my interest in cooking.

I seemed to spend most of my life anticipating Mum coming to collect me, and would become anxious if she was ever a little bit late. That empty, cold, sick feeling would start knotting in my stomach until I heard her footsteps.

I think a symptom of my insecurity manifested itself when I started biting my fingernails. I would happily nibble away at any part of the nail my teeth could reach, often biting them down until they bled. Mum despaired and tried everything she could think of, including smearing them with mustard and wrapping plasters right around them … but I continued regardless. I eventually stopped in my early teens through pure vanity and the fact that suddenly boys did not seem quite so 'yucky'.

After homework came the small chores. I didn't much like cleaning out the ash from under the fire grate or collecting the lumps of coal from the outside bunker, but I did enjoy scrunching up the newspaper to form the base of the new fire and laying sticks of kindling on top so that the air could get to them to catch. I always felt a small sense of pride watching Dad lighting my fire and it whooshing into life, spreading its warmth into the room.

Dad usually arrived home quite late, as he commuted by train to Slough, and Mum collected him from the station in our one car every evening, daughters and all. As I've mentioned, my mother was (and is) a very beautiful woman, and on one particular evening she was wearing a lovely white halter-neck dress and had her long black hair piled up on top of her head with one thick tress falling down her bare back. She was late for Dad, I remember, and put her foot down. A policeman clocked her speeding and, flashing his lights, gave chase to pull us over. Mum calmly got out of the car and I could see the policeman's jaw drop as he took in this vision of loveliness before him. He let her off without a ticket and we continued on our way. As Mum got back in the car she turned briefly and winked one immaculately made-up eye at me with a cheeky smile on her lips.

I guess we weren't too hard done by, as we were allowed a bit of TV before dinner – which we always sat down as a family to eat – and Dad often bought us a small bag of penny sweets each, from which Jane and I were given a daily allotment; Jane always gobbled hers down whereas I took my time over them. My approach to life hasn't changed much.

I looked forward to weekends with excitement, as it meant a walk down to the library with Dad to stock up on more books; on the way home we'd stop off at a newsagent's for our sweets and a comic each. Dad always raised his eyebrows when I chose the horror ones with tales of Dracula, Frankenstein and lots of blood. I wonder if he thought he might be raising a rather macabre child.

Outside of school, during the holidays, Jane and I spent some of our happiest times together at our grandparents' in Milford on Sea, often staying for a week or two. Milford was full of retired people – in fact, I can't remember seeing very many youngsters at all – and the children I spied seemed to be visiting grandparents, just like us. Nevertheless, I developed a strong fondness for the seaside and loved falling asleep to the sound of the waves crashing onto the pebble beach. Even now I sometimes take a day off just to rush back to Milford to recapture that feeling of total peace. Our time there was idyllic: Grandma taught us both to knit until we became proficient enough to purl and cast off our way to rather wiggly-looking scarves and gloves; Gramps showed us how to play 'Pooh Sticks' from the little bridge that crossed a stream on the walk into the village, and you'd see us tearing across to the other side to see whose stick would reappear first. We seemed to spend most of our time outdoors, either at the beach or in the forest, though if it was wet we'd play Scrabble, chess or card games. The sea air always made me ravenous, and the summers seemed full of sandwiches and salads, biscuits and cake.

One thing Mum always hated when we went to Grandma's was that, as an ex-hairdresser, my grandmother couldn't resist plonking a bowl over our long, straight hair (Mum liked us having long hair so she could put it up into ponytails or bunches) and literally cut around it so we returned home looking like two small page boys. I still recall the look of exasperation in Mum's eyes every time she picked us up.

Back at home, although never being aware of being poor, I remember money was always tight. Mum often made some of our clothes and we were always dressed in exactly the same outfits, just like twins, and our hair would be done the same way, too. Holidays with Mum and Dad were invariably camping expeditions, and with the typical British weather we were often cold, uncomfortable and damp – no wonder I have hated camping ever since.

On one trip to another favourite destination, Robin Hood's Bay near Scarborough, I showed off my first entrepreneurial skills by collecting pretty stones from the beach and setting about smoothing, polishing and varnishing them. I built a little show tray – similar to the ones usherettes used to have in cinemas for selling ice creams – priced up each stone and prepared myself to hit the street to try my hand at selling them. I was quite miffed when Dad then put a stop to my little enterprise.

Home life was never dull as Mum continually took in waifs and strays – usually friends who had fallen on bad times, were separating from spouses, or just needed sanctuary for a while. Many was the time I'd walk into the living room in the morning to find a sound-asleep body in a sleeping bag. It became the norm and we girls just took it in our stride.

As well as books, Dad introduced us to music, too. He insisted we learn to read sheet music and take up a musical instrument – descant recorders at this time – and plunged us into the wide world of classical music: Mozart, Beethoven, Handel, Holst, Vivaldi ... before he tried us on classical jazz. I've never been keen on it, and prefer contemporary jazz if I have to listen to anything, particularly as I'd discovered pop, rock, funk and Motown by then. Dad forever held his head in his hands as the bass pounded through the floors at home!

I developed quite an eclectic taste in music and used it to either reflect or alter my mood, to calm myself down or gee myself up. It's proven to be a very important part of my life. That's one of the ways in which the crash was so cruel to me: afterwards I discovered I couldn't concentrate long enough to read a book or a newspaper, and any form of music just jangled my nerves, making me agitated, even physically unwell. For a few years post-crash I was bereft of both books and music, and felt as though a huge part of my 'normal' life was missing. There are still times, even now, when I go through phases of not being able to listen to music – a sign all is not well with me – but, happily, I'm usually soon back to dancing around to the Who, Scissor Sisters, the Rolling Stones, Ricky Martin or Michael Jackson!

Richard was now, as far as I was concerned, my dad, though he and Mum were still not married, which was frowned upon by a lot of the other parents at school. However, soon after our move to Tilehurst he said he wanted to make things more permanent between us: 'Pam, how would you feel about me becoming your dad, officially … about me adopting you?' he asked. It sounded like a good idea, and the papers were filed.

It was customary back then for the child involved to speak directly to the judge at the adoption hearing. Dad explained that the judge would ask me a couple of questions, but it was nothing to be worried or fearful about. We duly arrived at Reading Civil Court and were escorted into a large room where a man sat behind what seemed like a huge desk.

'Hello, Pam,' he greeted me. 'I am Judge So-and-so.'

I stood shy and tight-lipped.

'Is there anything wrong?' he asked.

'Where's your wig?' I responded.

'Pardon?'

'I said, "Where is your wig?" You can't be a proper judge if you haven't got a wig!'

I might have been shy but when pushed would speak my mind. He chuckled, reached down into his desk and produced his white headpiece, which satisfied this young eight-year-old Perry Mason, and I answered his questions.

It wasn't until a few years later that Richard and Mum finally married, though sadly I don't have any memories of their wedding day. It was a civil ceremony and as it was 'a school day' both my sister Jane and I had to miss the ceremony. Being an A-grade student, my attendance in class was deemed more important.

Admittedly, I was very happy during my years at Springfield Primary, and easily passed tests. The kind and approachable head teacher, Mr Tutton, always seemed to take an active interest in me academically, and one day he took me, with a few select others, out to the other side of the school and to a mysterious door which I'd passed many times without knowing what was behind it. He unlocked it and showed us into a photography darkroom. It was like entering Aladdin's cave! There were photos hanging from string and strange bottles lined along the walls, and the bench had trays on it with weird, very smelly, chemicals.

Photography became the lucky lesson that I and the others were allowed to take up, as a reward for being top students. We learnt everything from how to take pictures to how to develop negatives, and all about 'fixing' the photos and hanging them to dry. It was fascinating and I loved the feeling of being closeted in that darkroom, with the red light on, turning clicks on a camera into finished glossy prints.

As you'll have gathered, everything in my little garden of life was rosy and set for the future. Or so it seemed…

Being an A-grade student meant I was put forward for Kendrick School, a secondary school for girls with a terrific reputation and academic record.

But I was at that age when it was so important to be with my friends and I, of course, wanted to go with the majority of them to Little Heath Comprehensive in Tilehurst. I persuaded, or rather wore down, my parents into agreeing to let me go there, despite them feeling it was a bit of a 'rough' school. I was nothing if not headstrong, and perhaps a little stubborn.

However, some bright spark in the education system decided it would be a good idea to mix the top students with the bottom students, with the intention that the A-graders would encourage the others to strive to achieve better results. The class I was placed in, Arundel 1, had some of the very worst students from the whole year and rather than all of us achieving a higher overall class average, the experiment backfired and the higher-performing students were dragged down to a much lower grade. You see, peer pressure is such that when others laugh at you, calling you a 'square', it's difficult to fight back and win ... so I thought, if you can't beat them, join them. It's funny, though: when some of them struggled with homework or couldn't get their heads around a particular topic, they were very quick to find me for help. Luckily, this meant I was never really bullied or picked on.

As though being a square wasn't bad enough, I had the added painful experience of having to wear NHS plastic glasses, flared skirts and sensible Clarks shoes – quite contrary to what the other fashion-conscious pubescent teenagers were sporting. As the years passed, and hormones started zipping around my body, my image, attitude and desire to be accepted by my peers at Little Heath changed dramatically as its environment worked its influence on me. I began feeling I was put upon at home as I was still not allowed out with my friends after school, and had an increasing number of chores, including taking on the cooking, keeping an eye on Jane, doing more of the housework – necessary as Mum and Dad both continued to work full-time. Mum also took on other work involving helping people with mental illness by way of therapy and mentoring, so spent even less time with us kids. Meanwhile, they introduced a very strict homework regime, with a minimum of two hours each evening and, being their 'sensible girl', I was continually asked to do more and more, while spending less and less time doing things other girls my age were doing. To this angst-ridden teenager, life seemed 'all work and no play' and I had no fun to counterbalance the workloads of school and my domestic responsibilities: I was not allowed to attend school discos, I was not allowed to hang out at friends' houses, and I was certainly not allowed to date boys. Though they did relent slightly and allow me to attend a youth club once a week which was run by a social worker, but only after they had checked and interviewed the organiser! Quite honestly, there appeared to be nothing to look forward to that might have made the mundane aspects of my teens more bearable.

Boys had by then also started becoming far more interesting to me but, of course, my appearance and geeky reputation meant my interest mostly went unacknowledged, or at least unreciprocated. There was one boy in my class of Irish descent who had lovely tousled black hair and bright blue eyes; he was athletically built, very white-skinned with the cutest freckles, and was one of the most popular members of our year. Oh, how I fancied him! I'd often sigh over him from a distance, never daring to say anything to him. Of course he never noticed me, but I carried a torch for him throughout my whole secondary-school stay. I still have a propensity for men of Celtic origin.

I've already mentioned how Dad insisted I learn a musical instrument at junior school. Well, I started off on the descant recorder and, as I grew older, moved onto the tenor recorder, then the oboe, before I tried the saxophone. Now, at secondary school, Dad was keen I continue and learn yet another, but my interest was waning. Keen not to disobey his well-meant wishes, *I know*, I thought, *I'll tell Dad I want to play the drums*, believing it would fox him.

But he called my bluff! The next thing I knew he'd arranged drum lessons, bought me a second-hand set and encouraged me to play and practise whenever I could – much to the distress of the neighbours. I thoroughly enjoyed the drums, though, and became pretty good on them, even bashing away for a school group in my teens for a while. The only problem was my shyness.

I hated being seen on stage, so the guys in the band came up with the idea of brushing my long hair forwards over my face whenever we played – all you saw were drumsticks sticking out of a mane of hair. They soon started calling me 'Animal', after the *Muppets* character.

My shyness wasn't helped in any way when, one day when I was about thirteen and I was walking home from school, which was just over a mile away from our home, I had only a few hundred yards more to go when I passed a group of young lads who were batting small stones into the road with a baseball bat. I didn't recognise them from school so quickened my pace, but heard them whispering as I passed. The next thing I knew they were closely following me along the road, with the leader swinging the baseball bat and smacking it into the palm of his hand – I legged it! They ran after me, waving the bat around and shouting 'Bash the Paki!', but thankfully I was pretty athletic and managed to outrun them. It was probably the only time I was glad to be wearing my sensible Clarks shoes rather than the fashionable ones my friends favoured.

I was pretty shaken by the whole experience and wondered what might have happened had I not taken to my heels so swiftly. Mum asked me why I was panting when I got home and when I blurted it out she jumped in the car and rushed off looking for the boys – luckily for them she didn't find them! By the time she returned I'd been through various thought processes and decided on my action plan: 'Let's just forget about it and move on.'

In subsequent years I coped with being called a 'nig-nog' and 'Paki cow' and – my particular favourite – being told, 'Why don't you go back to where you came from?' to which my reply was, 'OK, if you like – I'm English so I am where you want me to be.'

Relatively recently, I was talking to someone in my local pub and they started making derogatory comments about some of his darker-skinned colleagues. When I quietly pointed out he was being racist and I was the same ethnicity as some of the colleagues he was talking about, he said, 'Yes, but you're different. I don't think of you as black or Asian; you're just a nice coffee colour.' Needless to say, I excused myself and have not spoken to him since that day.

When I was fourteen, my parents were kind enough to pay for me to go on a school skiing trip to Foppolo, Italy. It was my first holiday abroad without my family and I loved the experience, not just because they were not around but for the excitement of visiting a new country, seeing the unusual scenery, trying the local food and struggling with the language barrier – it gave me a taste of what life might be like with more independence, and what was awaiting me in different countries if I were to explore more. Getting away from home also prompted us all to get to know our fellow pupils better; we got talking to each other as individuals and worked things out for ourselves, with a strong team spirit pervading our group. New friendships were formed and understandings reached which I don't think would ever have been possible back at home.

Happily, I took to skiing like a duck to water and, seeing my enthusiasm, my parents were kind enough to pay for a couple more trips. I soon picked up the name 'Kamikaze', as once I'd mastered the snow plough, been taught parallel skiing and could stop elegantly I was off, bombing down the mountain as fast as I could. Though, in my cockiness, I accidentally managed to ski right over some other guy's skis and duly snapped them in half, meaning a long trudge back down the mountain for him, for which I was very sorry but nevertheless found incredibly funny. On another trip I was silly enough to follow one of my fellow school pupils, Giovanni, who decided to take the 'black' run, which only experienced skiers were meant to attempt. We raced down, whooping all the way, until we saw that the slope in front of us was actually a jump which we had no way of avoiding. With a tandem scream of 'Shiiiiit!' we both shot over the jump, into the air with poles flailing, and landed in an undignified heap at the bottom. Luckily, without anything broken, we became legends with the rest of the group for the remainder of the week.

With a taste of greater independence, aged about fifteen, I decided to get a part-time job to earn a bit of money for myself. Mum, however, flatly refused to let me get any sort of work, and insisted that it would only detract from my studies. After a great deal of persuasion from Dad, who did see the benefits in my learning the work ethic, she relented a little but would only allow me to take on a cleaning job at the school – after school, on school premises, cleaning the classrooms I spent most of my days in. It wasn't quite what I'd had in mind but I knuckled down to it nevertheless and it gave me the spending money I craved – if not an independent personal identity.

The year before, aged fourteen, we'd all visited my mother's family in Vancouver, and I saw first-hand how my cousins had been brought up in a more traditional 'Indian' way: they were far more suppliant, quiet and prepared to follow their parents' wishes without question. Jane and I were much more Westernised and therefore more of a handful for our parents. A traditional Indian daughter had the role models of the older women who did not have careers and whose sole purpose was to tend, cook and care for their family. My role model was my mother, who by this time had become an extremely successful career woman, highly thought of by her colleagues – and you don't achieve that by being submissive.

However, Mum's hopes and expectations for me were poles apart from my own. She wanted me to concentrate on getting into university and I think may have liked me to become a doctor or lawyer, whereas I had no idea what I wanted to be but felt I was missing out on fun. Frustration, anxiety, awkwardness, rebellion and those hormones were a heady mixture; something had to give and that something turned out to be me – big time. My poor parents must have wondered what had hit them as this whirling dervish of a daughter tore through their home, telling them what was what: 'I've had enough of this. My life is so unfair. I'm not interested in being controlled by you anymore. I'm a free person, a free spirit. I'm a grown-up!' I shouted.

Alas, when you become a parent no one gives you a manual telling you how to deal with a raging teenager. Mum and Dad had no experience of an elder child, so sat dumbfounded and rather angry. They tried to win me back over by getting me another kitten – a little black kitten with piercing blue eyes which never changed as he grew older – as they knew I loved animals. But their ploy didn't work and Dad ended up looking after him most of the time, even naming him – Mingus, after the jazz musician Charlie Mingus. So was born a family tradition for naming pets after jazz players and singers that continues to this day.

I, meanwhile, was a truly horrible rebel. At home I skulked in my room, which I had decorated in dark colours. I didn't care about school and my grades slipped drastically. I was no longer a 'square' and instead became a ghetto-blaster-carrying, rivet-belt-and-hat-wearing would-be ghetto chick. Oh yes, I was one of the coolest girls in the school.

My sister, Jane, followed me to Little Heath Comprehensive around this time, but as I was four years above her in the school we didn't have much to do with each other; an age gap like that is like a chasm at that age. One day she sought out her big sister to tell me she was being bullied by one of the girls in her year. As I walked home with Jane that afternoon she pointed out the girl in question. I walked up to her and, even though I was diminutive in stature and the girl towered above me, I snarled: 'I don't know who you think you are,' as I jabbed my finger into her chest, 'but if I catch you ever bullying my sister again, you will make me extremely angry, and you won't like me when I'm angry.'

I think I had pinched the line from the *Incredible Hulk* series. I don't know whether it was the words, the anger that was showing on my face or the fact that I was older, and an older pupil could make a younger pupil's life hell at school back then, but she blanched, lost the cocky look on her face and scuttled away. Jane had no more problems with her after that time and for a while I was her hero.

Oh, another of Jane's classmates was a sweet, fair-haired little girl named Karen. Some years later, Karen married a young man named Michael Hodder. Michael became a train driver...

CHAPTER 5

ADOLESCENCE INTO ADULTHOOD

Aged fifteen, but going on twenty-five, much against my parents' wishes I started going out after school with my friends, though in fairness I did try to observe the curfew they later applied. I started lying about where I was going because I thought it would be easier than telling the truth and running the gauntlet of my parents' disapproval. However, they kept on catching me out, which sparked arguments.

For one such outing, I and one of my girlfriends decided to visit the family planning clinic to acquire a supply of 'the Pill'. How grown-up and sensible we thought we were! It was not that we were planning to sleep around – neither of us even had boyfriends – but we did know a couple of girls in our year who were pregnant and we didn't want to get caught out should 'something happen'. For us it was more of a rite of passage in that we were moving away from being mere girls and were metamorphosing into women.

HIV/Aids was a new disease that was attracting more and more attention. The government ran advertising campaigns featuring a rather scary gravestone, illustrating that there was no cure and you would die if you got Aids. There were many myths circulating about how you could catch the virus, and one of my more effeminate male friends at school was coming in for a lot of stick; I became so incensed with some of the behaviour towards him that, with the help of one of my teachers, I obtained explanatory pamphlets from an STD clinic which pointed out that you could not catch it from touching, drinking from the same water fountain, or breathing the same air as a homosexual man, and distributed them around the school. The Aids campaign did curb my curiosity as to what sex might be like, though.

Meanwhile, arguments with my parents were becoming commonplace, mainly based on them trying to enforce their rules and, quite rightly, trying to get me to refocus on my education. Mum and I just ended up shouting at each other while Dad stood back; when he did become involved, he would take me into the quiet front room and give me an icy look, before passing sentence as to what my punishment would be. Somehow, Dad's way of telling me off frightened me more than Mum shouting at me.

I found arguing with Mum highly emotional and exasperating; neither of us listened to the other and I was not very adept at getting my point across well. I desperately wanted and needed her help, understanding and guidance at this stage in my life but, at least as I saw it, I seemed unable to get it.

I always came away from our encounters shattered, downcast and in such emotional pain that even today I hate arguing and avoid it wherever and whenever possible.

Sadly – and some of it may have been down to my shenanigans – Mum and Dad were growing apart. Dad followed his own interests and hobbies and Mum followed hers. The only interests they seemed to have left in common were Jane and me.

Around this time I remember a school friend of mine, Matthew, learning to ride a 125cc motorbike, the one that makes that high-pitched 'eeeee' sound as it drives along. He had just graduated to a 500cc bike and called for me at home to show off his new acquisition, offering to take me out pillion for a test drive. Matthew was a thin, lean, lanky lad with no muscle on him that could be seen; the bike looked huge next to him, and I have to admit I chickened out and refused to go on it. Only a short time later Matthew was killed, having lost control, come off his bike and broken his neck – he was only sixteen. I was distraught. It was the first time I had ever had to deal with the death of someone I knew and I had no idea how to handle the grief. I wandered down into the kitchen and Dad asked me what was wrong. A few years earlier he had lost his elder brother, my uncle David, who had died in his early forties. I am not entirely sure what happened or how it happened but it had obviously affected Dad very much, and though he never spoke about it, I was aware that he was still extremely upset about his brother. We had a quiet chat where I talked through my feelings about Matthew's death and the waste it was, and for the first time ever he spoke about David's death and his feelings. It helped me hugely to come to terms with what had happened.

I was entered for ten O levels in my final year and struggled through, somehow managing to pass five of them. I didn't particularly care one way or the other. I had my mind on far more interesting things, such as meeting my first boyfriend, John.

I was hanging out with one of my girlfriends whose house conveniently backed onto a pub, and although we had only just turned sixteen we sometimes waltzed in, with a confidence that suggested we were old enough to be there, and ordered drinks. I don't know whether the landlord just turned a blind eye, or perhaps we looked mature for our tender years? But if underage drinking wasn't bad enough, I also took up smoking.

'Come on, Pam, try this, it's so cool,' my trendy friends would say.

To this day, I am continually trying to kick the habit, recently with more success, but I curse the day I started this merry-go-round of addiction.

Anyhow, one evening in the pub I saw a guy across the bar. He was in his twenties, I guess. I smiled at him, he smiled at me, we started chatting and he introduced himself as John. I have never at any point in my life considered myself an attractive girl or woman; if a guy starts talking to me, I simply assume they are being friendly. This may have something to do with me accidently overhearing, years before, Mum saying, 'Yes, Jane is my beautiful girl. Pam is more of a plain Jane but she is clever.'

I made no bones about still being at school, but John treated me as an equal and didn't talk down to me, which was a huge attraction, especially as he was working, had a bit of spare cash, owned a car and – to this impressionable teenager – appeared oh so very, very worldly wise.

I lost my virginity to John. Far from it being a huge earth-moving moment, it was a furtive, short-lived event which hurt like hell and was generally a bit disappointing. I couldn't see what the big deal was about sex.

My parents despaired when they found out I was seeing an older boy, though, of course, they didn't know about me sleeping with him – they would certainly have locked me away for good! Neither of them could understand why a twenty-something wanted to date a sixteen-year-old girl and, to be fair, in hindsight, neither can I.

It won't surprise you to discover that our relationship didn't last very long. After we slept together that once, he seemed less and less interested in spending time with me. I guess it's that old cliché: *Give a man what he wants and you'll never see him again.*

My parents had been in vehement opposition to me over my relationship with John and, after we split, all but threatened to ground me for life to save me repeating it, with Mum lecturing me about 'throwing your life away' and how 'he just wants to get into your knickers'.

'Yes, Mum,' I said innocently. She was right, of course, but I wasn't about to admit it.

In an attempt to placate them I agreed to return to school, albeit reluctantly, in the autumn term of 1983 to study for A levels. But I found the lessons boring and the routine stifling and decided further education held no interest for me. After just two months, I walked out. I knew if I told my parents they would explode. I certainly didn't need any more grief so I concealed my truancy for three months. Each morning I left home at the usual time, and each afternoon I returned home at the same time.

'How was school today, Pam?' Mum would ask.

'Oh, OK.'

'Any homework?' Dad would say.

'No, I did it in my free period,' I would lie.

Instead of going to school I went to another girlfriend's house, where we listened to music and hung out, drinking and smoking. It was just as boring as being at school but I had no direction, though still desperately wanted to continue being accepted by the 'cool' crowd.

I had no money of my own to pay for things, as I'd given up the part-time cleaning job I used to do, because 'cool' kids did not do cleaning, so, to my eternal shame, I began stealing from my mother's purse. At first it was only a pound or two but my habit then developed into £5 each time. I never spent the money on myself – no, I used it to buy things for my friends. I'm sure a psychiatrist would have much to say about me being insecure and wanting to buy friendship and, while probably true to a certain extent, I also think it was me genuinely wanting to treat people and make them smile. However, I should have waited until I had money of my own.

Maybe my turning over a new leaf at home aroused Mum's suspicions. Whatever it was, in one fell swoop she discovered I had been stealing from her, had left school, and that I was taking the Pill – which, of course, convinced her I was sleeping around.

She was furious and we had another blazing argument. All sorts of names and accusations were bandied around, on both sides, and I remained adamant I knew what was best for me – just as every other sixteen-year-old does. It all became too much for my mother to cope with.

'I've had enough,' she shouted. 'Either you leave this house or I will.'

I packed a bag and walked out. I was a sixteen-year-old child trying to emerge into adulthood and, yes, I got many, many, many things wrong. Though I'm certain I am not the only sixteen-year-old who has gone off the rails, nor will I be the last, I am deeply sorry for the heartache and anguish I caused my mum and dad. These difficulties during my teenage years were to have a profound effect on me and my relationship with my parents, until the train crash, really. I would deliberately avoid having much to do with them throughout my twenties and as my career began to blossom it was easier to put that before either them or my sister. Gosh, I could kick myself for being so petty and selfish for such a long period of time.

But back then, when I was still sixteen, with my mother's voice still ringing in my ears and a bag of possessions clutched in my hand, I marched off to the nearest telephone kiosk to call an old family friend, Kim.

Kim had lived with us for a little while – just as I had lived with Auntie Jubi – when she had first arrived in Reading. She was a beautiful West Indian woman in her early twenties, blessed with a superb singing voice, and we got to know each other well, with her even becoming a confidante to Jane and me, listening intently to our girlie secrets, offering advice and being a friend. I looked up to her like an older sister. Kim was then living in a rented house in Reading with her boyfriend and I persuaded her to let me rent a room from them. When I say 'rent', I had fully intended to pay my way, though at the time had no means of doing so. After a couple of days, thinking tensions might have calmed, Kim suggested I speak to Mum. I refused point-blank, and had no contact with her or the rest of my family for a very long time.

'She doesn't care about me,' I said to Kim, 'she only cares about herself.'

Unbeknown to me, however, even when I began paying a nominal rent for the room I was staying in, Mum was in regular contact with Kim, making sure I was OK and paying her some more rent and food money.

My tears soon dried when I moved into Kim's house. I was a sixteen-year-old independent woman renting my own accommodation and striding out into the big, wide, exciting world. I felt ever so grown-up despite having very little idea about fending for myself – but that didn't concern me one iota. My first port of call was the job centre; while I didn't have many formal qualifications, I considered myself quite smart and applied for a number of administrative jobs. The first two turned me down, but at the third interview I was offered the post of receptionist at a seating renovation company in Reading.

I worked hard and played hard, and topped up my social skills by meeting up with a few friends in the pub after work. One night, after a couple of my then usual tipple, Pernod and black, this guy, Sean, who had very dark hair and a black moustache, came in with a friend of his who was blond-haired with blue eyes. I said to one of my girlfriends, 'God, he's gorgeous.'

'Who?' she asked.

'The blond guy,' I replied.

We all got chatting and the boys offered to walk us home; my cute Blondie walked with me, and Sean with my friend. Then Blondie stopped near a shop doorway and grabbed my arm –

not to drag me in for an anticipated kiss but to hold onto as he vomited everywhere. My girlfriend dashed over and started fussing over him, while Sean and I were left squirming and trying not to look at the horrible puddle below. Sean and I decided to walk ahead, and when we started chatting it became clear there was a mutual attraction between us.

Just like my first boyfriend, Sean was older than me – he was twenty-three – and a former skinhead, who had since regained his hair and also lost the prejudiced views associated with his former image. Whatever he may have thought or whatever racist views he may have held in the past, he had obviously grown up and out of them. In fact, he was a very kind and gentle man, a sheet metal worker by trade, and in a very short space of time he seemed to become completely besotted with me.

I liked the attention he showed me, and I enjoyed his company. He made me laugh and he seemed to have a smile on his face all the time. He appeared to be very much at ease with himself, which was something I envied, and I wanted to be in his company every spare minute; I always looked forward to seeing him, with slight butterflies in my stomach. Yes, I think it was love, but perhaps a slightly immature love.

Some of his friends, who also frequented the same pub, were a different matter, as they hung onto their racist views and opinions, and only grudgingly tolerated me being around. But, over time, I believe they came to see that there was no difference between us and appreciated that I could be funny and intelligent and was not intimidated by them, and by the time Sean and I parted I genuinely felt that I might have changed some of their bigoted views.

Sean started visiting me at Kim's house most evenings. Unfortunately, when you are sixteen and 'in love' you are so selfish and exist within your own bubble, and while I paid every attention to Sean, I'm afraid I paid little thought to Kim or how Sean's presence might be encroaching on her time in her own home. Nor did I think about how it might affect my work: too many Pernods combined with late nights were not conducive to holding down a day job and I began to turn up late and throw the occasional 'sickie'.

Ironically, I enjoyed my job and the family who ran the firm were friendly, kind and good employers. What's more, they seemed to like me too. The only downside was the repetitious and boring reception work! I acquired basic bookkeeping skills, but I got through the work they gave me so quickly that there was never enough to fill the whole day.

'Pam, would you come into my office, please?' said the head of the company one afternoon. He was a man in his early sixties who took care of himself and his appearance, but he was no George Clooney.

'Come over here,' he beckoned, 'and sit on my lap.'

I was still only sixteen and not quite sure what to do. Naively, if somewhat reluctantly, I walked over and perched lightly on the very end of his knee. He tried to put his head on my chest but I pulled away sharply. Then, like some bizarre *Tom and Jerry* cartoon, he started chasing me around the desk. Luckily, I was a faster runner than him.

I was shaken and complained to my manager but it became obvious where his loyalties lay, and I was told off for my bad timekeeping and taking days off sick, and told I had an 'attitude' regarding the boring jobs I was asked to do. In the end, I knew work would never be the same again and was faced with no option but to leave.

Tensions started running high at home, too, as Kim grew frustrated with Sean always being around and, to add to her woes, I was now unemployed. I knew I couldn't keep up with the rent, but Kim didn't volunteer that my mother was actually paying it. I discussed it with Sean and he said we should find our own place together. We'd only been seeing each other for a few months, but nevertheless I agreed. When you are young and think you are in love you really don't think about the practicalities of your decisions, do you?

With a little state assistance we moved into a bedsit in George Street, Reading, which was quite frankly a hovel: one small, freezing, damp room in an old Victorian terrace devoid of any double glazing or insulation, with only a tiny one-bar electric fire for heat. I remember we bought rolls of cellophane to pin up over the windows to stop some of the draughts whistling through the gaps in the frames.

A family lived above us and we shared the kitchen and bathroom with them. They, unfortunately, owned a big Alsatian dog which was not at all house-trained and heaven forbid you made a dash to the bathroom in bare feet during the night is all I can say.

The road we moved into was a little scary, as it was frequented by drug users and dealers. Its pavements were also an open toilet for the local wildlife and not all were the four-legged Alsatian variety!

I was continually cold in that room, felt dirty all the time and never had the feeling of being particularly safe. Fortunately, we got to know some of the road's nicer inhabitants, one of whom mentioned he had bought the house across the road and asked if we'd like to move into a room there. It was still only a single room but it was palatial in comparison.

Still unemployed, I didn't really know what I wanted to do with my life and for three months, despite my best efforts of scouring the job vacancies pages, was without work. I lay around reading some Tolstoy, Dostoevsky and Shakespeare, authors Dad had pointed me in the direction of, as well as plenty of murder mysteries and historical novels, and listening to the likes of Soft

Cell, Talking Heads and Bryan Ferry. It was the one and only time I have ever been unemployed and had to claim unemployment benefit. The memory of the weekly trip to the benefits office to sign on, joining the long queues and feeling the human despair emanating from the pores of my fellow claimants, is one that still makes me shudder.

Money was hard to come by and we lived very much hand to mouth. After paying the rent and bills there was very little of Sean's wages or my benefit money left for food: I learnt rapidly how to cook cheap mince one hundred and one different ways and came up with a style of cooking that worked on the premise of *If it has not gone off, chuck it in the pot and see what happens.*

As the days, weeks and months passed Sean broached the subject of my mother. He knew we'd fallen out spectacularly but, believing time was a great healer, persuaded me that I ought to try to talk to her. He was a sensitive and caring soul and having come from a close family himself, he made me realise how important family should be. I hadn't seen my sister, Jane, for ages, and missed her terribly.

I knew it would be a difficult call to make but I screwed up my courage, trotted down to the street's only phone box and dialled… Fortunately, Mum didn't judge or castigate me, she just seemed genuinely pleased to hear from me. I told her about Sean, that we had a bedsit and were only a few miles away. She didn't seem too surprised, as I later discovered Kim had been keeping her in touch with what was happening with me, and we chatted a few times after that, until at Christmas Mum suddenly arrived at the bedsit and presented me with a really lovely grey woollen suit. Tensions between us began to thaw.

I was about to turn seventeen when a dose of reality hit me – or maybe it was me finally growing up and accepting responsibility for my actions? Whatever it was, I woke up one morning, took a long, hard look at myself in the mirror and the environment around me, and thought, *Come on, Pam, you're bigger and better than this.* It's a motto I have tried to use throughout my life since. I pulled myself up, dressed smartly in my grey suit and marched off to the job centre, single-minded in my determination to secure an interview; I didn't care what the job was, or how much it paid, I just wanted to be employed and off the dole queue. I duly lined myself up for a meeting with a small local firm of solicitors who were looking for a receptionist. I wore the only other smart clothes I possessed for the interview (determined not to wear the same outfit twice!) – my old school uniform – and turned up on time, eager and full of enthusiasm.

Something obviously worked in my favour, and they seemed to like me, immediately offering me the job. Better still, they soon recognised some potential in me, along with my having a modicum of common sense, and one of the firm's partners took me under his wing and started to train me as a legal clerk. It was interesting work, which left me with no fear of ever being bored – I loved it!

No two days were the same. I was running all over the place as the general factotum, and was involved in everything from divorce hearings to criminal trials, and even an intriguing visit inside HM Prison Reading to see one of my boss's clients – that was eerie and terrifying, but it fascinated me. I learnt a lot from watching, listening and generally just paying attention: the clients all had a different story to tell and all needed our help. However, no matter how rewarding I found the work, the financial reality of Sean's and my situation was a pressing one and, alas, the small law firm was unable to pay very much. They understood completely why I was considering moving on and provided a glowing reference, and I took another receptionist post, this time at a life insurance company which, in comparison, offered a handsome salary.

My life was about to be transformed forever.

As I've mentioned, I started work at the Scottish Life Assurance Company in 1984 at the age of seventeen. I guess it was about six months later, after I had turned eighteen, when I first saw Scott MacKay in the office, with his comical bouncy walk, and I was immediately attracted to him. Scott had relocated from our head office in Edinburgh; he was a tall, athletically built, blond-haired, blue-eyed, gorgeous-looking Scotsman and was nearly seven years older than me. His Scottish accent had a beautiful lilt, typical of Edinburgh, and made me quite weak at the knees – my fondness for the Celts!

'Nice tan. Have you just been on holiday?' he asked me in all seriousness in the coffee room.

I looked at him quizzically, licked my finger and rubbed it on the skin of my forearm. 'It's permanent,' I replied.

There was an embarrassing momentary silence which was soon shattered when we both broke into a fit of laughter. Scott told me he came from Leith, on the outskirts of Edinburgh, and that he'd worked his way up through the company and had moved to Reading for a promotion, but didn't know anyone.

'Well, you know me now!' I laughed.

I suppose it was the difference in our backgrounds that interested me at first – well, that, as well as his looks and his sexy, melodic Scottish accent. But it was also quite exciting getting to know and becoming friends with a 24-year-old successful businessman, a man who seemed to be heading places. Scott made it obvious that he was interested in our friendship 'becoming more' too.

I wasn't sure what to do next: I knew Sean would do anything for me, but in my heart of hearts I also knew we didn't have a future together. For some time I had known I wasn't in love with him, I was just fond of him. I felt I'd travelled a long way in two years, whereas I'm not sure Sean was any different than when we'd met. I'd grown up, and we'd grown apart. I wanted to work hard, achieve goals and have a successful career; Sean seemed happy with things staying as they were.

Sean came to one of my company's pub gatherings after work, and had absolutely no conversation with my colleagues as he felt he had 'nothing in common with them'. My colleagues tried to include him, but he became visibly uncomfortable and I ended up suggesting that we just go home. He never wanted to meet any of my friends after that.

I knew I couldn't continue living with Sean but I didn't want to hurt him. I thought about all the ways I could end our relationship – some cowardly, some even unfair or nasty – but felt I owed Sean the truth. I gently sat him down and explained it was time for both of us to move on. I was crying, and he became so upset, but there was nothing else I could do if I was to be true to myself and truthful with him. I sincerely hope Sean understood that I acted not from malice, but from the heart.

I packed my things and returned to live with my parents. They were delighted to welcome me back, and while I knew they never really approved of Sean I'm grateful they at least tried to understand my feelings and were considerate about our break-up. I never saw Sean again, but in recent years I have often said to Mum and my sister that if I ever met a man now as kind, loving and gentle as Sean was, I would count myself a lucky woman.

Scott and I started dating and he invited me up to Edinburgh to stay with his friends for New Year's Eve and to meet his parents. It was my first ever Hogmanay and it's since become my favourite part of the festive season!

Scott took me 'first-footing', where we visited various friends and neighbours immediately after midnight, taking a lump of coal with us; they, in turn, plied us with good Scottish whisky. We got happily and marvellously drunk and when it then started snowing everything took on an almost magical, surreal quality. I remember standing under an old-fashioned lamp post with the falling snowflakes lit up by the yellow halo from its light, and all sound around us was muted – much like the scene from *The Lion, the Witch and the Wardrobe* when the faun, Tumnus, is first introduced standing under a lamp post in the snow.

From beginning to end my relationship with Scott was always very tempestuous: we both had fiery tempers and passionate natures and were both very strong-willed. I have lost count of the number of times we broke up and then got back together again, but despite, or even because of, our volatile combination of tempers I fell very much in love with him. To me, he was an Adonis who made me laugh and cry in equal measure. I think he was in love with me too, even if my emotional temperament sometimes drove him to distraction. Neither of us was perfect, that's for sure.

Within nine months I left my parents' and Scott and I bought and moved into a two-bedroom flat in the Southcote area of Reading. It was the first home I'd ever owned and I became terribly house-proud.

Despite our ups and downs we had a good life; Scott did well as a senior pensions adviser at the insurance company and earned decent bonuses, which paid for wonderful luxuries such as restaurant meals and holidays. This was the time when I also moved on from being a receptionist to being assistant to Nick, one of the life insurance sales consultants.

One of our first holidays together was a trip around the Scottish Highlands. Scott was keen to show me how beautiful the countryside was further north of Edinburgh. We travelled by car and stayed in B&Bs along the way, visiting Drumnadrochit and the Kyle of Lochalsh, where Scott got me to try jellied whelks (disgusting), and crossing by ferry to the Isle of Skye where, in one of the pubs, the locals threw us an impromptu ceilidh and Scott tried (but failed miserably) to teach me Scottish reel dancing – after a few whiskies my head just spun.

It was on that trip that I realised there was a huge world out there. That whole trip was magical; I can still remember how much we laughed. Scott awoke a wanderlust in me: I wanted to see more new places. I discovered that I enjoyed meeting new people and listening to their stories and I loved finding out more about the history of the area we were in. This trait of mine and the sheer pleasure it gives me is one I have indulged ever since this trip.

Life was pretty good and by 1987 I was in line for promotion at the insurance company, which would have been the icing on the cake. I felt pretty confident I'd get it too, but at the last moment I was mysteriously bypassed. I was upset and annoyed that I obviously had no real chance of progression in what was still predominantly a man's world, but as chance would have it, that was when Peter Warren made his job offer to me.

My new duties were varied and my financial reward very satisfactory – so much so that Scott and I decided we could afford to move up the property ladder and bought a three-bedroom semi-detached house in an idyllic village just outside of Reading.

As I'd always had pets around while growing up, and as we now had a garden, I was keen to bring home two cats to complete our chocolate-box life. We found twin tabbies, from the same litter, at a local farm and named them Dizzy (after Dizzy Gillespie) and Sukie, which apparently was a Scottish term meaning cute, cuddly and affectionate. Sukie, the female, was the runt of the litter and did not live very long; there were sadly just too many things wrong with her for her to have much of a life.

In 1988 I turned twenty-one and Scott surprised me with a trip on the *Orient Express* from London to Paris for a long weekend. I can still remember how our luxurious compartment, lined in wood with exquisite marquetry panels, smelled and felt to the touch. Each coach had a concierge who was at your beck and call. Dinner was an event in itself, and was served in the dining car where, seated in armchairs at tables with chandeliers, we sipped champagne and ate quite possibly the most delicious four-course meal ever, while a pianist tinkled away on grand piano a few feet away. I had to pinch myself.

While I was still twenty-one I had a lovely home, a wonderful partner and two adorable cats, and both our careers were going well. Everything was perfect, yet strangely didn't quite seem as rosy as it should have done. I couldn't easily put my finger on an exact reason as on the surface all was fine, but I was uneasy and had a terrible feeling that complacency was now setting into our lives.

It was both our faults really: we both left for work early and, after a long day, returned late with just about enough energy to cook a meal before going to bed and then starting the cycle all over again. Friday evenings were the exception to the rule when we'd join some of the office staff and wander down to a nearby pub. Then our weekends followed a pattern: Saturdays were supermarket day, with a bit of socialising in the evening perhaps – always with the same friends – and Sundays held all the excitement of gardening and cleaning.

So much of our life seemed now to be set in routine; there was little spontaneity or excitement, and Scott never put much thought into being romantic – my previous birthday aside. He was rarely impulsive and if I ever suggested we did something other than go to the pub on a Friday, his response would be 'Why? What for?' So we never went to the theatre, rarely visited the cinema and restaurant outings were confined to birthdays and Christmases.

Understanding myself better now, I realise I was then experiencing the same feelings I'd had as a teenager when everything had seemed like it was 'all work and no play'. I don't want to sound like an ungrateful so-and-so, but I was doing what was expected of me by others and taking on my responsibilities with very few chances for me to cut loose once in a while and simply have fun for fun's sake.

I was still haunted by the insecurities of my childhood, and all I needed was an impromptu hug and to be told, and shown, that I was loved. But that never happened.

I still loved Scott so I would tell myself off for expecting too much – I always wanted more, and always wanted perfection. I'm often hard on myself, and can be hard on the people around me too, becoming critical of them, and it isn't an attractive trait. I greatly dislike myself at these times but, regardless, it was with this eye that I was now looking at Scott.

But before I had a chance to berate myself further, everything in my life ground to a halt when the property market collapsed.

It was late 1989 and recession had taken a firm hold, business had dropped through the floor and all our efforts and energies were solely focused on saving what we could from the country's financial mess.

The festive season didn't seem particularly festive that year, but as usual Scott and I spent Hogmanay in Edinburgh. The city I had fallen in love with now became the backdrop for a volcanic argument between us: a broken promise, business, money, the recession – everything.

The promise he had made me was over an ex-love; it had run its course, he said, always assuring me there was nothing to worry about. Of course, my insecurity alarm bells were ringing all the same so I asked him to promise me that if ever we found ourselves in her company, he would tell me. Some years later, during a party on this most recent trip, one of our friends let slip *she* was in the room and Scott had been talking to her, and it was 'nice that you don't mind him staying friends with her, Pam, especially after all they meant to each other'.

I could almost hear the thwack of the arrow piercing my heart. He had promised me – he had promised me faithfully – to tell me if she was there so I could at least make up my mind as to how I wanted to be – friendly, ignore her or even leave the vicinity. He had taken away this choice from me and I was livid.

I called Scott 'unfeeling', 'uncaring', 'blinkered', 'selfish' … along with several other, more choice names. The floodgates opened and the tirade between us was worse than I can even remember. Scott certainly gave as good as he got and I packed my bag, got in a taxi and headed for the airport. I flew home and saw in the New Year alone.

On Scott's eventual return home, we made up – as usual – and he asked me to marry him.

I'm not sure why I thought a marriage certificate with a couple of signatures on it would make things better between us, but I was excited and sincerely hoped marriage would recapture some of the intensity of feeling I had lost towards Scott. I even believed it would make me love him all over again, and I really, truly wanted that. Despite being just twenty-three I had always been quite insistent throughout my life that I never wanted children. I have never regarded myself as the maternal type and cringe when a friend or family member thrusts a newborn baby into my arms, expecting me to go all gooey-eyed. Maybe it's something that stems from my own childhood, or perhaps from me not being willing to give up my career to have children. Whatever the reason, I knew I just wasn't cut out to be a mother and Scott was aware of my feelings and said he understood. Deep down, however, I believed he wanted children; the things he said, the way he acted around children led me to believe he would be a perfect parent, but it was an issue brushed under the carpet as we started planning our wedding day.

Not being religious, I wasn't keen on a church wedding and ten months later I arrived at Henley registry office for the ceremony.

People always say your wedding day is the happiest and most memorable day of your life, but far from fondly recalling what I was wearing, how I arrived and who I was with, my abiding memory of the day is standing outside the room, thinking *What on earth am I doing? I'm not sure I want to be married,* while everyone, including the groom, was inside waiting. I had been told everyone has last-minute jitters, so I shrugged it off, opened the door, where I saw all my family sitting, and looked across to Scott, who looked back at me adoringly. I stepped forward, smiled and became Mrs MacKay.

Looking at the photographs, it was a beautiful sunny day and everyone was smiling widely and tossing rose petals in the air. I remember we had a great party afterwards too, at the George Hotel in Pangbourne. There were speeches of course, and Dad made a long one about marriage being like a hedgehog climbing up onto a kerb, although none of us quite got to grips with the analogy he was trying to make! The Scottish contingent soon took over the party; I still smile when I think of Scott, with his brothers and friends, all dressed up in full Scottish regalia, drinking their pints and then deciding to prove they were true Scotsmen by lifting up their tartan kilts. It was a sight which made many of the English lasses blush furiously.

Our honeymoon was spent in New England, USA. I loved New England in autumn – the full glory of the scenery set against the golden and rust-coloured leaves was spectacular. Scott was attentive and good fun to be with. We visited a comedy club and did a walking tour of Salem which focused on the famous witch trials of 1692 and taught us about the mass hysteria caused by a few unfortunate women. The old Mystic Seaport offered an intriguing insight into the past, and in Boston we even discovered the bar used in the sitcom *Cheers*. We made friends along the way, and Scott and I chatted nineteen to the dozen and laughed so much; I fell in love with him again and felt so very happy.

However, when we returned home everything settled back into the old regimented routine very quickly; the romantic gestures fizzled out and a huge feeling of claustrophobia engulfed me. Living together hadn't placed us under any pressure or constraints, but marriage was quite different; I'd made my bed and now had to be content to lie in it. I found myself beginning to resent the 'trap' of marriage and my rediscovered love for Scott began to erode.

Of course, children were expected to be the next step in our lives. Friends and family kept on teasing us about when the first would be born; Scott tellingly never said anything to the contrary. Maybe I was being very selfish, or maybe it was because I have always simply been too frightened to ever have someone dependent on me in the way a child would be? Though it was a subject never spoken about between us, as the months went by I became more and more aware that Scott really wanted me to think again about starting a family. It became an awful unspoken pressure which caused me to become even more emotionally erratic, and as though to redress the balance, Scott became more domineering. In public we were the charming newlywed couple, but as soon as we were behind closed doors I became shrewish and Scott began to belittle me and order me about.

By then I was twenty-six years old and was struggling with a failing business and the huge stress that brought with it, and Scott made it clear he wanted a simple life with a simple wife. Nervous exhaustion consumed me and I developed a huge rash all over my body; it was 'purely stress-related', the doctor said. From that moment on Scott could do no right as far as I was concerned; my mental state was one of paranoia, uneasiness and unhappiness. It all came to a head so quickly, and after only three years of marriage, Scott came home one evening as usual and I immediately greeted him with, 'Scott, I want a divorce.'

His stunned silence and quizzical facial expression made me realise he'd had no inkling as to the depths of my unhappiness.

'Pam, I know we've had some problems, but this … this … it's completely out of the blue. What has made you so angry?'

Strangely, I then became very calm, as if making the decision had released a huge pressure lock. I felt it was right not just for me but also for him. I explained I just wasn't cut out for family life, could not be the wife he wanted or deserved and could not give him the children I believed he wanted. He tried to argue otherwise, but in the end I think even he realised his reasoning was crumbling around him. Our split was very civilised, without any huge rows, and we just talked. For the first time in a very, very long time we actually appreciated each other's feelings; he admitted he did want children and I admitted my disillusionment with marriage and the fact I did not think I was in love with him anymore.

My split and divorce from Scott was a disappointment for my mother and led to further arguments between her and me. For the next twelve months we didn't talk; I got on with my life, and she with hers. When we did eventually start speaking again, primarily through Jane's intervention, I knew I couldn't let our arguments keep getting to me, so from that day to this, at the first sign of an argument or disagreement, whoever starts it, I either bite my tongue and keep quiet or stand up and walk away, trying to avoid any confrontation.

Prior to my requesting the divorce, when the business I ran with Peter Warren started failing, Scott kindly offered us space at his office in Twyford.

'Try to restart with the clients you managed to rescue from the demised business,' he suggested, 'and keep your overheads down.'

Now, I found myself in the difficult position of not only having to continue working with Scott around, but I had to live with him too – as neither of us had the money to move out of either the office or the house. For six months I occupied the upstairs rooms of the house and he the downstairs, and during the day we sat opposite each other in stony silence. I hated every single minute – it was awful. The empty, cold, sick feeling in the pit of my stomach was with me constantly. I worked so hard to block out my emotions that I would get home and be so tired that I'd just collapse into bed until the morning. My diet suffered as I avoided using the downstairs kitchen and I began to feel more and more unwell as the months crept by.

Scott was characteristically stoic throughout and as I desperately tried to keep up my facade, I selfishly paid little thought to how everything was affecting him. Until, that is, one evening when I heard him crying in his room. I had lost track of the date and couldn't think what had upset him so much but I fought my impulse to go to him. Instead I tried to ignore his sobs and to block out the sound by burying my head under my pillows, crying silently into the mattress for both Scott and me; eventually sheer exhaustion overtook me and I slept. Two days later, it dawned on me that it had been our wedding anniversary. I felt awful.

A few months later Scott moved out. It boiled down to simple mathematics: business was such that I could afford the mortgage while he could not. There was no equity in the house, only spiral-ling interest payments, so he signed the house over to me and left. Everything from then on continued to be very civilised; we compiled a list of assets and went through it, dividing it all in half. Our solicitors signed it off and that was that, my marriage was over.

Scott happily found love again soon afterwards, and is the proud father of at least two children. I wouldn't say we are friends, but when he heard about the train crash he was kind enough to visit me and asked if we might stay in contact. I thought, *How would I feel if I was his wife and he suddenly wanted to be friends with his ex-wife again?*

I smiled and said, 'I don't think that would be a good idea.'

I'll always look back on our happy times together with fond-ness and I hope he and his family are doing well, enjoying their lives. I really do wish them all the very best for the future.

After the divorce I did go out on a few tentative dates but nothing turned out to be serious and I certainly did not have any plans to start a new relationship; I was quite happy being a 27-year-old singleton in charge of my own life.

By 1994 I had known my business partner, Peter Warren, for ten years and had grown to like him as both a friend and a colleague. As a team we worked well together, both striving for bigger and better things, and both sharing grand designs for the future. Peter had been married twice already and had three children from his first marriage who were in their teens, and the next thing I knew Peter confided in me that his second marriage was 'on the rocks'. In fact, they separated very soon afterwards.

Peter needed somewhere to live and as we already worked together, having moved our offices from Scott's in Twyford into a converted garage at my home, and understanding what Peter was going through, I agreed he could move into my spare room for a while. It was then that our relationship changed from being businesslike into something far more intimate. We were both on the rebound from failed marriages, we had work in common and, from my point of view, I craved affection – though without necessarily a long-term commitment. If only I had recognised the 'rebound effect' for what it was, my future life would have been much simpler.

Peter was totally different from Scott, both in public and in private; he was very kind, charming, selfless, charismatic and dynamic. The age gap between us stood at eighteen years – far greater than in any of my previous relationships – but in a way I found it flattering that such a good-looking, tall man with silver-fox grey hair and twinkling blue eyes found me attractive; he had Irish blood in him too which sealed it!

'Pam, I can't make you love me. If ever you reach a stage when you can say to my face "I positively do not love you", then I will simply pack and walk away.'

'I've learnt that you have to work at a relationship to make it work,' was another of his assurances.

I believed him.

Was I in love with Peter? Was he in love with me? Probably not. In fact, I cannot remember one instance during our time together when either of us said 'I love you' directly to the other's face. Over the years we spoke around the issue of love; we referred to it but never actually said it. We developed a relation-ship forged from friendship, and while I have known couples who have made a marriage out of less, for us this wasn't going to be enough. Hindsight is a wonderful thing, isn't it?

Peter introduced me to a new circle of his friends; we went to some great parties and we shared fun times. Furthermore, he was always supportive of my work and the direction I wanted the business to go in – to specialise in pensions and investments – while he worked on any mortgages that were required by my clients and began to dabble in property development. Work aside, we had very little else in common and the age gap soon became more and more obvious; I was a sprightly young woman, still only in my late twenties, who wanted to go out and have fun after work, whereas Peter, at forty-six, was quite happy to just slump in front of the TV, saying he was 'feeling tired'. He was also beginning to let himself go and put on quite a bit of weight.

Oh no, I would think, *I don't want to get into a humdrum routine again. I want to enjoy what life has to offer!*

So I'd have to cajole and pester Peter into going out, or hosting a party, but cajole I did and normally, sometimes grudgingly, he would humour me and make the effort.

In late 1997 Peter asked me out of the blue if I would marry him.

My reaction was *Oh no, not again, I really don't want to be married*, and I turned him down flat.

A little while later he asked me again … and again … and again… In fact, he kept on asking me over the following few weeks and months. I even remember being at a party with friends and crying on one of the other women's shoulders as he'd asked me again. But over time his persistence wore me down and eventually I gave in. 'Oh hell, why not? It is just a piece of paper,' I said. How romantic.

Maybe because my divorce from Scott was so amicable I didn't consider the true consequences of another such commitment, nor did I realise that not everyone would act as graciously. Four years after Peter had moved in, in February 1998, I returned to Henley registry office to marry for the second time. However, I insisted

I was not going to be known as or called Mrs Pam Warren, I wanted to remain Pam MacKay; with Peter having been married twice already there was no way on earth I wanted the label of 'Mrs Warren the Third'. I had also been working under the name of Pam MacKay for years and didn't see any reason to change, plus I just liked the way it sounded.

I also made Peter promise that no one, aside from our witnesses, should know we were married, and I didn't want a ring. I think I must have felt that if we kept it private, as though nothing had changed, then nothing would change.

None of Peter's or my family were invited, nor were they told, and we followed our private ceremony with a quiet lunch at a restaurant in Reading. After all, it was simply a piece of paper that was keeping him happy, wasn't it? My actions really should have set huge alarm bells ringing. I should have had more backbone and stood up to Peter at the time, telling him I had no wish to marry him, and let our relationship run its natural course.

Our secret was kept for exactly one year, until one day when we returned to the restaurant where we'd had our post-marriage lunch with Peter's mother. The owner greeted us with 'Ah, Pam, Peter, how wonderful to see you again. Are you still enjoying married life?' I had never moved so quickly before, and almost flung Peter's mum into a seat across the other side of the room, hoping she had not heard.

We got away with it that day, but decided it was probably time to come clean with our nearest and dearest. My family met the news with a mixture of disbelief, concern and puzzlement – much as I would probably have done. They didn't approve of nor like Peter and no one would ever be as wonderful as Scott in Mum's eyes.

'I don't understand,' said Dad. 'The man's my age, for goodness' sake.'

Hmm, good point. Could it have been I was looking for a father figure to look after me?

We hadn't bothered with a honeymoon after we married, but having now coped with the after-effects of our big revelation we felt we deserved a break, and booked into a Sandals hotel in the Bahamas for two weeks of all-inclusive pampering. The one appealing advantage of staying at Sandals was that there were no children allowed! However, you were supposed to stay on the resort complex, not fraternise with the local Bahamians, so there was little to do other than eat, sit on the manicured beach and drink – all fine for a couple of days but I soon became bored. Bored on my honeymoon! Also, the resort was full of American couples who were, quite frankly, bloody rude to the staff.

I visited the on-site spa and got my first back massage from a lovely, very sweet Bahamian girl. It was so good that I kept going back every day. She and I became friendly and I moaned to her about being cooped up on the resort and not being able to see any of the real Bahamas.

'I am not officially allowed to do this but it's my day off tomorrow,' she said. 'If you like, I'll meet you outside the resort gates and take you to see Nassau and meet some of my people.' I leapt at the chance and the next day persuaded Peter to slink out with me. After a bus and taxi ride into the centre of Nassau we wandered about with our guide, being introduced to and greeting locals, and listening to the sounds of the local reggae music thumping out of small huts and houses which I'm surprised were not shaken apart by the pounding bass. We eventually ended up on the quayside where our friend introduced us to her aunt, who ran a fresh vegetable stall, and then on to a corrugated shack where fish were literally being plucked from the sea, cleaned and flung onto a makeshift barbecue. Oh, the smell – it was mouth-watering! We gladly accepted an offered fish cooked with fresh ginger, garlic and chilli and sat eating it with our fingers from a bending paper plate. The deliciousness of this simple meal was far above our five-star food at the resort. We ended up watching the sunset with our legs dangling over the edge of the quay. The day was heavenly.

Back at base, we became friendly with another British couple, Mike and Debbie, and hit it off so well that we spent much of the rest of our holiday together, laughing, lounging around, drinking cocktails at the pool bar and eating out at the various restaurants the resort provided. We naturally talked about work and Mike said he was a fireman in the London area, while Debbie ran a fleet of chauffeur cars. At the end of the holiday we agreed to stay in touch, which I am pleased to say we did. On a visit to see me after the train crash, they told me Mike was one of the first firemen on the scene at Ladbroke Grove, little realising I was involved.

Isn't it strange how you can meet random people in life and then cross and intersect with them again at any given point? Mike and Debbie are still very much part of my life and have proven to be great and understanding friends.

Having flown home to Britain, a spark seemed to disappear from Peter, and I watched as my once dynamic go-getter husband downed tools; he spent more and more time playing solitaire on the office computer, saying it helped him 'think', but I sensed he had lost his motivation. His property business was not going well: buildings were not being finished on time, he was often running over budget and the finished properties were not producing the levels of rent he had projected.

With no income from Peter's development company, and his mortgage commission income dwindling, my pension advisory service fees became our only reliable source of funds, which we had to use to buoy up his struggling enterprise.

Even then Peter wouldn't recognise that something needed to be done; he just flicked on his computer and sat staring at the screen and clicking the mouse.

When I took on outside consultancy work, looking into insurance company mis-selling practices, the time demands on me became immense; I had to concertina the rest of my own work into whatever free time I had – mostly evenings and the odd weekend. Consequently Peter and I didn't spend much time together, and even when we did it was to look after the needs and wants of his family. My life was quite literally spent either living and breathing work or entertaining the Warren family.

If that wasn't enough to contend with, I began studying for my financial exams and I was determined to excel. I suppose it did have the added advantage of meaning I could avoid thinking about how crappy my personal life had become!

It was at this point in October 1999 that the three-day course in preparation for my next financial exam, which would usually have been held in Reading, was switched to Moorgate in London.

CHAPTER 6

AWAKENING FROM
THE NIGHTMARE

For three weeks after the train crash I lay unconscious in a hospital bed, alone with my dreams, with all manner of machines beeping, pinging and pumping around me. I was actually in a medically induced state of unconsciousness, or coma, my breathing being done for me through a ventilator. My loved ones kept a 24-hour vigil by my bed, having been told I might not ever wake up.

Not only had my body suffered terrible damage, I had also experienced a massive mental trauma and was effectively in deep shock; inducing unconsciousness was considered by the doctors to be the best way of keeping me alive. It also gave my body a fighting chance and valuable time and energy to start its recovery process. In a way, you could liken it to rebooting a computer.

I remember, absolutely vividly, a number of my dreams. Some were quite bizarre: in one I was being held captive in a tent in the desert, with my hands tightly bound and some sort of chain or hook piercing my nostril which hurt when I moved, and I knew my family were held somewhere nearby so I kept trying to escape to try to reach them. In a second dream I found myself in Sydney, Australia. It was all very clear – the opera house, Sydney Harbour Bridge arching against a clear blue sky, the sunlight twinkling across the harbour waves – and yet I have never been to Sydney! Then in my next dream it was Paris, at the Moulin Rouge to be exact, where I was forced to watch performers dance and sing. There were also other scenarios where people around me wouldn't listen, or would talk over me as though I wasn't there. One common theme ran throughout my dreams – in some way I was being held against my will, could not get anyone to listen to me and felt an overwhelming need to escape.

In the last dream I recall, which might have been a final bid for freedom, I was strapped to a hospital trolley, trying to get up from it – the fact I was in a hospital must have filtered through to me in my coma – but then I found my bandaged hands couldn't open the double doors of the lift I thought I was lying next to. I could hear my family were close by and struggled to get to them but was gently pushed back on the bed by a Japanese doctor who said, 'Now you are prepared to help yourself, we are prepared to help you,' and a sense of calm descended over me. It wasn't long after I had that dream that I woke up.

I think when in a deep coma your brain can hear sounds going on around you and on some level you are aware of your surroundings; perhaps the human mind interprets these and tries to make sense of them? The last dream, I must admit, has affected me on some spiritual level in that I believe it was part of the reason I struggled to survive and eventually woke up.

Occasionally, there was another dream too, an all too vivid and all too real one, with fireballs, followed by darkness and smoke, the smell of burning hair, the sound of screaming…

Throughout all of my dreams I was aware of one sound – a constant and very menacing noise. I always wanted it to stop, but no matter how I tried it was always there; a monotonous sort of 'pshoo, pumpf, ptsch'. It was of course the ventilator that was keeping me alive but in my unconscious state, it simply frightened me.

I began my emergence from the coma, and drifted in and out of consciousness. My family was told to 'talk to Pam, let her know you are here'. I remember both seeing and hearing them in my brief conscious moments, but also remember feeling very cold and thinking I was in some sort of tiny box, claustrophobically tiny, and wondered if it was a mortuary. I seemed to convince myself that I had in fact died or was in the process of dying; the distorted images and sounds I was experiencing, coupled with feelings of looking down on my body, convinced me I was heading towards the hereafter. I then became aware of someone (it turned out to be a doctor, in fact) snipping at the skin on my face, and the physical sensation associated with it; the scissors felt cold, but before I could protest I drifted off into a dream world again.

Eventually, I awoke, properly registering my totally alien surroundings. Though I couldn't move my head I was able to move my eyes around most of the room. I had absolutely no idea where I was or what had happened, and then I saw my bandaged hands suspended from a sort of T-bar contraption directly above my head. *What the hell?* I thought to myself. It was obviously some sort of hospital, but why was I there? Why were my hands bandaged?

Just then, the ventilator next to my bed made one of its long exhaling 'pshoo, pumpf' noises, followed by a short sharp 'ptsch', and frightened the life out of me.

I caught sight of a small, somewhat stocky figure of a man sitting in the chair at the end of my bed. As I focused I could see it was Dan, my mother's new husband, hunched over a paperback and wearing a blue plastic hospital apron. He got up and rushed out to find a nurse. Just to the left of where he'd been sitting, I homed in on a pair of dark eyes, which in turn looked directly into mine; it was my sister Jane. I have never been so glad to see anyone in the whole of my life.

I whispered a barely audible, 'Hello.'

Jane all but fell from her chair as she jumped up and sprang forward; sinking down, she knelt beside me at my eye level. I will never forget the smile and look of relief on her face. It was Tuesday 26 October, three weeks after the crash.

'Hello, Pam, how are you feeling?'

My throat felt painfully sore, not only as a result of how badly damaged it had been from the fire and smoke in the crash, but also from the hospital having inserted a tube into it to open my airways for ventilator access. I also had tubes up my nose and all manner of sensors and wires around me.

My first thought was that I felt very, very cold; to this day I still curse the person who designed the hospital gown, which not only gives you the continuous feeling that your backside is hanging out, but because it is secured by loose ties down the back, has draughty gaps from neck to knee. In fact, I felt permanently cold for the whole time I had to wear one.

My eyes drifted to the left corner of the room where there was a television on. I could hear David Attenborough's voice.

He has such a lovely calm, reassuring tone, I thought to myself and realised the programme was *Walking with Dinosaurs*, which I'd been following before the crash. My interest perked up – this wasn't a weird dream and I wasn't dead.

'What have I missed?' I tried to ask.

Jane couldn't hear me as my voice was so weak, but perhaps that was just as well as it would have probably seemed quite absurd that my first words were of concern about a TV programme rather than about why I was in hospital. My voice was very weak for some time; anyone I tried to speak to would just stare at my lips moving and shake their heads in bafflement. Luckily, whatever connection Jane and I have as sisters meant she could understand me; she quickly became my interpreter.

'Do you remember anything?' she asked.

'No. About what?' I whispered, genuinely confused.

'Do you remember anything about the train?'

'Yes. I came home,' I replied.

I was thinking about the journey back from London to Reading on 4 October, the day before the train crash.

'No, no, do you remember being on a train going to London, but it didn't make it?' she asked.

'No.'

'Are you ready to know what happened, Pam?'

I nodded very slightly, and rather exasperatedly mouthed the word 'Yes'. I really wasn't sure what she was getting at. The realisation of 'something' having happened was dawning on me but the drugs coupled with confusion about why my hands were restrained served only to fuel my frustration. Jane went over to her chair and started rummaging through her handbag; she returned to my bedside and held up a newspaper. There was no picture – or if there was, she had obscured it – and its headline read 'Train Crash at Ladbroke Grove'.

'Peter took you to the station, Pam.'

'Yes, Reading...' I replied.

'You were going to Paddington.'

'For my training course...' I croaked.

At that very moment, I remembered what I thought had been a dream, an awful dream, and my blood ran cold.

'There was a jolting, a terrible grinding noise,' I said as images of the crash came flooding back, taking my breath away.

The jarring ... the braking of the train ... the deafening noise of grinding metal ... the interior of the carriage distorting as I looked down at the face of Keith Stiles ... the fireball ... the smell of burning hair, flesh and diesel ... it all became very real again and very graphic. Panicking, I began gasping for breath and flailing in my restraints, and I also started to sweat profusely.

Jane placed her hand gently on my chest to reassure and calm me.

'When did this happen? How long ago?' I asked, my brain racing.

'Three weeks,' she replied.

'Three weeks? It can't have been. It can't possibly have been three weeks,' I argued.

We fell silent as my brain tried to readjust to the loss of three weeks, and indeed attempted to take on board everything about the crash.

'Was anyone hurt?'

Jane played it all down. 'Some were, but they're all fine,' she replied.

'Did anyone die?' I asked.

Jane never answered; she was then saved from further inter-rogation by two nurses bustling into the room who immediately put a mask over my nose and mouth and connected me to the nebuliser – a piece of equipment whereby some sort of effer-vescent tablet is dropped into liquid and produces pure oxygen for inhalation quickly into your lungs and bloodstream. That was when I first realised my face hurt – wearing the mask was absolute agony and I came to utterly resent being subjected to the nebuliser. Every time a nurse came towards me with the contraption I glared at them, my eyes glowering with mistrust and thinking they were doing it deliberately to hurt me. But with my arms restrained in bandages there was very little else I could do, so on it would go and I indignantly huffed away while almost crying with tears of pain and frustration.

I began piecing together what had happened by talking with my family, via Jane, about the three weeks after the crash. My time in intensive care was just as much about coming to terms with the gap in my memory as it was treating my injuries.

Naturally, after the story Jane allowed me a glimpse of, I never saw any of the newspaper or TV headlines; I don't think it ever occurred to me that the crash was big enough to warrant much coverage and, anyway, the media wouldn't be bothered about ordinary people like me, would they? My family were very careful to keep the extent of the truth from me for as long as possible, and it was only much, much later that I discovered the immense media coverage it did indeed receive.

I had been first taken from the crash site to St Mary's Hospital in London with all the other survivors, but later that evening was transferred to Charing Cross Hospital where, on arrival, I was mistaken for someone called Evelyn – the lovely fair-haired woman who had wrapped her coat around me at the trackside. She'd left her work ID badge in the coat pocket and someone had read it and assumed... Well, her parents received a phone call to say that their daughter had been involved in a train crash and was seriously hurt in hospital, and that they 'should come immediately'. I can't begin to imagine what that poor couple must have felt in the time before Evelyn phoned them to say she was OK, and it was a mix-up.

Charing Cross, I discovered later, was where the 'no-hopers' were sent in the full expectation they would die. There were just the two of us: I was shipped there along with an American man called Michael Adams, who had been on the Thames Turbo train.

My family first went to St Mary's and panicked when the administrator said I wasn't there – with the identity mix-up, there was no trace of me. In the mayhem of admissions it was suggested they try Charing Cross Hospital, where of course there was still no record of me, though my mother – adamant I had been taken from the trackside by ambulance – was shown to a bed in intensive care, by which time they'd realised I wasn't Evelyn.

'It was impossible to tell from looking at you,' my mother said, 'whether you were my daughter or not. Luckily, I spotted the watch you were wearing – the one I bought for you.'

Having finally found me, my family were then told they should prepare themselves for the worst as the magnitude of my injuries were confirmed by surgeon Nicholas Percival.

He told them that I had suffered severe facial burns, both third-degree and 'full thickness' – which means all layers of skin had gone – with the same to my hands and right leg; the total area of burns covered 15 per cent of my body; I was also suffering from the internal effects of fire and smoke inhalation.

A secondary effect of the crash, Nick explained, was a reduction of synovial fluid in my joints; with the fireball's intense heat, the yolk-like fluid found in the cavities of joints, which reduces friction between the cartilage during movement, was severely damaged. This condition has led to arthritis in many of my limbs, where movement is often painful and difficult, particularly in cold, damp weather. That's something that will never go away and will only get worse as I grow older.

Added to all this, I developed pneumonia in one lung, which then spread to the other. It was at that point that my family and Peter were told to prepare themselves – I was almost certainly going to die.

Peter, Jane, my mother, my dad, and my mother's new husband all took turns to sit at my bedside throughout 'the coma weeks', as they became known. Jane recorded some of my favourite songs, including hits by Queen, Michael Jackson, Lenny Kravitz and Sister Sledge, onto a cassette player and played them over and over again in the hope they would aid my subconscious mind to fight – to fight for my life. Mum massaged my feet gently too, these being the only part of my body anyone could really touch.

During the three weeks of my imposed unconsciousness, I underwent a series of operations grafting skin from the inside of my arm to my face and from my thigh to my hands and legs. There were also daily sessions of intensive physiotherapy to begin the process of ensuring my hands would work again; the sessions continued for years afterwards too. Knowing the pain I suffered later, I am really glad I was unconscious as I can't bear to think of the intense agony I would have gone through in these early stages of treatment.

Apparently, on several occasions I tried to pull the two tubes from my throat, one by which I was being fed and the other which helped me to breathe. Jane said there was a male nurse who got quite cross with me and though he never spoke directly to me, he snapped at Jane that I was 'not allowed to remove the tubes' and was really very brusque. Jane didn't like his attitude and was convinced that I could hear, so asked for a more sympathetic and positive-speaking nurse to replace him. Maybe his attitude filtered into my dreams, and that's why I felt so constrained in some of them.

Against all the odds, I survived. I woke up.

On that first day of regaining consciousness, a nurse called me Mrs Warren. *Mrs Who?* I screamed in my head.

I looked at the white plastic bracelet around my left wrist suspended above me, and there it was: *Mrs Pam Warren. Oh well*, I thought, *there's not much I can do about it now.*

Although my re-emergence into the world was still a little hazy, I somehow knew then that boarding a train on that bright sunny autumn day, minding my own business, had changed everything in my life – my present, my future, the appearance of my body, the colour of my skin and even my name – though I did not know at the time to what extent and whether it would be for the better or the worse.

CHAPTER 7

FIGHTING BACK

If I had to be treated anywhere, then I am glad it was London's Charing Cross Hospital. All the NHS doctors and nurses were brilliant; they saved my life when there was thought to be little hope and looked after me so brilliantly during my recovery. I owe them so much.

I'm particularly grateful that Nick Percival was my consultant. Nick – a top plastic surgeon by trade, based in Harley Street – worked as an NHS consultant a few days a week at Charing Cross and it was my good fortune that the day I was admitted during that particular week in October 1999 was one of his days at the hospital.

Pretty soon after I regained consciousness the doctors said they wanted to get me on my feet. It's a proven fact that immobile patients quickly lose the ability to walk, and even though my ankle was still badly bruised and battered and my leg heavily swathed in bandages, they told me it was very important I get up out of bed. They produced a Zimmer frame for me to support myself with, but with the injuries to my hands I had to lean on the frame with my forearms and edge towards my sister, who was encouraging me with, 'Come on, Pam, you can do it. Just a few more steps…' I felt like a baby learning to walk for the first time, taking tiny shuffling steps, unsure of whether I had the ability to balance or stand unsupported. Plus I had the indignity of being forced to stoop forward as I shuffled along, which then meant my bare backside kept on popping out of the sodding bed gown!

The morphine which had kept the pain at bay since the crash was later replaced by an LSD-based pain-controlling drug, which probably explains why my early conscious memories of the intensive care unit (ICU) bordered on the surreal and outright psychedelic: at one point I remember thinking my room was a sweet shop and the doctors and nurses attending to me were in fact people coming in to buy chocolates and pear drops. I also believed I could see wriggling red, blue and green worm-like things being breathed in and then expelled by everyone around me, which sort of freaked me out at the same time as fascinating me!

Contrary to how you might think someone would react, I was actually very accepting of the situation and didn't at any point ask myself *why me?* or question the fairness of my situation. I had been told the extent of my injuries by Nick Percival, who also made it clear that recovery was very much down to me. I reasoned that there was nothing I could do to change the fact I was hurt, so I had to summon every bit of determination and my sheer bloody-mindedness to ensure I recovered as well as it was possible to. I focused on being positive, and on my over-whelming desire to go home, which undoubtedly helped speed up my recovery dramatically.

My stay in the ICU once conscious was short-lived, partly because of the speed of my recovery and partly because there was some sort of bug – though not MRSA – doing the rounds, which was considered potentially fatal to my seriously dimin-ished immune system. I was moved into an isolation room, and though it was technically on an NHS ward, it was actually rather sumptuous – a fully self-contained room with an en-suite loo, a nice television and my own window, although, as I was bedrid-den, I was unable to look out of it. Still, it was nice to see the sky and clouds, which served as a reminder to me that there was a life waiting for me outside. There was enough room for a mattress to be brought in too, so my mother and Jane took it in turns to sleep in my room, ensuring I was never alone.

There seem to be many differing opinions about how to best treat burns victims. I discovered that much of the thinking stems from the horrific injuries pilots suffered during World War II, who became known as the 'Guinea Pigs'. Some reportedly responded better when their wounds were left uncovered with air circulating around them, whereas others healed more quickly by being covered up. I don't think there's any one answer or best treatment, to be honest, as different people respond in different ways, but for my initial recovery, Nick Percival suggested my legs be bandaged and my hands entirely covered to just above my wrists. He said my skin had been in very good condition before the crash, as was evident by my looking much younger than my years – thanks to Mum's genes – so he felt confident I would make a good recovery this way.

As the right side of my body was burnt much more badly than the left, due to the position of my seat on the aisle in the train's carriage, I consequently had to endure more operations and treatment to my right side. With much of the skin on my hands frazzled, badly damaged or basically gone, Nick took grafts from my thigh to apply to them; but as the amount of undamaged skin was less than the amount needed, he used a technique of stretching the grafts on a board and then ran a perforator over them – a little bit like one of those gizmos you use to make latticework pastry – which created a mesh, or a net, of pure skin. It spread out much further over my wounds and provided a healing barrier. I still have a mesh pattern on parts of my hands now.

My face was next, but as leg skin is not sensitive or delicate enough, Nick said he would take grafts from the only other area available – under my arm.

'You have been burnt badly across the forehead, and bone is exposed. There is full burning around your eyes, over your nose and around your cheekbones and ears. The only part that seems to have come out fairly unscathed is your chin,' Nick explained in his blunt, but hugely sensitive manner. He told it as it was, that's for sure. He added that in practice 'the skin grafts probably won't take as well as I'd like them to'. In fact, I had to have four grafts in all on my forehead; after each of the first three operations bits of skin dropped off, and smaller grafts were used to replace them. I must have looked as though I had some awful flesh-wasting disease. To further complicate matters Nick explained there couldn't be any pressure exerted to the grafts as they took, but as they needed supporting he applied a petroleum jelly-covered gauze net, which had the added benefit of keeping the grafts moist but sadly offered little shielding from potential infection. Everyone coming into my room had to be screened and swabbed and wear sterile gowns and masks. Furthermore, anything coming into my room had to be new and in its sealed packaging and nothing could be removed from my room to be reused either – it had to be destroyed to ensure no bugs could be transferred.

I suppose it is surprising that I had paid no particular attention to my facial injuries up until this point. I can only explain this in terms of being able to *see* my other injuries, and they were bad enough. I was fearful of what a mirror might show me. I knew it was bad, but I didn't want to look. Nick did not seem to want to push me at this point; perhaps he too felt I had enough to deal with.

Trying to explain what my hands looked like is difficult, as it still makes me feel queasy. My arms down to my wrists were fine, but below that the only way you could tell my hands were actually hands lay in the fact that they were attached to my wrists and had ten separate fingerlike stump things hanging off them. While the bandages were on I could convince myself they were my hands and I simply could not move them, which, while odd, was not much different to the other bizarre things my brain was trying to come to terms with. With the bandages off they simply looked like encased hunks of meat, with deformed sausages that you might see on a butcher's block, but raw and swollen into grotesque shapes. I think the shock when I first saw them kicked off my survival instinct again: I watched and observed them in a detached way and did not allow myself any form of emotional ownership of them.

As well as getting my legs moving, it was considered imperative my other limbs should be exercised as much as possible too, particularly where significant muscle damage had been sustained – my hands and fingers being top of the list. The bandages on my hands and fingers took around ninety minutes to remove, not only for daily dressing changes, but also for physiotherapy sessions. Each day I endured the painful routine and despite copious amounts of morphine, it hurt like hell.

If that wasn't bad enough, soon after waking every morning I had to use the dreaded nebuliser for forty-five minutes. Although designed to help my lungs and breathing, the physical discomfort of having the plastic mask strapped around my head and pressing on my face was awful. No sooner had it been whipped off than a nurse would start taking my bandages and dressings off for Russell, my physiotherapist, to start an hour of digit and hand exercising; the sessions involved putting my fingers through their paces. I had no knuckles at this point and my fingers were completely straight, so to mobilise them Russell grabbed each joint individually and bent it – the pain was excruciating!

The dressing changes and physio were repeated seven days a

week and left me exhausted. But there was no rest as a nurse would then declare that it was time for 'lunch'.

They tried to spoon-feed me at first but because of the damage to my throat I couldn't easily swallow anything and would choke, so they introduced me to a marvellous protein drink, Ensure, which was quite delicious and I could sip it very slowly through a small straw. However, a side effect of my yummy drinks was that I soon piled on the pounds: on admittance to hospital I was 7 stone 9 pounds and when I left I weighed in at a hefty 10 stone.

An intravenous drip meanwhile was permanently attached to my body, though over time used up so many of my few good veins that it became virtually impossible even to locate a new one; when I attempted to be a good Samaritan and reported to give blood one day a few years ago, they spent ages trying to find a vein before sending me home, scratching their heads. I keep going to give blood whenever I can, as I think it is so important, and thankfully they have got used to me now – the more experienced phlebotomist can eventually track down a small vein somewhere.

The doctors eventually took me off the LSD drug because of its hallucinogenic side effects, and reintroduced morphine and a second painkiller, which I can't recall the name of; but such was the intensity of pain in my physiotherapy sessions that I needed the additional booster painkiller, and I used Entonox gas too.

Russell appeared daily to bend my fingers one by one, and with every one I would cry with the pain. He constantly reassured me that everything would be OK and that I was making good progress. The doctors meanwhile suggested I would 'hopefully' regain 50 per cent use of my hands and fingers. 'Hopefully?' I asked, with tears rolling down my cheeks. 'No, that isn't enough! I want a higher percentage – as near to normal as possible!' I'd lost all tactile feeling in both hands where the nerve endings had been destroyed – I still don't have a huge amount today, particularly in my right hand – but fearful that I wouldn't ever recover properly without my hands, I told Russell to keep pushing me more each day, 'regardless of the pain'. I had become acutely aware of how much we need our hands; stuck in my bed I watched everyone who came in – they used their hands to touch things, move things, manipulate things like levers, buttons, bandages, knobs etc., even accidently banging or knocking their hands. We don't always notice what we are doing with our hands or how much we use them, not just for practical things, but also for expressing ourselves, or communicating by touch and feel. Yes, I decided, I needed my hands back at all costs.

Every day I looked down at the puffed-up things at the end of my arms: they continued to look like raw sausages. Just to add to it all, every time Russell moved them blood squirted out from the ends of my sausages, er, I mean fingers. It was like a grotesque horror film! My fingernails had burnt to nothing, and the charred stumps at the ends of my fingers had to be amputated too, with the remains of nails on the few fingertips gradually dropping off – usually during my physiotherapy sessions.

Although the daily blood-squirting scene was both horrendous and painful I became rather blasé about it all, and far from envisaging myself in a horror movie, I thought of it more like a Mel Brooks comedy film. Oops, there goes another one! It could have been the drugs, but during one morning's squirt I began to laugh like a drain. A bemused nurse avoided my eye and fixed her stare on the morphine drip.

Even when the bandages had been replaced and Russell had left my torture chamber, I still had to continue little exercises such as touching my fingers to my thumb as often as possible; there was certainly never any let-up. But it paid off, as a couple of weeks later I saw a little crease in the middle of my fingers where the knuckles once were. My overwhelming feeling of elation was huge – it was working!

Pain control, dressing changes, physio and operations were now my daily routine. Gone was the pressure of the insurance and pensions advice business; gone was the threat of a looming exam; my life was now four hospital walls, a drip, a window and a steely determination to recover to full health.

Although my sister and mother took it in turns to stay at my bedside twenty-four hours a day between them, in between physio sessions I really welcomed the visits from the rest of my family and friends. Mum has never been comfortable with the sight of blood, so you can imagine just how pale she turned when witnessing my squirting sausage party trick, which I discovered could cover a radius of three feet from the bed!

It was around this time that I actually became very concerned about my mother. I knew the long vigils, coupled with caring for and amusing me every day, had been taking their toll on her; but now she was beginning to look ill and drawn and was becoming increasingly tired each day. I wasn't sure how much longer she could continue visiting without seriously affecting her health but then, purely by chance, a doctor noticed that some of my Entonox painkiller inhaler was escaping into the room – and my mother turned out to have an allergy to it. It was a relief to know what was to blame, but sadly from then on her visits had to be curtailed for fear of making her very ill.

Jane was living in Surbiton with her then boyfriend at that time, but spent most of her life in hospital with me, which I fear didn't do her relationship any favours. Shortly after I returned home she and her boyfriend split up; however, I was over the moon for them when they eventually got back together again and then eleven years later, in 2010, got married. They do say true love never dies, don't they?

The niceties of my daily hospital conversations with Jane about the weather, television and newspaper gossip soon gave way to me asking about the crash. I began to remember things which had happened, as far as my part was concerned, but I wasn't really aware of anything else or of how many others had been affected.

'Who died?' 'How many survived?' 'How many were seriously injured?' I asked. I also wanted to know about the three people who had helped me – could Jane track them down? I tried to find out how bad the crash had been but my family were still careful to give fairly non-committal answers, believing I had enough to deal with for the time being.

My whole family formed a support team every bit as important as the consultants, doctors and nurses who tended to me every day. Peter tried to help but quickly gave up his afternoon vigils, so Dad came to help out, giving Mum and Jane a break. Poor Dad. He isn't the most tactile of men, as I've already mentioned – I could see just how much out of his comfort zone he was, but still he came determined to do whatever he could.

A few old friends and colleagues came to visit meanwhile, one of whom arrived just when my gel net fell forward off my forehead. Without flinching, she leaned forward and replaced it. Unfortunately, not knowing what germs might have been trans-ferred, the doctors ordered it removed after she left, washed the injured area and replaced it with new netting. Fear of infecting and damaging the delicate grafted skin on my face, hands and legs was always at the forefront of my doctors' minds; visitors were only able to touch my feet, the one part of my body that was accessible and unscathed. My mother took to gently massaging my feet again every day, which I loved – it was so calming and reassuring and I swear I could feel her love being poured into her massages.

Throughout my recovery my greatest fear was being left alone in the room, which to be fair didn't happen very often. However, when I was, I developed heart palpitations and banged my foot on the bed to loosen the sensor attached to my toe (due to my fingers not being available), and duly set the alarms off so someone would come in and see me. The poor nurses must have cursed me but they always came running.

The graft 'donor sites' now became the most painful areas of my body, even in comparison to the burn injuries; if I moved and slightly rubbed them, I yelped with pain. I'm afraid the pain and tedium of everything was only really matched by the indignity of my position – with my hands bandaged so heavily, it fell to my family and the nurses to help me when I needed the loo … and more than once I had to complain about my mother's excessively long and sharp nails!

With the numerous feeding and breathing tubes that had been inserted down my throat, my airways now remained partially open all the time; I therefore wasn't allowed, or able to, drink water in any quantity. The few times I tried it went straight into my lungs and I ended up coughing it up. Consequently, I was constantly thirsty – perhaps more so due to knowing I couldn't really ever quench the dryness – and the highlight of my day was the treat of carefully sucking on an ice cube, from which a trickle of cold water would find its way down my throat, though not too much to be considered a problem. I had to wait many weeks for my throat and vocal cords to heal before I could eat solids again and take my first long, delicious gulp of cold water.

The hospital also had flat lollipop sticks onto which they could insert a sponge, dampen it and rub it around the inside of my mouth to help alleviate the dryness – that became one of Jane's jobs each day. We also discovered that during my three weeks in the coma my teeth hadn't been brushed – they were caked in plaque and gunk. Jane came to the rescue again and, ah, the pleasurable feeling of a toothbrush gently rubbing against my teeth and gums was a simple yet uplifting one.

Equally uplifting were the bundles of cards, letters and messages from friends, neighbours, colleagues, former classmates and even complete strangers from all over the world wanting to wish me well, which Peter brought in with him every day; people of all faiths – Anglican, Roman Catholic, Hindu, Jewish and Muslim – told me to keep fighting and that they were praying for me. There were prayer groups and meetings held for me and distance healers sent me their healing energies, apparently. Reading through the letters was hugely comforting and humbling and often brought me to tears. I realised how lucky I was to be alive and how extraordinarily kind and beautiful humanity can be. I still keep them all in a big box I call my memory box; I don't go in it very often as it also holds some painful memories, but very occasionally I look at a few of the letters and they still move me to tears.

Bizarrely, amongst all the get-well wishes was a card from the examining body responsible for the financial exam I was due to sit at the end of October, the one for which I had been travelling to London to attend the training course on that fateful day, wishing me all the best for it. I don't think anyone had bothered to tell them that I was otherwise engaged. Still, it made me smile when I read it.

Though my family had kept me in the dark as to the extent of the crash and how many people had died and were injured, I began to realise how serious it must have been as the letters and cards started to pour into the hospital for me. The messages from all over the world indicated that the effects of the crash, and the people it had touched, were not just confined to the UK. Details were not contained but from the sentiments expressed in them I came to know that many people had died and many more, like myself, were injured. Who were they? How many had died and how many had survived? What had happened exactly? Why had it happened? The one headline that I had been shown was a newspaper that was asking whether the rail industry had put profits before the safety and lives of their passengers. Was this true? The questions began to filter into my brain but there was little I could do to find out, confined within the walls of Charing Cross as I was.

True to her word, Jane set about contacting my trackside heroes. The dark-haired lady, who had called Peter's mother on the phone from the trackside at Ladbroke Grove, was the first to visit. Unfortunately, due to the heavy medication I was on, I can't recall exactly what we talked about, but do remember we were both moved to see each other again. I hope I got across my heartfelt and deep thanks for all her help.

Next came a tearful reunion with Matt, the man who was the very first to my aid; without him being so quick to help I'm not sure I'd have ever made it. We chatted about various things, including what had happened on the day. Of course, before the crash these people were complete strangers, and I knew nothing about them; it was nice to learn about his family and work. Again, because of the medication, the details of our long chat are blurry but I did have the opportunity of meeting Matt again, along with his wife, a little later when I returned home. We stayed in touch for a while afterwards and I can never really thank Matt enough for what he did for me.

The third person, Evelyn – my fair-haired helper who poured water on my hands and for whom I had been mistaken when first admitted to hospital – I wasn't destined to meet until a few months later. I was not quite as doped up on painkillers by then so I remember that get-together more than the other two, and the uplifting conversation we had. She became a good friend and hugely important in the (later) campaign to improve rail safety.

Thirty-one people lost their lives in Ladbroke Grove on 5 October 1999: twenty-four people on the Thames Turbo train and seven on our high-speed train heading into Paddington. Figures vary for the number of injured, but the last statistics stated that 227 survivors were admitted to hospital, and a further 296 'walking wounded' were treated for varying degrees of lesser injuries.

Back in hospital, I was lying in bed feeling a little sorry for myself after physio, when the most peculiar (and offensive) smell came wafting down the corridor. I honestly thought someone was wafting dustbins around – it was absolutely foul.

'What on earth is that?' I asked.

Jane stuck her head outside the room. 'Er, it appears to be your lunch.'

By this time my throat had recovered enough for me to eat solid food slowly and a plate was deposited in front of me, with a brown, lumpy liquid sloshing around which in turn had white lumpy stuff in it – not the most eloquent sentence, I know, but there is no other way to describe it. The menu declared it to be cottage pie.

'How am I supposed to get better on food that smells like sewage?' I asked indignantly.

Jane couldn't believe it and from that day on Peter and the family started bringing in food from local takeaways and restaurants. I later made a bit of a noise to the powers that be at the hospital about the food and my next meal arrived from the top floor – the private ward. It was delicious! That made me think: if the food is better up there, then maybe other things are better too?

Bernard Clarke was a solicitor and a client of mine; Peter had a word with him and Bernard said he'd look into the private healthcare issue with Railtrack. I was quite happy in my NHS room and hadn't really thought about it until the food issue arose, but as soon as Bernard contacted Railtrack they said they'd happily pay for my transfer upstairs – they hadn't offered before because no one had asked!

I was swiftly moved to a lovely spacious room with a TV and carpet on the floor, and lovely, edible food was cooked daily by a chef who consulted about what I fancied to eat; had it not been for the hospital bed in the room I could have easily convinced myself I was in a hotel. I even had a comfortable chair positioned next to the window which afforded me a beautiful view over west London – what luxury! Although I soon discovered that when it was dark you could also see right down into one of the operating theatres ... it became my own private production of *Casualty*.

I then received news of my first setback: some of the early grafts to my face and hands had failed and I needed further surgery to remove more 'donor skin' to replace them. I felt a bit like a leper, with skin peeling off everywhere. Still, what could I do? There was really no option but to keep on accepting the medical advice and enduring the operations, so I faced them with resignation and as much fortitude as I could muster.

One day, coming up in the lift to the top floor, Peter said he was joined by a chatty woman who was 'six foot three, with big shoulders, huge feet and a large Adam's apple' – he thought it was a man in drag. He was almost correct as one of the nurses told me that as well as being a centre for acute burn victims, Charing Cross was also the centre for sex change operations. Now, that's what I call diversification!

It was after that lift journey up to see me that Peter announced he could not keep coming as it was 'too far to travel' and he was henceforth 'cutting back' on his visits.

I was upset beyond measure. I took it personally and wondered what I'd done to make him feel this way. Of course, I understood travelling to Charing Cross for weeks on end must have been tiring, *but I don't have any choice about the matter, do I?* I thought. *It's not as if I can just choose to get up and leave.* I didn't say anything or argue with him – I didn't have the energy to – and so Peter just became another occasional visitor.

About six weeks after the crash I was allowed to have a bath and have my hair washed for the first time. Jane accompanied me into a cavernous bathroom which had a hoist to lift me in and out. I became quite excited as I was lowered into the lovely clean, warm water waiting below me. Unbeknown to me, I didn't really have any hair to wash, but Jane said nothing and the feeling of her fingers gently rubbing my head coupled with the smell of the shampoo was so wonderful; it restored some of my dignity again. Speaking of which, another victory came when I got rid of the hospital gown in favour of some baggy tracksuit bottoms and jumpers several sizes too large, which Jane bought from a nearby Tesco. Wearing those warm, sensible clothes made me feel like a human being again – and it was such a joy not to have my backside permanently exposed to the world!

Ironically, considering I had always been a shy and sensitive soul, I fast became used to being examined, prodded, dressed, undressed and operated on, and all feelings of embarrassment about nudity left me. This happened to such an extent that one afternoon when a male nurse took me for a bath, he turned his head sideways as I undressed, like any gentleman might, and I said, 'But you're a nurse! You've seen all this before, for goodness' sake! Come on and help me get my trousers off.' I then continued talking to him very matter-of-factly in a nude state.

Aside from moving upstairs, and being taken down to the operating theatre, my trip to the bathroom was really the first time I'd thought much about life outside my own room, and normality. I knew I wasn't the only survivor of the crash still at Charing Cross, as Mike Adams, the American who had been on the Thames Turbo train, had suffered horrific injuries, including a broken back, and was in intensive care for a great deal longer than me. I made friends with his wife, Natalie, who visited him regularly and acted as go-between for discussions between Mike and me, as I was not allowed to visit him in isolation. Mike and I really identified with each other's physical and mental anguish as we'd both been through the same terrible ordeal. I tried to send him messages of hope and titbits on how recovery might feel once he was out of intensive care. Unfortunately, I never met Mike, and I believe he was transported back to the USA once he was medically stable enough. Very sadly, he ended up a paraplegic, and I lost touch with him and Natalie once they had gone.

One thing that I was told – though I don't know for certain – was that Mike, as an American, was treated very differently from how a British patient would be. Natalie explained that the American embassy could not have been more helpful in ensuring Mike received every care and attention he needed; she received regular enquiries for updates from the embassy, and even a personal call from President Clinton. There was no comparable support for British survivors in any hospital, although I believe the Duke of York did visit some. No, for us Brits there was no one authority coordinating and ensuring our needs were taken care of; no phone calls were made to me or my family, and it was left to us to ask for and find things out for ourselves, such as me asking to be moved upstairs to the private ward.

In fact, it was worse than that as when I regained consciousness I was assigned a police liaison officer. Keen to interview me for my version of events, she was pushy and rude, paying little or no thought to my condition. After several 'spats', which completely jangled my nerves, I asked the hospital to stop her coming to see

me. Perhaps aware of this lack of interest my family were experiencing from our own country, the American embassy visitors
said to Jane, 'Right, what do you need? What can we get you?
Who would you like us to call?'

Makes you think, doesn't it?

I know I've written about skin grafts, my hands, having a bath
and so on, but the one thing I haven't mentioned – because I put
it off for as long as possible in my recovery – is looking at myself
in a mirror. There are not usually many mirrors in hospitals, least
of all on a burns unit, so I easily avoided the issue, even managing
to shy away from the one in my en-suite bathroom. I certainly
knew there was something wrong with my face as it felt tight and
peculiar, but in truth I was completely and utterly afraid about
what I might see staring back at me from my mirror.

Nick Percival visited me regularly, often with his registrar in
tow, who had in fact, under Nick's supervision, conducted one
of the operations on my hands, and I often teased Nick about
my left hand looking better and less scarred than the right, and
asked which one he did. He refused to answer! However, Nick
explained that a second skin – a glue-like substance – had been
painted onto my face which when set had covered up the burns
and kept out infection. I had then undergone the various graft
operations, which had had a petroleum jelly-covered gauze laid
on top of them. I could certainly feel the effects of what he was
describing, but throughout said to myself, *Oh, I mustn't look at my
face. It's more important to concentrate on getting my hands working.*
It was just something I refused to think about. So far Nick had
never pushed the issue, but one day roughly three weeks after
the operations on my face he just came right out with, 'Have you
looked at your face yet?'

My blood ran cold.

'You need to look at your face. You must look at your face,' he said. I am not sure what Nick was expecting; I suspect he thought I would tell him or one of the nursing staff when I was ready to do it, so they could be with me. Not knowing what the normal procedure was I decided it was my face, my fate, and it was down to me to deal with whatever I might find. I had to confront this last demon, so I might as well just get on with it alone. I waited for one of the rare occasions when there were no nursing staff in my room and my family were elsewhere for a few minutes and snuck into my bathroom.

I glanced over to the mirror above the washbasin, gritted my teeth and very, very slowly lifted my head and looked up into the mirror.

I was absolutely horrified. Horrified.

My skin was a crusty mess of red, black, purple, pink and yellow; my eyes were drooping; there was gauze on my face hiding more damage, but through it I could see pus oozing out of lesions; my lip was hanging down, too. In fact, it was impossible to see where my lips started and ended. I then saw my left ear was completely coagulated, and that my hair was burnt to nothing with just tufts of matted strands left on my dark scalp.

I burst into tears, which only made my face hurt even more. I was devastated. I simply couldn't believe what I was looking at. I don't think I'd ever really imagined what my face might look like. Yes, I had seen my hands, but had somehow come to terms with them. I feared my face would never heal and that I would never again look like the Pam who used to stare back at me in the mirror. I was so frightened – would I always look like this? Was this to be my window on the world forever more?

I returned to my bed and sobbed my heart out, though I wouldn't tell Mum or Jane why I was so upset when they returned.

I wasn't ready to discuss it with anyone until the following day. I wanted time to assimilate my own thoughts.

The next day I managed to briefly push aside any feelings of anger or self-pity. What was the point? The evidence was staring back at me from the mirror and nothing was going to change it. I tried to use my emotional detachment, which had served me well with my hands, but it was difficult to take in the damage and in the end detachment eluded me and I cried once more. Nick, having been told what I had done the day before, decided I'd recovered my composure enough for him to talk to me further and described the plan for the next round of skin grafts to my hands and legs that I would need once they were healed enough not to require bandages. They would be protected by pressure bandages – very, very tight material that applies constant pressure to the grafts – because, Nick further explained, hypertrophic scarring – the unsightly over-knitting and bubbling up of grafted skin and wounds – occurs in most burns victims and was always treated this way.

'However,' he concluded, 'you can't use these bandages on a face and now the grafts are taking hold, I suggest we look at an alternative treatment for your face. It will help the skin heal and minimise hypertrophic scarring,' he assured me.

It involved me wearing a clear plastic mask.

CHAPTER 8

JOURNEY HOME

The perspex mask was made in the maxillofacial unit at Charing Cross Hospital; Colin Haylock, the head of the department, explained how it worked:

'Now, Pam, it's made of a rigid transparent acrylic material. It looks like a see-through theatrical mask and the way it works is by effectively acting like a greenhouse, keeping the skin moist and hot, which helps the grafts to take hold. I have to make it quite tight but this is necessary to apply pressure to the skin, which will push the scabs down and in turn improve the appearance of the scar tissue you will be left with on your face.'

To say having the mask fitted was a terrifying experience would be an understatement. I have always loathed having anything on my face, be it a party mask or a face pack, and my daily routine with the nebuliser had only strengthened my loathing. The first stage involved making a cast of my face from which the mask was to be moulded; Colin covered my head with a horrible inch-deep jelly-like substance which looked like algae-infested mud and smelled, well, not much better. I could feel it tightening and setting almost immediately, and had to keep my eyes closed, but as the thick jelly was smeared across my nose and mouth I began to panic and hyperventilate.

'It's really important not to move,' Colin said with his calming voice, but I felt I was suffocating in darkness, and my every thought and impulse was to move and free myself. A sense of dread engulfed me.

The five minutes my face was covered seemed an eternity, and this was only the beginning. The mask was ready to be fitted a week before I left hospital. I say 'left' as it was actually my decision and not the doctors', in part due to a physio lady forgetting to visit me when she was supposed to be covering for Russell one day. I thought *They obviously don't care that much about me now I am out of danger* and convinced myself I'd recover better at home. I was certainly desperate to return home, and perhaps this was the excuse I needed. I'd been at Charing Cross for over two months by this point and had begun to feel institutionalised.

On the day of the fitting I was wheeled down to the maxillofacial unit in a chair and placed in the waiting room, where Peter sat with me. Unlike the rest of the hospital, which was all hustle and bustle, this room was very quiet and calm. I looked around and realised that all eyes were focused on me – some glanced surreptitiously while others blatantly stared, gawping at me.

I leaned forward to Peter. 'Why are they all looking at me?'

Peter didn't reply. He didn't know what to say, but his expression said it all, really. The people were of course staring at the face I had seen in the mirror, which, though healing, still looked pretty grotesque – the face of Pam Warren after the accident. It was an unnerving moment; the first time I had encountered a reaction from the 'public', from people who were not my family, doctors or nurses.

I felt I needed to hide my face to avoid upsetting people or, worse still, making them feel sick, as I first did when I looked in the mirror. I hunkered down in the wheelchair as Peter looked on quizzically, and curled up as much as I could. In truth, I wanted to cry and run, and it took all of my resolve to stay in the waiting room while frantically hoping Colin wouldn't be much longer.

A nurse finally emerged to take us through to the consulting room-cum-laboratory where I was ushered into a chair while Colin disappeared to another part of the room to get the mask. It was akin to sitting in the dentist's chair, knowing that he is about to appear with a big drill – the dreaded anticipation of knowing it's for the best, but it won't be very nice. Colin reappeared and started walking towards me with a clear plastic mask in his hands, which he then gently placed over my face. I winced, as I had always done when the nebuliser was attached, in anticipation of discomfort and pain, but strangely I felt neither. The contours of the mask matched those of my face, and consequently any pressure it exerted was spread evenly and comfortably over my whole face. Colin shook his head. 'The mask is too big,' he said. You see, since making the first cast from the awful, thick jelly the swelling on my face had reduced as my skin and muscles had continued to heal and the shape of my face had changed.

He hurried away to another corner of the room from where I heard an odd buzzing type of sound: Colin was working the mask with tools to alter its size. He used heat to soften the perspex and then snipped at it before running it along the outside of some grinding tool. And I thought hearing the dentist's drill was bad enough!

As achieving the correct balance of pressure was a major factor in reducing scarring Colin needed to judge where to attach the bands to hold the mask around the back of my head; he had to pull the perspex tight against my facial skin at the same time as ensuring as much as possible of the developing scar tissue was covered by the mask. I spent a lot of time sitting and waiting that day as Colin disappeared to make alteration after alteration at his workshop bench; he wanted everything to be perfect and took huge pride in his work.

As I sat in my chair awaiting Colin's next alteration, my eyes wandered around the room: there was a fascinating array of books, medical equipment and instruments – a cross between a workshop, a surgical theatre and a branch of B&Q. But then my focus settled on something altogether different: a whole row of specimen jars along a shelf. In them were what looked like pickled body parts – eyeballs, ears and even a nose. I wondered if I had stumbled upon Frankenstein's laboratory for a moment and began to giggle.

Realising what I'd seen, Colin shared a story of when he was once travelling abroad and met a local who had an ear missing, which caused him great derision from others. Colin became fascinated as he knew he could build him a new ear – and that is exactly what he did when he returned to the UK. Hence his motley assortment of jars.

A few hours later my mask was finally fitted. It was hot, uncomfortable and unsightly, and I was faced with wearing it for twenty-three hours a day for at least eighteen months. Colin saw I looked unsure and said, 'It will work, Pam, just give it a chance.'

I smiled, turned to Peter and said, 'I'm vain enough to put up with anything to get my face back.'

Actually, it never ceases to amaze me just how adaptable the human body is, and I started feeling comfortable with the mask very quickly. I even learnt how to sleep fairly well with it with my head propped up on two pillows.

As my face healed, so the swelling reduced further, meaning I needed to revisit Colin for new casts to be made and fitted; in all I had three made over eighteen months.

There was still always the question of my hands. As the grafts healed the new skin became quite tight, behaving a bit like a chamois leather – when moist and exercised it was soft and pliable, but when left alone it hardened and stiffened. My physio sessions did a good job of moving my finger joints but my wrists were a different matter: they very quickly stiffened and started painfully pulling my palms down towards my forearms. To overcome this Nick Percival made hard plastic splints, a bit like large shoehorns, which were attached by straps around my forearms and effectively forced my hands back into a straight horizontal position.

The top joint in my right thumb was also completely burnt through and destroyed in the fire and was deemed completely unsalvageable, but again Nick came up with the idea of inserting a stiff piece of wire through the top of my thumb, down through the damaged joint and into the base of the digit. Apart from it looking a little odd that I had a piece of wire sticking out of the top of my bandages, it worked well and enabled the bone to fuse around it. After a few weeks the bone had healed and the wire was due to be removed. Nick sent one of his registrars into my room with what looked like the largest pair of pliers I had ever seen!

'Is it going to hurt?' I asked, eyeing the chomping jaws with suspicion.

'No, the bone's fused so there'll be no pain,' he said as he firmly put my arm into the crook of his and held it fast. With one swift movement he grasped the wire with the pliers and tugged. I thought my thumb was going to come off completely, and the pain! Oh boy, the pain made me cry.

'You lied to me!' I said when he had finished and was brandishing the wire triumphantly.

'Yes, but you wouldn't have let me near you if I had told you the truth,' he replied. He had a point.

Prior to my discharge, my hands were measured for the pressure gloves I needed to wear; the highly technical procedure involved was a nurse drawing around my unbandaged hands with a pen, just as I am sure we all remember doing at primary school. This was then sent off to the 'pressure garment factory' where my bespoke gloves were made from a strong nylon-type fabric, with a side zip to help get them on and off; the same material was also used for a pressure bandage for my right leg.

As my physical recovery was on the up and life was becoming bearable again, I learnt that Peter had used our savings, along with money he'd managed to winkle out of Railtrack for his own expenses and more he had borrowed by way of a mortgage, to buy a tall, run-down town house with the aim of renovating it into several self-contained flats and renting them out. This was intended to deliver a stable income and do better than his previous property development projects. He'd been encouraged by his daughter, who felt he 'should go for it'. It would mean his few remaining weekly visits would be further reduced.

'What do you think, Pam?' he asked.

I didn't know what to say. I tried to see it from his point of view – yes, he had to keep a business going – but I felt his timing was hardly ideal for starting a new project and we were by no means cash rich. Peter was committing to a renovation he would have to tackle personally, and I feared we risked losing everything we'd worked so hard for. Furthermore, I had no idea how long it would take me to recover properly, or even if I ever would. I realised the drive to and from London was tiring, and I wasn't exactly a bundle of laughs for him, but for better, for worse, I was his wife and I had nearly died. I was still very sick and needed support and strength from my loved ones. But I didn't have the energy to argue and as I still couldn't speak very well I couldn't articulate my fears. So I let him get on with it.

After Peter had gone I began to worry that if I didn't get back home soon things might go badly awry, particularly with our finances, so I asked to see Nick Percival. He came up to my room quite late after an evening operation and was visibly exhausted, so I decided to keep it short and point-blank asked him if I could go home. To my pleasant surprise, he didn't argue or even try to talk me out of it. Realistically, I was no longer in danger and my ongoing therapy schedule could be done as an outpatient.

Also, as my medication regime was fairly standardised and future operations could be arranged whenever they were needed, there was no reason for me to stay in hospital.

'As long as you've got your mask, and you promise to wear it twenty-three hours a day, and you keep up the physio, then you can go,' Nick said.

I promised.

The next morning I excitedly told Jane they were letting me go home, but far from jumping up and down with excitement as I thought she would, the blood drained from her face. 'Who's going to look after you? How are you going to manage at home?' she asked.

'Well, Peter will look after me,' I replied.

'No, he simply won't be able to cope,' she said. 'He won't know how to treat or deal with your grafts, or how to manage your pain or be able to help you when you have been woken by nightmares and flashbacks.'

Jane then matter-of-factly said, 'OK, I'll leave my university course for a year. I will come home with you and look after you.'

I tried to protest that she had her own life, her university course, a long-term relationship, and that she shouldn't put any of this on hold to look after me; she wouldn't listen.

'I almost lost my sister once. I want to make sure there is no danger of losing her again.'

And that was that – Jane was coming home with me.

Preparing for discharge from hospital was actually rather complicated, and because of my poor health and general lack of immune system, coupled with all the medication I was on, I became exhausted very quickly. Realising the daily trips to London for therapy would be difficult for me, Jane set about finding centres closer to home.

On discharge day – 20 December, I think it was – I woke with a feeling of excitement and anticipation that I hadn't experienced in a very long time. After almost three months in hospital, I was finally going home. I had hoped to leave early in the day, but unfortunately the paperwork wasn't ready right away and my prescriptions needed to come up from the pharmacy, which took hours. By the time I actually left it was dark and freezing cold.

With my big coat on, collar pulled up and plastic mask in place, I stepped out and into Peter's car and entered a strange world, a much faster one than I previously remembered, with lots of people everywhere, and it was quite unnerving. It wasn't a comfortable drive home either, and I remember groaning in pain as we went over humps and bumps, and coupled with cars zooming by with their headlamps blazing, I felt quite spooked. I pushed myself back into the seat firmly, convinced we were going to crash.

Oblivious to my worry, Peter drove so fast in the outside lane that I became near paralysed with fear, pulling my coat tighter around me and my floppy velvet hat as far down over my eyes as I could, while redirecting my consciousness inwards. I closed down to such an extent that I didn't even realise we'd pulled into our driveway.

Mum, her husband, Dad and Jane had gone home ahead of me and gave me a cheer as Peter ushered me through the door. One of my cats, Dizzy, rubbed back and forth across my ankles, delighted to see me again, as I was him. The emotion was huge – I realised just how lucky I was to be crossing the threshold of my house again. I was home for Christmas, when so many others on the train never made it home alive.

CHAPTER 9

HOME, THE PSYCHOLOGIST AND THE SURVIVORS' GROUP

The first thing I did was to totter about the house looking in each room, visually reclaiming my home; it was such a treat to remind myself that there was life outside of hospitals, nurses, drips and medical machines. I poked my head around the door of my office and glanced at my desk, which was piled high with mail. *Ah well, the world keeps turning*, I thought. It's funny that while you get on with everyday 'normal' life and work there is a tacit assumption that you are indispensable or everything would come to a grinding stop if you were taken out of the equation; that is, until something momentous happens to you which does exactly that and you realise how truly dispensable you are and that things have a habit of continuing on without you. It was a valuable lesson which helped take a lot of stress out of my life thereafter.

One of the most moving things that happened to me the day I left hospital was when a parish council delegation turned up with a huge, beautiful fruit basket from all the villagers to welcome me home. I didn't think they'd know what had happened, and it was a kind and caring gesture on their part which deeply moved me. I love my little village, and with good reason.

I was then completely exhausted by the day's events and desperately needed to go to sleep, but there was the question of our sleeping arrangements. I still had to have my hands hooked up and suspended at night, and couldn't risk being in a bed with Peter in case he rolled over and knocked me. So I offered to take the smallest bedroom and its single bed, and Peter and Jane rigged up some makeshift hooks, suspended from an old floor lamp stand, to support my hands. Being in a single bed didn't unduly bother me, nor did the bijou nature of the room – I much preferred its décor and views to those of my most recent accommodation. Meanwhile, Dizzy, my old tabby cat, wouldn't leave me alone: he stayed with me every hour of every day, save only going downstairs to eat or pop outside for a few minutes. He curled up beside me on the bed and never let me out of his sight. It was almost as though he knew I'd been very ill – he was affectionate but extremely gentle. It was bitterly ironic that just as things started improving for me, Dizzy's health began deteriorating. A few weeks after my homecoming, he became so ill that the vet advised that the kindest thing would be to put him to sleep. Sadly, he was an old cat – he'd been with me for almost fourteen years – and his body was beginning to fail him.

I defy any animal lover to say putting down a pet is an easy decision to make. I knew the vet was right, but even so I found it particularly tough thinking of how I had been so close to death myself, and how Dizzy had massively lifted my spirits when I returned home. Now there was nothing I could do for him, except to end his pain. Peter kindly took him to the vet's for me and followed my wishes that he stayed with him while the injection took effect. Peter returned with a sad air about him, and I cried myself to sleep that night, feeling bereft for days and weeks afterwards.

As you'll have noted, my sister Jane had been a key part of the family team that helped me in hospital, diverting much of what should have been study time for her university course to me. I will never forget how she looked out for her big sister. Before I left hospital, Jane and Mum had planned that I would not be left alone at any time when I returned home; Jane moved in, gave up her university course and said she was there 'to help Peter care' for me, despite me protesting that Jane should live her own life and that none of us knew how long it would take for me to get better, so it was unfair on her to take it all on. In the end she compromised a little, living in with me during the week and returning to her partner for weekends. I must admit I was secretly relieved she was going to be with me so much as I had become very reliant on my sister's care and love. She had become my principal carer.

Peter helped out with the cooking, but was preoccupied with the building project and other business opportunities or watching Reading FC play. At weekends, when Jane was away, he brought in an outside nursing agency to cover his absences. The nurses were very good and extremely kind, but they were strangers in my home and the agency could never guarantee the same nurse each weekend. I'd had my fill of strangers in hospital, and as my sensitivity about my wounds and injuries grew greater, I began to hate new people poking, prodding and cleaning them. I always hated feeling unclean and ill-prepared for the day ahead, and this was made worse because Peter would often leave things like helping me have a shower or get dressed in the morning until the nurse arrived, whatever time that might be.

My homecoming apparently signalled to Peter that I was well enough for him to continue with life as near to normal again. I understood his need to get into a work routine, and to enjoy himself too. I knew I was a burden and was very aware of how draining caring for someone like me could be. But I quickly began to feel like an inconvenience.

New Year, and indeed the new millennium, fast approached, and as it had always been one of my favourite times of year, I wanted to mark it in some way. My next door neighbours, Mary and Simon, came over for the evening and we toasted the beginning of the year 2000 with champagne, although I was only able to sip at one glass because I was still on heavy doses of morphine and various other medications, which was a real bummer!

With a new leaf turned over in the story of my life, I began thinking about work again. I'd been out of the loop for four months and was worried about my clients and their financial affairs, and felt it unfair to leave everything in limbo any longer. I told Peter there was no way I could return to work for the foreseeable future, so wanted to sell off my side of the business. He understood and said he would help with the arrangements.

I felt Peter overestimated what I could actually cope with, with me sitting through meetings he had arranged with potential buyers in my dressing gown and bandages, my face covered with scabs and the plastic mask, wilting in a chair at probably one of my lowest ebbs. The meetings were sapping me physically and I was anguished meeting all the strangers. There was a succession of meetings, until a financial adviser friend of Peter's struck a deal to buy my client base. I duly arranged a personal introduction to each client, only for the friend to then let me down on the financial side. After the awful, stressful experience of reaching a deal, the company I had worked so hard building up was handed over for a fraction of its value.

I plumbed new depths when Peter invited one of his clients to come into our home, past where I was lying in my makeshift daybed downstairs, without warning. When this guy came back past me on his way out, I heard him say, 'Yuck! What the fuck happened to her?'

Understandably, Jane became more and more concerned with what she was seeing on a daily basis. Peter was carrying on as though virtually nothing had changed and didn't realise I couldn't behave like I had or have the same energy as before. And I couldn't. In fact, I was weakening to the point where I became so sick I couldn't keep down food or liquid and my temperature soared.

Jane rang my GP, who in turn called an ambulance. I was rushed to the Royal Berkshire Hospital in Reading.

By the time I was admitted, my body was hurting and aching all over, I wasn't very lucid and I couldn't talk much.

I began drifting in and out of consciousness but do remember them trying to get a drip into my arm as I was dehydrated, and they struggled as my veins had collapsed. Doctors were asking me questions but I couldn't respond. Peter caught up with Jane at the hospital, sorry that he had been so blasé about my ill health. The doctors told him I was completely exhausted, both physically and mentally. I'd obviously picked up a bug, and with my immune system suppressed by all the painkillers I was on, I couldn't fight it off.

Thankfully, after a few days I regained my strength sufficiently for them to allow me to return home and Peter fussed over me and made sure I didn't lift a finger, insisting I just watch TV. Mind you, there's only so much daytime TV a sane person can take! After a few days, I realised I needed something positive to focus on, something to do and to aim for without tiring myself out. It was then that I looked around my room and paid closer attention to the hundreds of cards and letters that were still pouring in to me from well-wishers who were, in the main, complete strangers – people from as far away as Canada, the USA and Australia, and all over the British Isles and Europe too. I even received a 'psychic painting' from a kind lady in Sweden who said it would help me heal. To say I felt humbled by everyone's kindness would be a massive understatement; some of the letters moved me to tears, just as the ones I'd received in hospital had done, and it still gives me a warm feeling to think that there are so many genuinely nice people in the world.

That's when it struck me: I would reply to as many people as I could who had included their addresses.

Jane kindly had some cards printed for me:

'Thank you very much for thinking of me. I am now out of hospital and doing well...'

As I dictated, Jane added a handwritten note personalising each card, and then diligently wrote out envelopes before trotting out into the village to post them all. It gave me enormous satisfaction to let those people know how much their words had helped and that I was on the mend. I was one of the lucky ones...

We must have sent out hundreds of the little cards and with each one Jane wrote and mailed, I thought of the other survivors and what they might be going through. How were they coping and being cared for? I remember, a few days after leaving hospital for the first time, that I received a general circular from a group called STAG – Safety on Trains Action Group. It was a campaign group formed after the Southall rail crash, and inside the letter was an invitation for me to attend their London meeting, in January 2000. I decided to accept.

Both Peter and Jane told me I was in no fit state to consider going up to Baker Street for the meeting, but I was adamant I wanted to. They eventually agreed, providing I let them both accompany me.

When we arrived at BDO Stoy Hayward's accountancy office there were around forty people waiting – mainly the bereaved of the Southall crash and three survivors and bereaved from the Ladbroke Grove crash. I was introduced to Maureen Kavanagh and Carol Bell, two of the founders of STAG, who ran the meeting in a very businesslike manner, forming committees and setting up management structures for their campaign. Maureen was automatically proposed and seconded as the group's chair and then various others were invited onto the 'board'. I spent my time, as did most others present, listening and watching rather than talking.

I don't doubt for one moment that STAG invited me to the meeting with the best of intentions, but throughout there was something which made me feel very uneasy about my being present, although I couldn't put my finger on what it was at the time. I later realised those assembled were further along the road to recovery than I was – at that point I could still barely speak with any volume, so had no choice but to listen – and I also saw there were more bereaved than actual survivors, and that the former didn't seem to be listening to the concerns of the latter. Their agendas seemed very different, even to me walking in and not knowing much about any of them. It was only my personal impression that they were two separate bodies of people, each trying to achieve a different goal, but it made me unsure as to whether it would be possible for the two diverse points of view to harmonise and achieve tangible benefits.

I wavered about how the group might help me and whether I should join STAG in their quest to ensure the UK's rail system was made safer. I certainly agreed with their aims, but it seemed to me that survivors wanted answers, whereas the bereaved wanted justice and accountability – or for heads to roll. The survivors wanted accountability too, but mainly answers and a safer rail network.

This subtle difference in their attitudes played on my mind, and in turn made me decide to speak to other survivors of the Ladbroke Grove rail crash.

I asked the liaison officer from the British Transport Police, a large West Indian woman who regularly came to my house to ask questions, if I could have a list of survivors' names and addresses, only for her to tell me the Data Protection Act wouldn't allow her to divulge such personal information. By the time she visited me again, I'd thought of a Plan B.

'How about I draft a letter and the British Transport Police send a copy on to each survivor?' She asked me what exactly I wanted to write to them about, and after some discussion (and some obstinacy on my part!) she agreed.

I dictated a letter to Jane which basically explained how I had been involved in the crash and asked, if they felt able, for those who had been involved or affected to contact me. I'm not really sure what I was expecting as a result. Perhaps a letter or two? A phone call? Or maybe nothing at all? Nevertheless, I felt it was something I needed to do and maybe, just maybe, it might provide some answers to the many questions I had.

Five days after passing the letters on, I received a telephone call from a man named Denman Groves, who explained that his daughter, Juliet, had died in the crash. He told me about her and everything he had been going through since hearing the news. He sounded so gentle, yet so very obviously distressed and, like me, he was trying to make sense of what had happened. We talked for over an hour. It was an emotional conversation, but it also made me realise that other people had been deeply affected and had their lives changed forever by the crash too. The next morning Robin Kellow phoned; his daughter Elaine had died in the crash.

They were bereaved, but for the next few days my phone rang incessantly with calls from survivors too. Most resulted in long conversations at the end of which I asked if they would like to stay in touch, and duly dictated their addresses to Jane, who was sitting beside me, poised with a pen in her hand.

Four days after hearing from Denman Groves, I'd received a total of thirty-five calls and found myself listening to thirty-five very different and heart-rending stories and relating my story thirty-five times over. It was emotionally draining, though I did draw some strength and sense of comradeship from talking with other survivors. However, I realised my approach of long

LEFT My biological father, Yogash Tewari, taken before I was born.

BELOW The day we moved to Cookham. Richard, my new dad, bought Honey the ginger cat for me when we moved into the village.

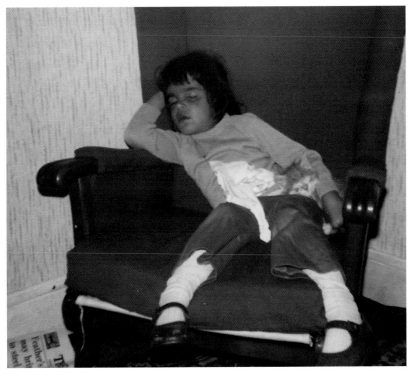

My sister and I. Mum liked to dress us in identical outfits.

My geek days at Little Heath.

When my Indian grandmother came to visit us in the UK she dressed me up in a sari. I felt very uncomfortable.

Towards the end of my teenage years. They had been hard and this picture sums them up.

Team paintballing while at Scottish Life. I used to have such elegant hands.

Move over Joan Collins! Embracing '80s style in a shoulder-padded suit.

Thirty-one people died and more than 500 were injured when the trains collided at Ladbroke Grove on 5 October 1999.

The Queen visiting the crash site.

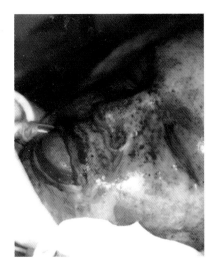

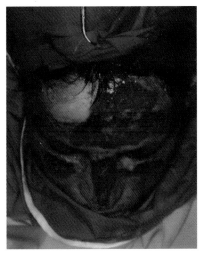

In hospital in the aftermath of the crash. I was fighting for my life.

Before the grafting operation. All the layers of skin on my face were gone. Thankfully I was unconscious throughout this period.

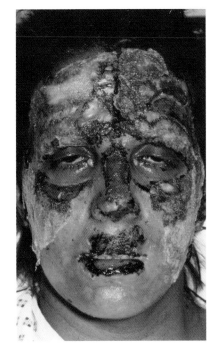

Out of the coma.

Thursday May 11 2000

Mirror

www.mirror.co.uk

PADDINGTON CRASH FURY

Profits before safety

By HARRY ARNOLD

RELATIVES of the 31 victims of the Paddington rail disaster yesterday heard of a catalogue of blunders and warnings that went unheeded.

The first day of the inquiry into the tragedy was told how the rookie driver who went through a red signal had a conviction for assault and should not have got the job.

Senior counsel Robert Owen accused Railtrack of putting profit said there had been "a conflict of issues of operational safety and commercial considerations".

He was echoing an allegation made earlier by crash survivor Pam Warren, 31, who wears a mask over her horrific burns.

At an emotional news conference before the London hearing began, Mrs Warren said survivors were now

MASK: Pam Warren

From the *Mirror*. I don't have any personal photographs of me wearing the mask because I refused to have them taken.

Swindon, October 2000. The AdVan during our campaign on the first anniversary of the crash. I am hidden by the media mob.

2001. Out of the clinic – and the mask comes off.

ABOVE My first appearance with make-up on after the mask was removed.

MIDDLE At the Women of the Year awards in 2001. The lovely Marie Colvin became a dear friend. She is sadly missed.

BELOW Presenting medals to members of the emergency services in Harrogate.

LEFT The tenth anniversary of the crash.

BELOW Simon Weston has been a tower of strength for me in the past. I count myself very lucky that we are such good friends.

telephone conversations followed up by a letter was simply not practical. I had sent out four hundred letters in the first instance, and wondered how I would deal with it if over a hundred people called me. Thirty-five had been difficult to cope with. I decided the best way forward was to arrange a meeting at which we could all talk face to face.

However, the STAG meeting I'd attended had given me food for thought.

Before arranging my first meeting, I contacted a psychologist friend who specialised in the after-effects of disasters. He confirmed and re-emphasised what I had thought about the STAG meeting: 'Do not mix the bereaved with survivors, Pam,' he said, 'they have different emotional needs and agendas. If you do, you may come to blows in the future.' I heeded his advice and only invited the survivors who had contacted me.

While all of this was going on, I was also coming to terms with my own problems, albeit not physical this time. You see, straight after the train crash there had been a team of counsellors and psychologists brought in to help people with the mental trauma of what had happened, but by the time I'd left hospital, the counsellors had all but disappeared. I was effectively left to cope alone with my mental recovery and was suffering terrible nightmares – a nightly reliving of the crash, which soon became more and more intense. While my family were a great support, I didn't feel they really understood the mental anguish I was encountering each and every night; I was terrified of closing my eyes for fear of what might appear. It was my idea of what purgatory must be like. I was being tortured night, after night, after night.

As if night times weren't bad enough, during the day I began having flashbacks where the real world would disappear and I found myself back in the crash, experiencing the same feelings and sensations I had on the train. This often culminated in me physically seizing up, sweating profusely and finally violently throwing up. I couldn't even escape by reading or listening to music – that was probably the morphine. I turned to my GP, Dr Oppenheimer, who suggested I meet a psychotherapist called Dr Suzanna Rose. For the next nine months I visited Dr Rose, a well-proportioned, fair-haired, gentle woman in her early fifties whose clinic was near Twyford in Berkshire. She started off by asking me to talk about the crash but as she was a stranger I didn't feel comfortable opening up to her; I found it too painful to relive. So she tried a technique called 'Rapid Eye Movement' – basically getting me to follow her finger with my eyes as we talked about the crash, supposedly to desensitise me. I'm afraid the technique didn't work, though I did try to play along for those few months. My conscious mind simply couldn't accept how REM would work or help and, perhaps, put up enough of a barrier for it not to be effective in my case.

Meanwhile, the first meeting of the survivors was held at the Posthouse Hotel in Swindon on 8 April 2000. I arrived early with Peter and Jane to look over the function room I'd hired, having no idea how many people might turn up, what their attitude would be or what we were going to do or say. All I knew was that it felt like a positive step to be taking.

Just before 11 a.m. the first people arrived, wandering into the room quietly; there was no animation, no chit-chat, no normal first-meeting enquiries. I look back now and realise we probably all looked very grey, subdued and even haunted. As a few more came into the room I tried to smile and put them at ease, though I'm sure my appearance didn't help matters with my face distorted by sores and my skin grafts grotesquely displayed through my plastic mask. Not to be perturbed I continued my role as hostess: 'Tea, coffee, water?' I asked. 'There are nibbles at the back of the room.'

I must have said, 'Hello, I'm Pam Warren' two dozen times. 'Hello, I'm Pam Warren. Nice to meet you. Thank you for coming,' which was playing havoc with my vocal cords as they tired very quickly. I followed each introduction with a nervous laugh and an explanation as to why I couldn't shake their hands, quickly waving my own, encased in the black pressure-garment gloves to demonstrate the point. I can't recall exactly how many there were, but I think about fifty-odd people.

We arranged the chairs in the room into a semi-circle facing a table at the top of the room and sat down, just looking at each other, until I forced myself up and said, 'Well, thank you all for coming. I don't know what to do now ... erm ... I suppose one of the things we ought to do is talk about what happened?'

There was a deafening silence, and my nervousness and uncertainty grew by the second, until someone asked, 'Do you remember the smell? That awful smell after the crash?'

It was as though a giant 'on' switch had been flicked, as everyone suddenly started talking. 'What train were you on?' ... 'Where were you?' ... 'Which carriage were you in?' ... 'Do you remember this?' ... 'Do you remember that?'

We all left our chairs, moved towards each other and broke off into little groups, all talking, all very animated, with gestures, hand movements, a few quiet tears and even some smiles. I moved between the huddles of people, listening and chipping in. Nobody had to explain anything – the mere mention of diesel, or the fireball, or the wreckage was enough. Everyone knew what it meant, looked and felt like – we had all shared in it first-hand and now seemed to have a tangible bond that needed no verbal explanations. The meeting ran for the rest of the morning and into the afternoon. I had only booked the room for a couple of hours but the Posthouse staff were brilliant and understood what was taking place. However, I don't think any of the people assembled noticed the time, we were just so enthused.

I came away feeling an overwhelming sense of relief. There were people there who completely and utterly understood, and there were so many of us – none of us were alone.

Having called the meeting to some sort of order, we all agreed to meet again. It was at this point that someone suggested we form a group – my blood ran cold as I remembered the STAG meeting.

'What sort of group?' I queried.

'A support group,' one of the others responded.

'Somewhere we can get together and chat, exchange ideas, pass on experiences,' another replied.

'Where we can help each other,' came another.

I relaxed and my blood flowed again. Although we had a mixture of ideas, we all wanted to be an emotional support for each other. I don't believe campaigning was even mentioned at this time, simply that questions needed to be posed to the rail industry – to Railtrack – regarding their safety record. One or two of us were to go away and look into the Clapham rail disaster report and the findings of the Southall rail crash. It was early days for the internet, but the HSE and Railtrack preliminary reports into Paddington were already available online. For anyone taking the time and trouble to root around, to talk to survivors of the crash with significant experience of railways, there was plenty of information to be gleaned. We were about to become rail industry experts in a very short period of time.

'OK,' I said, 'but this has to be done on a bit of a proper footing, otherwise our meetings might drag on for hours. Can we agree that whatever happens we are a democratic group so everyone has an equal say?'

Everyone agreed.

I mentioned that I absolutely loathed committees (which I

still do), but felt we needed to appoint someone to arrange the meetings and be a sort of coordinator. As the words left my lips I sensed all eyes were on me, though with friendly smiles, swiftly followed by fingers pointing at me. I had no choice but to agree. As for what we might call our meetings? We decided on 'The Paddington Survivors' Group'.

CHAPTER 10

THE LADY IN THE MASK

Ever since my discharge from hospital my home life had seemed to revolve around therapies and medical appointments. I had to visit a physiotherapist, Kate, every single day to have my hands and fingers manipulated and bent throughout their full range of movement; the searing pain, tears and teeth-grinding became routine. I also had to see an occupational therapist, Meryl, who helped me work on the muscles in my hands to make my grip stronger, which is actually very important in day-to-day life – I had to relearn how to hold a knife and fork, a cup, a plate, a saucepan … everything, without dropping it. It was just like being a toddler again. For a while I even had a plastic 'tippy cup' as I kept on dropping my best crockery at home.

I knew it was going to be a long, slow process as I'd lost all feeling in both hands, making my sense of touch non-existent. I had to concentrate on my exercises so much that on occasion I noticed my mind disassociated itself from my hands, meaning I could look at them dispassionately, as if they were separated from the rest of my body, and observe with total fascination what they were trying to do and the improvements they made as the months went on.

I also saw a speech therapist each week to try to strengthen my voice again. In the early days I could barely speak above a whisper and in the weeks and months that followed my vocal cords still felt weak. The therapist taught me a technique for using the flow of air to project my voice more without putting unnatural strain on my vocal cords. I guess she effectively taught me how to breathe again.

I also still had to attend outpatient appointments with Nick

Percival so he could monitor my progress and deal with new operations as problems occurred. Although I had lost the tips of most of my fingers I still had the vestiges of my fingernail beds so shards of nail kept trying to grow, but the nails were too damaged to retain so these beds had to be removed. I then had a procedure called Z-plasty to cut into the webbing between my fingers, which was overgrowing and restricting movement. There were also a few more graft operations to go through for my face, and some laser surgery to smooth some of the scar tissue on my face that had not been caught and pressed down by the mask and some that was bubbling up on my legs.

In hindsight, I should have realised the treatments alone were enough to deal with, but of course the Survivors' Group now figured too. 'It will only mean arranging the odd meeting every month or so,' I told everyone. How wrong was I!

I've already mentioned my solicitor friend Bernard Clarke, whose timely intervention ensured I was switched to a private ward in hospital. Well, Bernard became an increasingly important part of my recovery, and, boy, was I grateful he was on my side. With an intimidating physique, not unlike a Maori rugby forward, Bernard has an intellect to match and can crunch facts and arguments into a logical order, wiping the floor with ill-prepared challengers.

By early spring 2000, Bernard had gathered and marshalled a lot of evidence for what we all knew would be a long and drawn-out battle to win adequate compensation for the injuries I had suffered in the crash. Not that any amount of money could ever compensate for what I'd been through, but there was the issue of my ongoing medical treatment and needs, plus of course the question of whether I'd ever be able to work again, and without me bringing an income home, there was no way Peter and I could carry on living in our home – the mortgage payments were too high. This battle was also about the authorities responsible being called to account.

In late April 2000, I met with Bernard in his dark oak-panelled office in Crutched Friars near Tower Hill to review progress and prepare for the government's own inquiry, chaired by Lord Cullen, into the crash, which was due to begin on 10 May. Near the end of our hour-long meeting, Bernard leaned forward across his desk and looked me directly in the eye: 'Pam, when the Cullen Inquiry kicks off the media are going to have a field day. My advice is that you need to appoint someone, a media consultant, to stand between you and them – someone to help you handle it all.'

I was a bit perplexed as I couldn't understand why the media would be interested in me. However, I had already learnt to take Bernard's advice seriously, so I merely asked, 'Who?'

'I have someone in mind. I've worked with him before, but why don't you see what you think of him? His name is Martin Minns.'

Two days later I received a call from a man with a pronounced West Country accent. There was something in his voice that I liked – it was calm and reassuring – so I invited him to meet me at my home the following afternoon. I still didn't believe I really needed his services but again trusted in what Bernard had advised me to do.

At 4.30 p.m. the next day, a fair-haired, slightly dishevelled man in a blue blazer arrived, looking far younger than I had anticipated and reminding me a little of Boris Johnson. Peter ushered him into the room where I was sitting curled up with my feet up on the sofa. Martin sat down opposite me, with a coffee table in between us and Peter in an armchair to my right. Within a few seconds, Martin noticed an ashtray and a packet of cigarettes on the coffee table.

'Good oh! Smokers! Marvellous!' he proclaimed. 'Do you mind if I light up?'

Martin later confided that he was relieved to discover we both smoked as he was worried about meeting this badly burnt woman and having to excuse himself for a ciggie every hour or so. He seemed to relax instantly and feel at home with us both, and that was a major factor in my liking him right away. His accent, by the way, wasn't so much Somerset as a 'knackered Norfolk accent', he said. I was struck by his lovely sense of humour – it had been some time since I'd laughed, and to find myself having a conversation about quite sombre and serious subjects, but able to smile and see the funny side of things, convinced me that I might indeed welcome a Martin Minns around. As for the media interest in me, I genuinely believed that I would be wasting Martin's time but, hey, if he said he really wanted to shield me from media intrusion, who was I to object?

At the next meeting of the Paddington Survivors' Group (the PSG) at the Posthouse Hotel in Reading, I introduced Martin to the group and it was unanimously agreed that he should be our media consultant, although in our naivety we simply didn't grasp how much interest the media would start to take in us. Of course, Martin needed paying for his services and Railtrack, who at the time had agreed to fund our support group meetings, agreed to pay him a small amount to act for us and, in a way, protect us. They at least seemed to appreciate how the media would react and agreed that none of us were savvy enough to cope with it.

I think it was also at this second meeting that we all discussed using our experience to make a difference in bringing about some of the changes that the rail companies had promised in the past – after the Southall crash, for example – but had not delivered. As things stood, commuters couldn't travel on trains in safety. Every survivor in the group, without exception, thought and felt the same.

It was just four days until the Cullen Inquiry and with little time to waste, Martin suggested we hold a pre-inquiry press briefing so the media would have material for the opening day. It was to be my first experience of the media feeding frenzy, and the group's first lesson in how to handle it. We decided to blend our early thoughts, internet research into the shelved Clapham report and the testimony of survivors into a hastily drafted ten-point plan for rail safety.

In a nutshell, the plan called for driver training in the UK, which was some way behind that of Japan, France and Germany, to be improved; it also highlighted the need for improvements to the rail infrastructure in Britain, which was not in a good way – safety and signalling equipment was something less than state of the art, and improvement work was being carried out under the shadow of government levies and fines for any late-running projects, which we felt encouraged Railtrack and their contractors to cut corners to get the work done on time; trains needed to be fitted with sprinklers and more adequate emergency exits (and means to exit); there also seemed to be no system in place to stem overflow or 'peak loading' of carriages. The ten-point plan called for the restoration of the public subsidy to railways to immediate post-privatisation levels, some form of direct accountability or 'corporate killing' legislation, the implementation of fail-safe signalling, and the suspension of all profits and bonuses and punitive fines for late running until an 'auditable safety system' had been installed by Railtrack. Given we'd only been at it a month, we felt we'd made good progress, and our objectives were clear-sighted and reasonable. It didn't take a genius to ascertain that the railways were in a mess.

By now I had formed strong alliances with many of my fellow survivors, who were to become pivotal to the public face of our campaign. Because the media always wanted me (because of the mask) all of the following guys became very protective of me and deflected the media from me whenever they could:

– Richard Castle was a wing commander in the Royal Air Force. He had received burns to his body, hands and face and wore pressure bandages, much the same as I did, though not the mask. Richard was the quiet voice of reason within the group and came across as a very unassuming man. He was good with words and expressed himself to the media in an understated but effective way;

– Tony Jasper, though not physically damaged, did a lot of running around from interview to interview. Again, he was quiet but had a good way of getting his point across with the media and worked tirelessly to keep the media pressure off me;

– Jan Vaughan was also not physically damaged but was, again, a great advocate for the group (Tony and Jan were single when they joined the group. During our campaign, circumstances meant that they found themselves together a lot and they fell in love, married and eventually moved to France to start their lives afresh);

– Evelyn Crosskey, the survivor who had helped me at the trackside, had only recently been married when the crash occurred. She became my media partner in the early days of the campaign as the media naturally liked to pair the two of us together. She was always by my side and added her voice to mine. Behind the scenes she was, for a while, my second in command at the PSG, and attended all meetings with me. If members couldn't get hold of me, she would step in and deal with it all. She continued to support, act and advocate the PSG's aims until she reached a point where she wanted to move on with her life, which may well have been down to the intrusion that the publicity was placing on her life and her recovery;

– Andrea Bryce, a beautiful, calm and understanding young Scottish girl who helped out with the media in the early days. She eventually returned to Edinburgh and is now happily married;

– Helen Mitchell, another stalwart of the initial media campaign who gave of herself tirelessly. An erudite speaker, she got our points across effortlessly. She became a close friend for a while, though we have lost touch in recent years;

– Janette Orr remains a good friend to this day, having said to me at one of the early meetings, 'You may not want me in the group.' When I asked why, she replied, 'Because I work for Railtrack.' I had to reassure her that it made no difference – she was a survivor the same as the rest of us, had a voice (she wanted to find out what had happened) and had a right to know why and what would be done about improving things. She became a real demon with the media, not taking their unreasonable demands, shielding me from their questions when it became too much for me, and partnering me in interviews and meetings after Evelyn had gone;

– Colin Paton (a guard on our train) had originally joined STAG but decided to throw his energies into the PSG as he found, the same as I did, that he was not listened to by them as a survivor. Colin was a strong advocate for our cause and was able to describe things from a rail worker's point of view. Straight and to the point, blunt even, but avuncular and with a great sense of humour, he eventually married a few years on and emigrated to Greece;

– Colin Field was also burnt badly on his hands, face and body. Like Richard, he was not given the plastic mask, and had to wear pressure bandages on his torso and hands which I know gave him a lot of pain. This didn't stop him always being good-humoured but direct and to the point with the media;

– Simon Benham became the PSG chairman after I left, and was quite a young man when this all happened. Even so, he contributed his opinions and got stuck into helping with the media and coming to various meetings with the politicians and trade unions. He went on to marry some years back and is now settled with a baby;

– Jonathan Duckworth became chairman of the PSG after Simon and was part of the group who took over when most of us had moved on with our lives. He then took on all of the media requests and coverage while we all dropped out of public sight.

There were, in total, eighty-one members of the PSG, and although many were not keen on dealing with the media and the publicity it entailed, all were supportive of our entire approach and campaign. The guys mentioned above and I initially formed the core of the PSG media team with others helping out whenever and wherever they could.

Two days before Lord Cullen opened his inquiry, we all returned to the Posthouse at 10 a.m. and as Peter and I arrived we saw people milling around with cameras, tripods and microphones while vans and estate cars were being unloaded of equipment in the car park. There, flitting between them, was Martin Minns, with his mobile phone firmly clamped to his ear, finding out who wanted what and when. The press turnout was overwhelming. I was a little startled and bewildered at first – a bit like a rabbit caught in headlights – but before I had time to think, Martin whisked me off to what was to be the first interview.

I had never known anything like it before; to say I was scared to death would be a mild understatement, partly because I'd never been in a public arena with my mask on. All of the media seemed to gravitate towards me. In my mask, the old adage of 'a picture paints a thousand words' was very apt. I was so grateful that Martin stood in between us and handled everything so expertly, and thank God for the other guys from the PSG sharing the journalists' demands. Privately, I hated the attention and wanted them all to go away, but I knew I had to use the opportunity to try to do some good and perhaps attempt to bring some positive meaning to what had happened to me at Ladbroke Grove. I squared my shoulders, bit my lip, stuck my chin out and strode into the fray.

Over the next two hours, Martin kept popping up each time I'd concluded one interview to move me over to another waiting journalist or camera. 'Pam, the gentleman over there is from Meridian TV, and would like to interview you under the tree outside. Are you up to that?' Martin asked. He then drew a quick breath and spun around to Tony Jasper.

'Tony, there's a guy here from BBC Radio Berkshire – that's your neck of the woods. Would you mind…?'

Then he turned again to Richard Castle. 'I've told the people at *Channel 4 News* you're a whizz when it comes to the details of rail safety. Would you mind…?' and so on and so on.

I remember Tom Heap, then the BBC's transport correspondent, making me walk up and down the lawn in front of the hotel as the camera rolled to establish some shots, followed by what he called the 'Noddy shot', in which the cameraman filmed Tom first and then me nodding slightly as if taking in a point in the interview. Both scenes were then intercut into the final piece. I'd never realised before that these little bits were actually staged, filmed separately and cut in … And so it all went on. It was energetic, lively and educational and I also found it strangely comforting that there was such a massive interest in our campaign to improve rail safety.

When it was all over I thought about how much I had learnt that day, and though it had been hectic and tiring, I said to myself, *Well, it's over and if that's it, I can cope. It's not too bad.* Little did I realise then that this was just a tiny foretaste of what was to come in the weeks, months and years ahead.

Lord Cullen's inquiry into the Ladbroke Grove rail disaster began on 10 May 2000 at the Methodist Central Hall in Westminster, directly opposite the Houses of Parliament. Louise Christian, the lead solicitor representing some of the bereaved and survivors of the crash (though not me), had organised for a press conference to take place in a subterranean meeting room next to the café in the hall immediately prior to Cullen opening the proceedings, and she asked Martin if I would attend. As I was going to be called as a witness, I thought it might be a good opportunity to check out the hall so I would not be overawed when I took the stand.

The drive up to London that morning on the fast-moving M4 motorway had already exhausted me and, as sometimes happens when I am anxious, I withdrew into a shell – I seem to disappear deep inside myself, and although I am still moving, walking and talking, I am not mentally engaged, which in turn means I don't feel any threats which might otherwise engulf me. One of my psychologists labelled it 'disassociation'; I just call it 'gone'. It's a trick the brain can play if it perceives that you are under threat, and although it's not an unpleasant feeling, it does mean you have to concentrate very hard on what you are trying to do or say until it passes.

It was in this state of mind that I entered the press conference, and the moment I stepped through the doors I was hit by an intense feeling of great anxiety and claustrophobia. There were five television cameras, seven or eight photographers and an equal number of journalists, together with survivors and their families, bereaved and observers, all confined in an oblong room of perhaps 30 by 15 feet. At the far end, a table was set up and was the focus of all the attention; Louise Christian sat at its centre and was to be flanked by three Ladbroke Grove survivors – me, Evelyn Crosskey and Emily Hoch (who had broken her back in the crash and received 30 per cent burns; she had not joined the PSG) – and three bereaved family members – Robin and Diane Kellow, whose 24-year-old daughter, Elaine, had died, and Birgit Andersen from Washington DC, who lost her daughter, Emily, in the crash. We each said our piece about our hopes for the inquiry, and Louise made various points along the way, as well as introducing all the speakers to the press.

Just as I stood up to speak the photographers suddenly moved forwards to kneel and crouch down in front of me with cameras whirring, snapping and flashing, unlike at any other time that morning; others moved to the side of the room, to stand on chairs and angle their lenses down on me. The television cameramen, who had seemed quite relaxed, now moved forward, intently pressing their eyes into their viewfinders. It struck me that my mask and I had become the centre of the press conference, which was both unnerving and intimidating. I heard myself say something along the lines of 'The rail companies are being allowed to get away with running a Third-World rail system', and about how angry I was that the Crown Prosecution Service had decided no rail official would be brought to task, and that 'there is a chronic need for the rail industry to develop a culture of safety'.

I sat down and the cameras flashed even more, making me feel quite disorientated and nauseous. My 'gone' state deserted me and all of a sudden the world snapped back into focus; I panicked and had an overwhelming urge to just run out.

Martin meanwhile sat at the back of the room taking everything in, gauging the reaction to what was said. He told me that as soon as the press conference started he had no doubt they were all waiting for me to speak; the one photo they wanted to tell the story was seemingly mine.

The next morning was a particularly lazy one as I was completely exhausted. Ever since the crash I had found early starts were almost impossible, and at 10.30 a.m. I shuffled into the kitchen wearing my pyjamas and dressing gown, and heard the phone ring. It was Scott, my ex-husband: 'Pam, I've just walked across the petrol station forecourt near my office and I glanced across at the newspapers in the rack. Your face is on the front page of virtually every one of them!'

I took a few steps back, stunned and staggered at what I'd just heard. I felt a huge wave of anxiety come over me, and without being able to speak or react just put the phone down and walked, subdued, to the sofa where I just sat, staring into space.

By the time Martin Minns called some fifteen minutes later, I'd curled up on my sofa with a mug of tea Peter had made me; the curtains were closed and I'd basically switched off into my 'gone' state again. It was just as well Martin called as Peter didn't really know what had happened.

'Hi, Peter, have you seen the newspapers this morning? Pam's face is front page, and she's covered on the inside of all of them as well.'

Peter dashed out to the newsagent's and returned with an armful, which he showed to me; but as soon as I saw my face in full colour on the front of the *Daily Mail* with 'Agony of the woman in the plastic mask' underneath, I had to turn away.

Up until this point I'd been relatively unknown and was able to recover in private, amongst my friends and family and in the isolation of my home. Now, all of a sudden, it had become very public and I felt my life, my privacy and my identity had been taken out of my own control. So many other people had been affected, hurt, killed, bereaved by the crash, and I couldn't understand why it was my face that dominated the newspapers and not theirs too. I hadn't appreciated what Martin had said about the media interest in us … and me.

For two days I didn't leave the house and only spoke to Peter and Jane sporadically. The emotional strain was debilitating and adding to it was the fact that I knew I had only one week before giving evidence to Lord Cullen.

With everybody's help and support, I somehow managed to refocus my energies and attention on being a good witness, as it was important I presented my testimony in a clear, concise and professional way. I knew the whole process would be highly emotionally charged.

An inquiry is really no different from normal court proceedings, though less formal, so there was very little preparation to do for it. All I knew was that I was being called as a witness to answer questions that would be posed by barristers for the interested parties from the rail industry, the survivors, the bereaved and Lord Cullen, the inquiry's chairman.

Peter and I were picked up at 8 a.m. on the day I was due to give my testimony by a police officer in an unmarked car.

Martin was waiting for us as we arrived in Westminster, and ushered us past the waiting photographers. With only a few minutes to compose myself, I was led through large double doors into a cavernous waiting room and to a seat between Keith Stiles and a man I later realised was Andrew Rosenheim, another survivor of the crash.

I started shaking with fear (forsaken by my 'gone' state this time). I was still on heavy medication, including the morphine, so my brain felt like it was wading through mud. The large public room was packed with many other people I'd never seen before too, which was also disconcerting.

When I was called, Peter had to physically help me into the witness box as I felt the strength draining from my legs and arms. Morphined up, I had to concentrate hard on the questions. I tried to focus on what I was being asked and answer as clearly as

I could. As far as I can recall I was simply asked for my account of what had happened to me and what I was aware of during the crash. In the briefest of pauses between questions, I glanced down to my right and saw a large-scale model re-creation of the crash site, and it winded me like a punch in the stomach; I'd still not seen any photographs or news reports featuring the wreckage, but now, looking down at the model carriages lying at absurd angles to the track, the true horrifying extent of the disaster was clearly visible. I retold the story of the crash and my ordeal, but my voice kept faltering. It was the first time I'd talked about what had happened in such great detail and all in one go. I felt sick. Each time my voice gave out, Peter raised a glass of water to my lips, which I sipped at, but I didn't have the strength to hold the glass myself. In an effort to get through, I concentrated on Lord Cullen himself, who was sitting high up on my left; he eased my nervousness by smiling kindly at me.

I was asked to clarify a few more points before being let go with the barristers' and Lord Cullen's thanks. I remember being bemused as I quit the room but hoped I had given a helpful account and that it might do some good. When I finished speaking, a man from Thames Trains rose and said, 'I want to express my admiration for your fortitude.'

Lord Cullen smiled again and simply said, 'Well done.'

I took Peter's arm and we left the room. We were met by Martin, and walked out towards the back door of the building where I nervously reached for a cigarette to calm my nerves. Martin then briefed me on what was coming up next: he'd set up an interview with Valerie Grove from *The Times*, after which I'd have to leave the building by the front entrance for a photo call ... and then walk across to the green in front of the conference centre for interviews with various television news channels.

I didn't really want to do any more, I just wanted to go

home. Giving my evidence had drained me to what felt like breaking point.

'Pam, you can cut and run now but you will probably have the media looking for you at home, doorstepping you and popping up when you least want them. We will effectively lose control of them. If you give them a few minutes of your time now, they will respect your privacy and leave you alone later,' Martin said.

My trust in Martin was total, so I (a little reluctantly) agreed to his proposal; the thought of media turning up at my home was also enough to startle me into submission. Martin was to be proved right time and time again over the ensuing years. 'I promise I'll keep it as short as possible,' he further reassured me.

He led Peter and me out to the front steps, where I stood for what seemed like ten minutes as the cameras flashed. 'Got everything you need, gentlemen? Thank you very much,' he said, and ushered me across the cobbles to the triangle of grass beyond.

'You have Tom Heap from the BBC first, and then I'll take you over to do a live interview with Sky News, and once you've done that we'll see where we are, OK?'

For about an hour, I was placed in front of one camera after another, and along the way was taught how to handle a live interview, listening to the disembodied voice of an interviewer in the studio through an earpiece, and learning I had to 'look at the red light' on top of the camera. These technical details were interesting and actually helped distract me, though I swear I could hear my body creaking like the planks of an old ship as I forced it to go on!

I tried to avoid watching the news that night, though the next morning did see *The Times*, which was headlined: 'Masked victim relives horror of Paddington', with a subheading of 'How one woman's dignified account moved the rail crash inquiry'.

Martin had also arranged a more in-depth television interview for me, before the inquiry opened, with Sir Trevor McDonald on ITV's *Tonight* programme, which aired the day after my appearance in front of Lord Cullen.

'The inquiry into the Ladbroke Grove rail disaster has been dominated by the image of one woman,' Sir Trevor said in his programme introduction, 'so badly burnt that she now has to wear a plastic mask…'

Some have thought (and indeed a few have said) that after the initial media frenzy and the image of my masked face in particular becoming a 'symbol' of what had happened to us, I became influenced by the spotlight and press attention. I certainly wasn't aware of it; I had very strong principles about what I was and was not prepared to do and didn't go out looking for attention – it was *they* who kept coming looking for me – and I never took one penny piece for anything I did. Each and every encounter with the press left me shaken and exhausted, making me only want to scurry back to my lovely warm home and curl up on the sofa. But, with Martin around, I became media savvy very quickly and did realise that, if handled correctly, the press could play a powerful part in the PSG campaign.

In fact, in a little over three weeks an obscure collection of people thrown together by a tragic coincidence had become a nationally recognised group whose utterances were sought on an almost daily basis by the country's media. I had ceased to be either Pam MacKay or Pam Warren, but was simply 'the woman in the plastic mask'.

CHAPTER 11

TAKING ACTION

O ur next PSG meeting was taken up with discussions about what had happened during the Cullen Inquiry. After a while a general consensus came to the fore: if we could harness and utilise some of this interest, surely it would be possible for us to campaign for a safer railway system and maybe, with a bit of luck, actually achieve this goal?

My own view was: *Well, we might not achieve anything but at least we can always say we had a go.* It was more important to try and fail rather than not to try at all; luckily my fellow survivors agreed. Well, I say my fellow survivors agreed… However, there was one, only the one, who really didn't see things the way the rest of us did and became quite militant, even suggesting 'setting fire to [Railtrack's] Gerald Corbett on the steps of the inquiry to see how he likes it'. Needless to say, we were horrified with the very thought of it, let alone him saying it publicly. He may have been angry at what had happened to us but, in my view, that did not excuse such vile thoughts of revenge. It wouldn't change what had already happened. We all remonstrated with him and he grudgingly sat down quietly. Quite soon afterwards he left the PSG and joined STAG instead.

STAG's main priority in their campaigning was to get the government to pass corporate manslaughter laws. Their focus seemed to be that individuals in corporations should not be allowed to hide behind their company's persona and avoid prosecution. While in theory I agreed with this principle, I could not see how in our case you could point to a person and allege that they had deliberately set out to cause harm or death or that they were personally responsible for the actions that had led to the incident. There were so many factors and failings that had contributed to what had happened to us at Ladbroke Grove – how, then, could you point the accusatory finger at one lone person?

All of us at the PSG felt it was more important to campaign to identify and change the industry practices that had led to our train crash and ensure things became safer for those travelling on trains in the future. We couldn't alter what had happened to us but we might be able to change things tangibly for others. We had realised that there had been public inquiries and recommendations made after both the earlier tragedies. Large reports from the Clapham Junction and Southall inquiries had been given to the rail industry and government, but not many of the recommendations had been implemented and, in the main, the reports were overlooked, ignored or just left on the shelf. The only way to stop the same thing happening to our public inquiry report and recommendations was for us to keep asking and checking up on what improvements had been made. We decided that, for us, this was our priority and where our energies should be directed. Corporate manslaughter legislation, while needed, was too large a subject for us to encompass in our campaign and would not have the immediate tangible benefits we were after.

We next discussed how best we could approach any campaigning. What had other campaign groups tried? Where had they failed and succeeded? What was the best way to proceed and how could we be most effective? I had done some background research and had been in touch with some other groups that I admired, such as the Omagh Support and Self-Help Group (OSSHG), and we used their valuable advice to devise a strategy. As I have mentioned, the Paddington Survivors' Group was run on a democratic basis and therefore everyone had a say. Although unanimous agreement was not possible on everything, the majority vote was always carried and, I'm pleased to say, it was always constructive.

Our plan was quite simple: we didn't want anyone else to face what we'd gone through.

The first of our objectives was to bring about immediate safety improvements; we knew it would take Lord Cullen at least a year before he published any findings, in which time the urgent subject of rail safety improvement might have been ignored, or even forgotten. There were measures which could be taken immediately based on the recommendations of previous reports (Clapham and Southall included) and what was already known about how the Ladbroke Grove crash came about.

Objective number two was to make sure that, upon publication, Lord Cullen's recommendations would be implemented in full. From the outset we had little doubt Cullen would include most of what we wanted in his report; our concern was rather – as had happened before – that the government of the day and the rail authorities would not take the full level of recommendations on board and/or thoroughly enforce them. We didn't want Lord Cullen's report being placed on a shelf somewhere to gather dust.

We felt by keeping Ladbroke Grove and its aftermath in the public eye through the media, and with pressure on politicians and the rail industry's leading figures, it would prove tougher to ignore us, our aims, and those of Lord Cullen. After all, nobody likes bad press. Of course, we turned to Martin Minns to spearhead matters. Martin had in fact drafted a campaign proposal for the PSG and right at the front he said the group should 'use Pam Warren as the focal point'. Martin knew, and indeed had witnessed, the power of 'the woman in the plastic mask'.

I never ever considered myself a celebrity, but from the moment I agreed, saying, 'If it helps?' I did suffer the feeling of becoming public property, and with it I lost a little of my own life. But at least I had the trust and support of my family, who knew me better than anyone else and understood why I felt I had to do this and, in particular, my husband Peter ... or so I thought.

I approached my media role as I would have a job, though I must admit I continued to question my motives each and every time I was asked to do an interview, which I think in fact proved helpful in keeping me focused – why was I doing this? And what might it help us achieve?

On 12 July 2000, Martin told me he'd heard John Prescott, the Deputy Prime Minister and Secretary of State for Environment, Transport and the Regions at the time of the crash, was going to announce his ten-year plan for transport in just six days' time. Martin said it was imperative that the PSG got its proposals out into the public domain before Prescott, in the hope of perhaps influencing some of his policies. What puzzled me, though, was that part one of Lord Cullen's inquiry wasn't coming to an end until late July, so why was Prescott making long-term transport announcements before he heard any of the report findings? It gave me an uneasy feeling the powers that be might be making moves to pre-empt or, worse still, ignore Lord Cullen's findings in favour of their own thoughts.

The day before Prescott's announcement, on 17 July, we called a press conference at the Methodist Central Hall in Westminster; our campaign was entitled 'Action Now on Rail Safety'.

It was the first time the PSG went it alone without the bereaved and without their lawyer, Louise Christian. Martin stressed it was important that the difference between survivors and bereaved be addressed at this point for fear of blurring what could be our most important engagement with the media to date. Unlike many of the bereaved, we were not searching for the guilty.

The day started very early, and soon after 7 a.m. I found myself talking to BBC Radio Five Live, followed by BBC Radio Wales, and then I was live on television on *BBC Breakfast* and *BBC London News*. Evelyn Crosskey, Andrea Bryce, Tony Jasper, Jan Vaughan, Richard Castle and I whizzed all around London in black cabs from the White City studios to Aldwych and Millbank and then back to Central Hall for 9 a.m. and the awaiting radio cars. By the time the press conference got underway all the major television companies had their cameras in place, transport correspondents from the major newspapers were poised with notebooks and pencils in hand, and multiple tape recorders were positioned with their microphones on the top table – behind which we survivors sat.

The thrust of our speeches was really to get John Prescott to meet us and declare his support for our proposals to improve rail safety. Evelyn, Andrea and Tony took it in turns to introduce each section of the proposal document before I concluded with a challenge, looking directly into the lens of the cameras: 'So what's it to be, Mr Prescott? Will you stand by the promise you made at the time of Ladbroke Grove that "Money is no object" to ensure it never happens again?' I finished by saying, 'As things stand today it is not a question of *if* Ladbroke Grove could happen again, it is a question of *when* it will happen again. It is time now for action on rail safety.'

It was a direct and deliberate throwing down of the gauntlet to government. We were certainly cavalier about it, and a modicum of apprehension did hit me as I heard the words coming out of my mouth – I was worried they might pick up our gauntlet and slap us in the face with it.

At midday we headed up the stairs and outside onto the green in front of the conference centre for various live interviews. I was paired with Evelyn Crosskey, partly because it was she who helped me at the trackside, and partly because she was so nervous she felt more confident being with someone (and it was nice to have her company too). We'd just finished one interview when, to my great surprise, Louise Christian, Maureen Kavanagh and Carol Bell of STAG stormed up beside us and Louise started wagging her finger in my face. 'How dare you hold a press conference without consulting us,' she shouted. 'It was always agreed that we'd hold press conferences together. How dare you not invite me and the bereaved!'

We'd never agreed any such thing, but my stomach tightened with anxiety. Inwardly, I cursed myself. Of course I should have at least told them what we were planning to do – that would have been the polite thing to do. But with hindsight I realise that I viewed the unfolding events with my survivor's mentality and with the objectives of the PSG's campaign at the forefront – other groups, such as STAG, did not really enter my head as by now I did not consider their aims to be the same as ours. Diplomatically, organising the press conference had probably not been a good move; but I guess it is better to make a decision, even if it is the wrong one, rather than not make a decision at all.

Louise's aggressive body language and tone made me want to turn and walk away, but being aware of so many TV cameras and microphones in front of us I thought for a moment, and then replied, 'I think we'd better take this off the street, Louise.'

'The bereaved want to see you,' she literally spat at me – indeed, some of her spit did fly out and hit my mask – 'and they're in the upstairs meeting room in Central Hall,' she shouted, as she pointed her finger across the green.

I told her, very politely, that I had one more interview to complete and would head over to see them all directly afterwards. I certainly hadn't expected this confrontation. Her determination to try to pick a fight with me in the full glare of the cameras would have sparked a PR disaster for our campaign and, to be honest, it seemed she'd have been quite happy for that.

From the time we formed the Paddington Survivors' Group we'd been quite clear it was a support group for *survivors* of the crash, and that our primary objective was in campaigning for improved rail safety. Some bereaved felt excluded and angry, but we put the matter to a vote amongst all our members and 90 per cent voted in favour of maintaining our stance.

To compound our differences, STAG and the bereaved had attended each day of the Cullen Inquiry with T-shirts emblazoned with the word 'Murderer', which was intended for the rail professionals. Neither I nor others in the PSG wanted to be seen to be party to this kind of behaviour and felt it too aggressive an attitude to achieve anything.

When I walked into the meeting room in Central Hall, a number of the bereaved immediately, slowly and very deliberately, turned their backs on me. Only Denman Groves remained courteous and gave me a welcoming half-smile. After minutes of silence, punctuated only by muttered comments, I decided I'd had enough and walked out. How could I have a discussion with people who kept their backs turned and refused to talk?

I went downstairs to the coffee bar, shaking with anger.

Ten minutes later, Evelyn came down and saw me. She'd gone into the meeting room with me and had stayed behind, but had obviously been crying. She said once I'd left the room, the bereaved turned on her and complained, bitterly saying I'd held a press conference without telling them because I and the PSG had no idea, and didn't care about, what they were going through. Evelyn had tried to respond when someone shouted 'fuck off' at her.

I was livid and headed straight back to the meeting room. Every step of the way, we survivors had gone out of our way to be sympathetic to the bereaved. It was clearly a one-way street.

This is bloody ironic, I thought as I returned to the room. *They're accusing us of having no idea what they are going through when they are showing a singular disregard as to what we might be feeling. Besides, how dare they feel entitled to swear at a person they know nothing about, and not even allow her to speak?*

'What on earth are you doing?' I shouted as loudly as I could as I re-entered the room. There was silence. I told them how upset Evelyn was downstairs, and that the reason for the press conference was to pre-empt John Prescott and, hopefully, put rail safety at the top of the government's agenda. It was not a personal PR crusade of mine or the PSG; we were not out to collect scalps and we had not it done deliberately to exclude or upset them.

'We want these people sent to jail for what they have done,' one person shouted out. The atmosphere in the room then turned ugly and threatening.

It was clear to me that there was so much anger amongst them that any attempt of a rational discussion would be futile. I swallowed, bit my tongue, apologised and said that the next press conference would be a joint one. But inside my old worry that we were two very different groups of people with very different agendas resurfaced, and it could actually all explode if we weren't very, very careful.

Ten days later, and just prior to John Hendry QC, the lead barrister for the victims of the crash, making his closing speech to the inquiry, we held a joint press conference – the PSG, the bereaved and STAG together. I took my place at the table in the meeting hall next to Robin Kellow, Denman and Maureen Groves, and Louise Christian.

The format was much the same as at the other joint ones, where Louise started by introducing each person and making a speech of her own between the other contributions, along with a closing speech. Louise spoke at great length and she did this five times during the press conference, managing to repeat herself so many times I was not entirely sure she was aware of what she was saying. During each of her speeches I looked around the room; by the time of the fifth, I could see the cameramen and reporters becoming restless. Having become a little more savvy to the media in recent weeks, I knew the press conference was close to running past the deadline for lunchtime news bulletins and felt Louise's poor presentation was now actually becoming counterproductive. I began shifting uncomfortably in my chair, and thanked the heavens when it was finally over.

I knew politically it was best to try to maintain good relations with STAG and the bereaved, and I still had no desire to offend or upset any of them. So a week later I wrote an open letter apologising unreservedly if it had been felt that I or the PSG had ignored or excluded them from our campaign. I reiterated why and on what basis the PSG had been formed, what we were trying to achieve and how we were trying to achieve it. I hoped they might see the bigger picture. In a further attempt to build bridges, I invited Maureen Kavanagh and Carol Bell of STAG to my home, where Evelyn and I could discuss things in more depth with them and see if we might find some common ground to work from. The meeting was not a success.

Maureen and Evelyn sat on the sofa, with me and Carol in separate chairs opposite them. After teas and coffees had been produced Maureen started talking about how disappointed and angry STAG were that the PSG had acted alone and without consultation. I could see her point of view but Evelyn and I tried to explain our position: that we did not feel the two groups' campaign objectives were the same, and that survivors did not seem to have much of a say in STAG, who were predominantly bereaved from the Southall train crash. The PSG's offers to work in tandem with STAG in the past had been met by an unenthusiastic response, and downright hostility in some cases. Surely, I tried to reason, it didn't matter who raised the issues of rail safety in the public's awareness, it was more important that they were raised.

Maureen seemed to get more and more irate as we spoke. Her tone became adversarial and increased in volume and, as I could still not talk very loudly because of my healing vocal cords, I had little option but to drop out of the conversation and simply listen and watch. Evelyn kept on trying to reason with Maureen and tried the conciliatory approach of offering that we work together in the future. Maureen was having none of it by now and, red-faced with anger, kept on talking about 'slights', 'exclusion', how we were ignoring her authority and claimed that 'the PSG want all the glory' while jabbing her finger in Evelyn's direction and calling her 'dear' in a patronising tone. Carol and I simply watched with growing alarm.

How Evelyn managed to keep her temper I do not know but it was admirable as she maintained her calm and carried on trying to talk in an even and controlled tone. Eventually, though, it obviously became too much. 'Don't call me dear – I am not your dear,' Evelyn shouted at Maureen, who was so taken aback she actually stopped mid-flow in her rant.

I could see her gathering her breath to shout back at Evelyn, so I did the only thing I could think of: I slammed my half-empty cup of tea onto the table with a bang and said, 'That's enough,' as loudly as my throat allowed.

We all paused and then Maureen stood up, picked up her handbag and, still enraged, shouted, 'Yes, it is quite enough,' before storming out of the house with Carol following in her wake, shooting us an apologetic look backwards. Carol appeared just as aghast as I felt.

After she had gone Evelyn and I looked at each other, both puzzled and shocked by what had just transpired. We could not understand where Maureen's rage came from or why she felt that way. I was even more convinced that my decision not to defer to STAG had now been proven right. Evelyn and I reported to the other PSG members what had happened and the majority decision was to continue campaigning alone.

By mid-summer 2000, the day-to-day requests for comments and interviews had tailed off after the closing of Lord Cullen's first phase of his inquiry, but I was still inundated with calls from television producers, in particular those making documentaries and other programmes to be screened on the first anniversary of the disaster. There were just too many requests to assist with them all, but I did agree to take part in the BBC's *Panorama* programme and another for Meridian TV. Much of my August was spent filming and keeping up with therapies and operations, while all my friends took off for their annual holidays in the sun. I knew where I'd rather have been!

Though, as stated, we were not on a witch-hunt, we did believe that safety on the rail network could be improved only if the individuals in charge of it could be held responsible for their actions, or lack of them. As such, we did incorporate into our campaign a call for the introduction of a corporate manslaughter charge, leaving no one in any doubt that we felt Railtrack was guilty of a crime. Even though I was uneasy having done so, I had stated that 'someone was responsible for two trains running in opposite directions on the same line at the same time, and for that they ought to be accountable'.

I didn't want us to be seen to be pursuing individuals to bring to justice, as I don't believe any human being would turn up to work and deliberately want to cause death and injury; this was more about ensuring individuals could no longer hide behind their corporations and companies and shrug off responsibility when they made mistakes.

Similarly, at no point did the PSG blame Michael Hodder for what had happened. OK, he was the driver who made the physical error, but it was the rail system that had let him (and us) down with their penny-pinching on safety systems and lack of suitable driver training. It was said at the time within the industry (or so we heard) that it was deemed cheaper to pay compensation to potential victims than spend the money on expensive safety equipment and systems. This is what we were angry about. We weren't out to get one lone, inexperienced man who made a terrible mistake.

On 23 September 2000, I again travelled with my fellow survivors to the Posthouse Hotel in Reading, though this time it was not to convene a meeting of the PSG but to meet with Sir Philip Beck, the chairman of Railtrack, and Gerald Corbett, its chief executive, along with the chairmen of Thames Trains and Great Western. We had extended an invitation to these people as we wanted them to face us and understand we were determined that things had to change. Bang on 11 a.m., a balding, short, pugnacious man breezed into the ground-floor reception room and held out his hand to shake mine. He was Gerald Corbett. I duly held out my hand, but recoiled in terrible pain as, although it was still encased in a black pressure glove, he had gripped my hand with considerable force. I yelped. 'Arrgh!'

'Oh God, I am sorry!' he responded, immediately letting go of my hand and raising his left hand to my shoulder in an apologetic gesture.

In an instant, I noticed that the anxiety and tension that had built up in the room before his arrival all but melted away, for Gerald Corbett was not the great corporate 'I am'; he was in fact a very nervous, anxious and incredibly friendly man. When Sir Philip Beck arrived, he immediately took the lead in the discussions, very much from the Railtrack side as you might expect. He seemed ill at ease and struggled to be coherent and after his fitful performance had continued for a few minutes, Gerald Corbett interjected and, turning to us, said, 'Well, actually, you're not here to listen to us primarily. The important thing is for us to listen to you first of all.'

With that, Corbett took over the running of the meeting.

We talked at length about what had happened at Ladbroke Grove, the impact of the crash on our lives, the problems with the rail system and what needed to be done. As we told our story, made our points of view clear and raised questions, Gerald Corbett listened intently with his eyes cast down at the table in front of him, almost shamefaced in demeanour. He answered our questions directly and, as far as I could tell, honestly, as a human being and not just as the chief executive of Railtrack.

Before meeting the Railtrack executives I was aware that the day could easily have ended in acrimony: it could have been an opportunity for us to vent our anger, and a chance for Railtrack to say they had met with us, listened to our concerns and ticked that box on their list of things to do that week. It actually turned out to be a day that I think subtly changed us all.

I have no doubt that, until they met us, Gerald Corbett, Sir Philip Beck and all the others from Railtrack had not fully comprehended the human consequences of Ladbroke Grove, and thought the PSG were, dare I say, like STAG – a group of people clamouring for justice and compensation. However, after meeting us they realised we were a serious, pragmatic and constructive campaign group. From our side, the perception of the 'faceless, uncaring and dissembling corporate suits' had been challenged, and we all agreed to meet again.

All of the above happened in less than a year from the train crash. I was not only coping with my ongoing medical interventions and recovery, I had also been in an absolute whirlwind of activity for the group and our campaign. After each and every press call, conference or interview, I would be wrung out like an old dish cloth and would collapse into bed, often unable to rise again properly for days afterwards. If a call to arms came on behalf of the campaign, I would have to force myself up and out by my sheer mental will. Deep down I knew I was overdoing it and my mind and body would probably stall at some point. However, we were making progress and the people who could change things were listening. I felt I had to keep going no matter what the personal cost.

CHAPTER 12

A DAY TO BE REMEMBERED

With the first anniversary of Ladbroke Grove looming, and I and the others being unable to think of little else, the PSG decided we should use the date as a focal point of our continued campaign and stage a series of events throughout the week in which the anniversary fell to highlight our aims, aspirations and work to date. Although we knew it was going to be an emotional week, we also recognised it as a chance to capitalise upon intense media interest and it was an opportunity the campaign could not afford to miss.

We dubbed the period 'Rail Safety Week' and busied ourselves checking artwork for stickers, leaflets and posters, while agreeing media schedules with Martin Minns and determining who in the PSG would do what, and where and when. It was very much a military exercise and one that actually helped us all keep sane at a time when I know I personally could have quite easily tumbled into a depressive spiral. A strong sense of obligation drove me on and I said to myself: *Idle hands are the devil's tools.*

On a cold autumn morning, Monday 2 October, with the sun occasionally breaking through the clouds and drizzle, I found myself meeting with Tony Jasper, Jan Vaughan, Evelyn Crosskey and Andrea Bryce from the PSG on the short road in London which runs from Ladbroke Grove to the north of, and parallel to, the rail tracks where twelve months earlier our lives had changed forever. It was an eerie experience to say the least, and a hugely emotional one, and I kept feeling vomit rising into my throat, which I had little option other than to keep swallowing back down.

This location had deliberately been chosen to unveil our

AdVan mobile billboard; made up of two side-by-side panels, the huge poster on the side of the van depicted a train emerging from the barrel of a revolver. Above was the line, made famous by Clint Eastwood in the *Dirty Harry* films, 'Do you feel lucky?' along with 'Action now on rail safety!'

Next to the central image, set against a red background, were four lines:

> 10 trains pass a red
> signal every week
> Paddington one year on –
> nothing's changed

It was short, sweet and brutally to the point.

The television cameras and press photographers gathered in front of the van as I pulled a rope to reveal our poster from underneath a large tarpaulin. I was encouraged to stand directly in front of it by the assembled photographers: 'Stand there, Pam…' 'Look this way, Pam…' 'Turn to your left, Pam…'

I should add, when we formed the PSG there were costs involved such as paying for our meeting room, refreshments, paper for the minutes which were sent to all eighty-one members, postage etc. We decided at an early stage in our campaigning to never take any money from the media as we did not want to stand accused of having 'personal agendas'. Instead, we had asked the rail insurers whether they would fund our minimal costs, which they agreed to. Being frugal, we managed to save a little money from the insurers' allowance and used it for the first anniversary campaign, added to which Martin pulled a lot of strings with his contacts to provide services for free.

After the initial photo call we broke off, under Martin Minns's direction, to take part in individual interviews with the awaiting journalists. The questions came thick and fast, asking everything from 'Why do you feel nothing has changed?' or 'What should the government now be doing?' to 'Just how safe are our trains?'

It was a whirlwind, and one I wasn't sure I could carry on being a part of. I took a deep breath. *Just take each hour at a time*, I told myself. *It'll all be over before you know it.*

Just as I completed my last interview I was bundled somewhat unceremoniously into the passenger seat of the AdVan for a half-day trip along the route taken by the First Great Western train – my train – stopping off in Reading, Swindon and Cheltenham rail stations, meeting up with other local PSG members for more photo and filming sessions with local news and television crews, before then rushing home for a live interview with the BBC's evening news. It was so cold in that van – boy, oh boy, I can still feel it now! I'd fortunately thought to wear some fluffy bed socks under my boots so I could at least try to warm my feet, but I had forgotten about my hands; the cold went straight through my (inadequate) gloves and my grafts hurt like hell. Consequently, I wasn't in the best frame of mind at each stop-off, although I had little choice but to grin and bear it.

Tony Jasper and Martin Minns meanwhile headed off to meet with yet more PSG members and set up a stall on the concourse of Paddington station, which was to be manned each day throughout Rail Safety Week, collect`ing signatures for our petition and handing out our leaflets to passengers; Paddington had somewhat reluctantly agreed to our stall, but I think they felt it diplomatic to cooperate.

Throughout the week, we kept up a round of TV and radio interviews on as many programmes and channels as possible, from *GMTV* to ITN, *Central News*, *Sky News*, *Channel 4 News*, *Channel 5 News* and so forth, with all of them preparing individual reports on Paddington one year on. How we managed to keep going I am not sure; some of us, me included, would end up in tears at the end of each day. But as our press momentum grew, so did the feeling that we should hold a one-minute silence at 08.11 on the Thursday to mark the exact moment of the crash, and remember those who were not lucky enough to survive. Many rail companies agreed with us, as indeed did other companies and organisations around the country, as into the late hours of the Wednesday night prior, Martin Minns continued to receive faxes and emails of support.

I knew I'd previously been the focus of the bereaved's vitriol and was painfully aware I should not do anything to further exacerbate their ill feelings towards the PSG. I said that if my presence on the memorial day at the site of the crash, which was where they were gathering, could be perceived as me seeking publicity at the expense of the bereaved, then I'd rather stay away. It was decided a more sensitive move for everyone would be if we assembled at Paddington station instead of at the Ladbroke Grove site.

Just after 8 a.m. on the Thursday morning about twenty PSG members gathered at Paddington station with Gerald Corbett and other Railtrack officials, along with representatives from First Great Western and Thames Trains. I didn't really feel comfortable with Gerald Corbett standing so close to us on such an emotional occasion, and I was growing ever more apprehensive about the emotions welling up inside me: a mixture of anger, fear, resentment, frustration and uncertainty – all the stuff I had been pushing to the back of my mind, refusing to feel or deal with. My stoic front crumbled when a woman came over to me and said how much her thoughts were with us; I could only blurt out a curt 'thank you' before turning away. As she walked away across the concourse I realised she was someone I had been at school with, someone I had once been quite close to, and I had neither recognised her nor been pleasant to her, which caused me a huge pang of remorse. My emotions were all over the place, as was my head. Then, at 08.10 precisely, a disembodied, vaguely scary, monotone voice announced over the station speaker system that there would be a minute's silence for all those killed at Ladbroke Grove.

The whole of Paddington came to a standstill as all the commuters stopped what they were doing, bowed their heads and observed the minute, even though it was at the height of the rush hour; it was very eerie and surreal. Apparently this scene was repeated at all the main train stations along the First Great Western route that our train had travelled through. It was an act of solidarity that astounded our group when we found out about it afterwards. The minute ended with another announcement and an explosion of flashbulbs from the assembled photographers.

As we broke away, I burst into tears, hugging Peter and some of the others for support. The anniversary was hugely emotional and far from time being a healing factor, I have found each subsequent anniversary equally difficult, though perhaps I am now better able to control my feelings and memories. But I always make a point of stopping at 08.10, quietly paying my respects to those who lost their lives.

The next day, the last of Rail Safety Week, culminated with me leading a delegation from the PSG to deliver our petition signed by thirty-six thousand people to 10 Downing Street. As I walked those fifty or so yards from the security gates on Whitehall up towards that famous black door I remember thinking this was the completion of a journey which I had started a year ago. It wasn't one I had ever intended to make, but at least now I felt I had reached a meaningful destination. For a brief moment I allowed myself to believe that the worst was behind me, that we could all move away from such relentless campaigning and could start moving towards our futures.

The physical and mental toll of Rail Safety Week left me utterly exhausted. I retreated to my home in the country with Peter and quietly started recharging my batteries, feeling we had accomplished something very worthwhile and had got somewhere with our campaign. My respite was brief, however, as the following Tuesday, along with members of STAG, the PSG had a meeting with Deputy Prime Minister John Prescott (now Lord Prescott), the Secretary of State for Transport, Lord 'Gus' MacDonald, and others at what was then the concave, glass-fronted headquarters of the Department for Transport not far from Victoria station in London. The meeting was billed as an opportunity for STAG and the PSG to ask the people directly responsible for transport matters what was being done to improve rail safety. Our joint delegation numbered some twenty people, so it was far from a cosy gathering, and in fact we all sat behind small cylindrical microphones in order that anyone speaking could be heard by everyone in the room. Lord MacDonald chaired the meeting with the strangely quiet, hunched, looming figure of John Prescott to his left. Anyone aware of John Prescott would know he is usually one of the strongest and loudest of personalities; he seemed quite different this day.

Both men made the appropriate noises about rail safety issues being central to all of their transport policies, and while they could not pre-empt Lord Cullen's findings, they would deliver on any measures recommended in his final report. However, something in the way they were saying it made me disbelieve their intent and I began to lose interest. I wasn't the only one. As the meeting went on, I became intrigued by the figure of the Deputy Prime Minister, whose face – which had been propped up by his splayed fingertips – gradually melted into his left hand, like a bored schoolboy at the back of the class on a hot afternoon. A little while later I thought he looked like he'd nodded off as he had his eyelids closed, though it probably was not the case.

I didn't quite hear what Colin Paton, the guard who had been on our train, said at first from the seat next to me. I heard the words 'not caring about safety', at which point I literally jumped in my chair when John Prescott, with his eyes flashing open and his head springing up from his hands, shouted at full volume, 'How dare you tell me that I don't care! I've been fighting for better safety on our transport system since I was a trade union activist. So don't you tell me I don't care!' He continued to shout in quite an aggressive tone for a while. It was so unexpected and so at odds with how his body had been behaving that it took me quite off guard. In fact, outside on the pavement afterwards we PSG members looked at each other and asked, 'Did that just happen?'

Though the outburst did little to impress us, Prescott and MacDonald did both restate that the government would 'deliver any further measures arising from Lord Cullen's inquiry'. From our point of view, one of the main aims of our campaign was to 'deliver Cullen' so this undertaking seemed like a major step in the right direction and we hoped with all our might that they were being sincere.

A few days later a small delegation from the PSG met again with Gerald Corbett, though this time at Railtrack's offices above Euston station. Again, Corbett grew on me and I personally came to like the guy; there was no shilly-shallying with him, he never attempted to blind us with science or statistics, and he seemed genuinely disturbed by what had happened to us. More importantly, the personal rapport we had established with him so quickly really did lead us to believe we were making practical and positive progress with Railtrack towards delivering a higher standard of safety on the railways. We discussed reaching an 'arrangement' with Railtrack as to how to deliver new measures, including providing the PSG with a formal role to consider proposed changes and monitor progress.

On Tuesday 17 October, still feeling pretty good about things, my sister Jane called me at home. I sensed something was wrong by the tone of her voice. She asked if I had seen the lunchtime news. I hadn't. She broke it to me as gently as she could – a Great North Eastern Railway train had come off the rails on a bend near Hatfield, travelling at over a hundred miles per hour. Some people had died, many were injured, but how many was uncertain. Stunned, I dropped the phone down and ran into the living room to switch on Sky News, where I sat glued to the screen, appalled, for the rest of the day and most of the night. Between fits of tears I spoke to friends from the PSG; we called each other non-stop throughout the day, all despairing over what had happened.

Though my thoughts lay first and foremost with the people on that train and their families, especially of the four people who had died, I began to hear myself saying the unfortunate phrase I'd coined at the Cullen Inquiry: *It is not a question of if it will happen again, it is a question of when.*

It went round and round my head all day and I felt absolutely sick to my stomach that I should have in some way predicted such an awful, awful thing as what I was watching on the TV screen. It was a phrase used many times in the press since I had said it and now, although I realised it was illogical, I felt I had somehow brought this accident on by tempting fate.

Gerald Corbett called me. He sounded in shock and I thought I heard the crack in his voice that people get when they have been crying. He told me a lot more than the TV news stations were revealing and explained that a track had broken, before talking more about what they knew so far. To be honest, it wasn't possible to take in what he was saying as my mind was in turmoil. He offered to send his car to pick me and any other PSG members up to drive us to his office at Railtrack when we were ready and felt able to talk, and he said he would explain to us again what Railtrack knew so that we would be properly informed about any rail safety implications.

The Hatfield crash was devastating, and we PSG members knew all too vividly just what the people in that train had gone through, what they had heard and what sounds and smells they had experienced. It brought our own memories to the surface and opened up many healing wounds. Our one small mercy was that we could at least talk to one another about it – we understood and drew comfort from each other. Our first action was to contact the British Transport Police to offer our help to the survivors.

My tears at seeing the pictures on TV turned to anger. *For goodness' sake,* I thought. *How much more needs to happen before someone, somewhere does something tangible rather than just sitting around talking?* It was akin to a hellish form of Groundhog Day.

On the day of the Hatfield crash Gerald Corbett offered his resignation immediately. From our point of view it would have achieved nothing and would have only served to remove our one point of human contact in a corporate machine. My reasoning was not based on personal likes or dislikes of the man, it was more pragmatic. Corbett had been in charge at the time of our crash, as he still was when Hatfield happened, and he appeared to have been deeply affected by both. With his deep emotional response I thought he was in a position to really affect the imple-mentation of better rail safety. Any new chairman would not have such an emotional link and might therefore be less inclined to treat rail safety with the impetus we felt it needed. If he left, I was worried that everything we'd achieved so far would leave with him. I knew that my reasoning would not be understood by those on the outside and, indeed, might seem incomprehensible to many but surely it made sense to use the weapons we had to best effect change. Gerald Corbett knew us, he knew we were not a hysterical group and he knew we researched and deliberated over everything to do with rail safety; we were familiar with the hierarchy of UK rail ownership but were independent with no vested interest in the actual rail system itself. Maybe this could work to our advantage as we brought pressure to bear on him to push safety along at a faster rate.

After our very first meeting, Gerald Corbett had given me his home telephone number, so the day after Hatfield I used it. His wife answered and said that he was still too distraught to speak. She also mentioned that upon hearing the news of the crash the previous day he had left the room and just wept, before picking up the phone to call me.

More than ever, I felt that the PSG needed to back Corbett in an effort to safeguard the progress we had made with our campaign, but I needed the views of the other members before being able to act so I began phoning around as many as I could get hold of to canvass their views and decide upon a line we should take. With only a couple of exceptions, the feeling was that Gerald Corbett should not be hounded from office – and we knew a board meeting had been scheduled for the next day, which we feared would result in Railtrack allowing Corbett to fall on his sword and deflect the blame from them. We had to act fast and I was the only one available to do it…

I was in no fit state to travel to London, so Martin Minns immediately booked a room at the Madejski Stadium in Reading to hold a hastily convened press conference at 4 p.m. As I arrived Martin was finishing off a handwritten draft speech for me to use as the basis of a PSG statement, which I read and made a few notes on as the press were setting up their cameras and micro-phones. It really was a back-of-a-fag-packet-type affair and the notes were simply key words, emphasised by underscoring, trying to get across the reasons for us standing up for Corbett and reit-erating our main desire to stop members of the public having to put their lives in danger on our railway system. Hatfield was unfortunately yet another example of what we had been saying for over a year. I was angry on behalf of the people who had been caught up in Hatfield, thinking to myself *How dare this happen again?*, and used this anger to lend weight to my few words and keep myself going.

After the press conference I stayed back for two or three indi-vidual television interviews before then heading outside to talk on my mobile phone to other TV and radio stations. There were just so many requests that I couldn't possibly handle them all, and Martin Minns suddenly found himself having to step in on a couple while I was on another interview, including one with Radio Sheffield. Martin had just begun arguing our strategy for Gerald Corbett to stay on in his job when another voice came onto the line arguing for him to resign – it was Louise Christian.

Whether our support made any difference I do not know, but the board of directors at Railtrack refused to accept Corbett's resignation that afternoon.

It was a week before we met with a pale, ill-looking Gerald Corbett again. A group of us from the PSG travelled up to his Euston office and, by that time, the cause of the crash had been identified – a rail had sheared as the high-speed train had rounded a bend. Corbett showed us a shredded rail and explained just what had happened, ending with a huge sigh. 'And it happened on my watch again.'

Tony Jasper, Jan Vaughan and Helen Mitchell from the PSG were with me at that meeting and while we were all upset, angry and indignant, I think we were also affected by the way in which Corbett was taking it, which did much to soften our words towards him. We cast glances at each other when, in this room full of his own board members, Gerald Corbett vowed to get the rail track system safe, ending with the comment 'In a strange way, the PSG are our bosses now. You'll be acting as our conscience to make sure we get it right.' It wasn't the most diplomatic thing to say in front of his own board and from the looks on their faces, they didn't like it.

Following the Hatfield crash Railtrack published a list of eighty-one potentially dangerous stretches of line and imposed speed restrictions to lessen the danger to passengers. They may have made train travel safer but with the rail network in a state of near gridlock in places where the improvements were being carried out, there was huge pressure from the travelling public and politicians alike, which obviously made the board of Railtrack nervous. On 17 November, one month after Hatfield, Gerald Corbett offered his resignation as chief executive again and this time it was accepted.

Two weeks later on 29 November, the *Daily Mirror* ran a story stating that I was to accept a paid position within Railtrack. The PSG as a group had discussed having a presence on a national rail safety task force and Rail Safety Ltd – a temporary body set up by Railtrack – but at no time was the mention of money made, and we were only considering it. Even if money had been offered, I personally would not have accepted as for one thing I would have felt compromised. To me, it would have been a step too far. I wanted a safer railway system, not personal gain or gratification. Yet here was the *Daily Mirror* saying I was to be paid £29,000 by Railtrack.

I immediately issued a statement utterly refuting the allegation and sought advice from Bernard Clarke, my solicitor, about suing the Mirror Group. Unusually for him, he was not in a combative mood, saying we probably couldn't prove 'injury' to my reputation. I duly backed down, but it left a very bitter taste in my mouth; someone, somewhere, had obviously fed this false story to the newspaper and it had to be someone who did not like me or what I was standing for. I will never understand how people can be so malicious as to tell blatant untruths about others.

A week later, again without my participation, I was in the *Daily Mirror* once more, under the headline 'Pam's Mask Agony'. The newspaper reported that my mask would not be coming off before Christmas and that I faced more operations well into 2001. This time they got their facts right but I still have no idea where they got them from.

As the year drew to a close and Lord Cullen ended the first phase of his inquiry, I felt we had moved three steps forward between May and October, and then two steps back after Hatfield. None of the immediate improvements we had called for had been implemented, and another fatal crash had taken place. Our working relationship with Railtrack vanished overnight with Corbett leaving (as I had been worried about) and it appeared someone was feeding journalists with malicious and untrue stories about me.

I was totally fed up, disheartened and utterly spent. I had been working flat out for months, scurrying around promoting the PSG's campaign. It had partly been my way of coping and I had thought it would help me in my recovery by adopting a 'back on the horse' mindset. But the Hatfield crash in October, followed by the events leading up to Gerald Corbett's resignation in November and our loss of direct contact with Railtrack, all of which might have been just disappointments to someone else, were devastating for me.

I was still having to cope with ongoing operations as an

outpatient on my grafts, scars and other injuries and the recovery after each procedure was a further drain physically. I was still attending physiotherapy for my hands, at the Hand Clinic in Windsor, although I had reduced this to three times a week as my hands were gradually improving, but they were still bloody painful treatments and I was still on heavy medication, including several doses of morphine each day. To make things even more difficult, the flashbacks and nightmares were really beginning to assert their presence, which deprived me of the sleep I needed to counterbalance my other activities. I was existing in a constant sleep deficit.

Looking back, the effort of dealing with all this was too much for anyone to cope with. Something had to give.

CHAPTER 13

ON THE EDGE AND
THE CLINIC

As Christmas loomed large on the horizon it looked as though we might all be able to finally take some time off from campaigning and regain some of our energy. Peter decided it was a chance for us to escape for a while and organised a long weekend away, with a couple of friends, to the northern part of Majorca. I know Peter was trying to be thoughtful, but the idea of catching a plane scared me to death!

We arrived at the check-in at Heathrow, with me wrapped tightly in my large grey wool coat, scarf, gloves and floppy hat, although my mask was still pretty obvious, of course. I stood to one side of Peter and our friends, who happily chatted with the lady on the desk, unaware of the huge nausea and panic that had suddenly engulfed me. Then the check-in lady looked over at me and exclaimed, 'Oh, it's you! I've been following you on the news. You are such a brave lady.' I smiled weakly back at her, merely trying to keep myself together, but the next thing I knew we'd been upgraded. She'd obviously added notes to our boarding details too, as we were treated like royalty by the cabin crew on the plane.

However, my biggest fear still loomed large: I would be putting my life and safety in the hands of the unknown person who was flying the plane. I reasoned to myself, *Planes don't often crash. Regulations are so vigorous that planes are much safer than trains, and even if the worst happened, I am not going to survive it so won't suffer anyway.* I kept on repeating this to myself all the way there and all the way back when we returned. It wasn't so much the fear of crashing, more the fear of surviving a crash. Strangely, by convincing myself any crash would undoubtedly mean death, I could handle the situation easier.

I can't remember that much about Majorca apart from the north being quite mountainous and pretty; it was winter, so everything seemed very grey, cold and dark. Peter ferried me around everywhere by car, and I just looked at things through the window.

I was mightily relieved to touch down again at Heathrow – I felt like kissing the tarmac!

Right before Christmas, at the next meeting of the PSG (we were still a support group as well as a campaign group so we continued to meet even when not campaigning), I was talking with a few of my fellow survivors when the subject of Peter came up. He had to drive me to the meetings and, of course, was a family member who had been affected too. However, his comments within the group were sometimes very insensitive, sometimes patronising and sometimes downright hurtful. I'd winced a few times in the past, like on the occasion he'd commented to us all, 'If you act happy, you will be ... you need to pull your socks up and get on with it,' or another time when he had said, 'In years to come you'll be able to put this all behind you.' But now it had unfortunately reached the stage where he had upset quite a few others. So much so that they asked me to speak with him about leaving the group. Well, what could I do? I understood how they felt and could sympathise as I had heard his remarks about pulling ourselves together, or depression being 'a state of mind, not really an illness', and how his life had been disrupted, and so on. But all the same, he was my husband. Feeling as though I had split loyalties, once I was back at home I tentatively broached the subject with Peter and suggested I might make my own way to the PSG meetings so he wouldn't have to sit in on them all as he obviously felt frustrated by what he heard at times. He reacted badly, but after an hour or so calmed down and no more was said on the subject. But he never attended another PSG meeting.

Nick Percival told me I could now withdraw from the daily doses of morphine that had been keeping my background pain at bay for the previous fifteen months; I was to stay on morphine, but only when I was having my physiotherapy or found myself in extreme pain. He came up with a withdrawal plan to wean me off gradually as morphine is no different from any other class-A drug and has a number of withdrawal side effects. Unfortunately, the first withdrawal plan was too fast and I developed extreme symptoms which were akin to having really, really bad flu and feeling as though my skin was crawling with bugs. I felt extremely yucky and was prostrate in bed until the doctor was called. I was immediately reintroduced to morphine for a while, and then withdrew at a much slower rate over a couple of months, which seemed to work.

Though physically improving by then, I'd recently started experiencing nightmares that were more terrible and vivid than ever before. Flashbacks featuring intense and graphic memories of the crash increased in regularity and severity too, striking at any time during waking hours. Any sense of reality would melt away and I would find myself back on the train, feeling, hearing and smelling the crash again, unable to focus on anything around me. It was almost as though the crash was happening all over again, which was very disorientating and distressing for me. Each time I had a flashback, I felt completely drained. I still get them, even now, but mercifully they are much fewer and farther between.

Although there was no real trigger to the flashbacks, I did discover that a smell of burning (which does make barbecues a little tricky), a loud crash or bang, or the sound of metal grating against metal certainly contributed to them. However, if I am tired or feeling stressed about something, then I'm particularly vulnerable. They often start with just an uneasy feeling, though sometimes I will break out in heavy perspiration as if I am very hot, or I might hear noises or smell burning. The worst symptom of an attack approaching is when I seize up – I literally become stiff, unable to move, swallow or talk properly. Then, as it eases, I panic, hyperventilate and throw up. I have to leave wherever I am and go outside for fresh air and space; it isn't a case of 'Would you mind excusing me?' so much as 'Get out of my way!' so I dare say some people have found my behaviour rather strange and rude at times.

Stupidly, in 2000, I kept all this to myself and refused to admit to anyone how bad the flashbacks had become. You see, pre-crash Pam would have seen flashbacks as a sign of weakness, to be hidden at all costs, and in trying to be my old self again that was the attitude I tried to take. Everyone, including my family, kept on saying how well I was doing and I naturally wanted them to continue to think that. Bottling up my problems, fears and demons didn't do me any favours at all, but I say that now from the wonderful position of hindsight.

One thing I did tackle, however, was my relationship with my sister Jane. Without question, I would never have recovered so quickly and returned home without her care, love and sacrifice. And the latter was what concerned me now. She had given up a whole year of her life and, along with the pressures of looking after me, her own relationship was now suffering and her university course was still on hold. I tried to persuade her the time was right for her to return to her own life, and that I was well enough to continue with Peter's help. She can be as stubborn as her big sister at times but after a long talk she agreed to move out.

With another new year looming, and another tough one

behind me, I was determined to celebrate a happier year ahead. I wanted at least to make a start on getting back to a normal life and routine again, and with that in mind invited two friends – Michael and Jean – to join Peter and me for dinner on New Year's Eve, and to stay over afterwards. They brought some lovely nibbles and a bottle to start the evening off and I cooked a red Thai chicken curry, with Peter doing the chopping and me combining and stirring the ingredients in a large wok. This simple act of cooking again was a huge step forward; I've always loved cooking and found it relaxing, and now I felt I was recapturing a small part of my past life. We all mucked in with the accompaniments and it was huge fun, just like the good old days.

I began the evening sensibly, with just two glasses of champagne – I still had to be careful with my prescribed mix of painkillers and sleeping tablets. However, as the evening wore on we all became rather jolly in our conversation and mood, and Michael rolled a joint. I hadn't smoked pot in years, and it was madness for me to do it, but some cussed part of my brain egged me on and told me I would enjoy it ... I did!

When midnight struck, we clinked our glasses and welcomed in 2001. Not long afterwards Michael, Jean and Peter went up to bed but as I still felt wide awake and chilled (due to the pot, no doubt!) I put some music on and tackled the pile of dirty dishes and pans, as I hate coming down in the morning to a filthy kitchen. I popped a sleeping pill, thinking I'd head upstairs soon, and set about cleaning up to the rhythm of my Lenny Kravitz CD through my headphones. By all accounts, Michael looked in on me as he went upstairs and said he smiled widely when he saw me looking so happy.

A few minutes later, while standing at the kitchen sink, that all too familiar awful feeling of uneasiness grew in the pit of my stomach and seemed to flow into every pore of my body. The ensuing flashback which engulfed me was the worst ever; I think I even gasped out loud as it hit me. Everything in the room around me vanished, only to be replaced by images of the crash. I found myself back in coach H, jolting, with an orange and black fireball in front of me. I heard the crackling of burning hair, and the stench of diesel fuel and burning flesh was overwhelming. It was all followed by total darkness. I came round, my body bent over double, my face screwed up in agony and my hands hanging onto the edge of the countertop. It lasted for perhaps only a few moments, but left me nauseous, sweating profusely, shaking like a leaf and utterly exhausted.

I managed to straighten up, open my eyes and look at the few remaining plates and dishes in the sink, which I focused on in an attempt to remind myself I was back in the real world.

Of course, I was left feeling shaken, and despite the hour felt more awake than ever; yet I also felt an overwhelming desire to go to bed and sleep. It had been quite a while since I'd popped the sleeping tablet, and given the jolt to my system, I thought it unlikely to now kick in, so I grabbed the packet and took another one.

I waited, hoping the urge to close my eyes would soon arrive so that I could climb the stairs and just fall into bed and into a deep sleep. But the second one didn't seem to work either. Mind you, it had probably only been five minutes since I'd taken it and not long enough for it to have an effect, but I took another … and then another. I was certainly not thinking straight and everything seemed so far away from me, so unreal and surreal.

Then I began to feel my legs start to buckle. Then it was as though my body was shutting down, from the floor upwards – my waist became numb, then my stomach, and then my arms started feeling odd. I clicked back into reality and realised what I'd done. Somehow I managed to make it upstairs, and dashed into Peter's bedroom, hitting the light switch full on and shouting as loud as my (still damaged) vocal cords would allow, 'Pete, I've taken too many pills! Help me!' Somewhat dazed initially, Peter then sprang out of bed and rushed towards me … and that's the last I remember before falling unconscious.

Poor Michael and Jean had been woken up by all the commotion and I hate to think how they must have felt – a blooming great way to start their New Year!

My next memory is of waking up in the Royal Berkshire Hospital, with two very stern-looking nurses glowering down at me.

'Why did you try to take your life?' they asked.

'What? … Pardon? … Sorry? What are you talking about?' I asked while trying to focus my eyes, my sore, dry throat aching with every word – an after-effect of the stomach pump administered to me a few hours earlier.

'Why did you try to commit suicide?' they asked bluntly.

I was totally bewildered and couldn't answer. I didn't know what they were suggesting. I knew I'd taken too many pills, but it wasn't to kill myself – was it? They told me I had in fact taken eight pills over a period of about thirty minutes, but that no harm had been done and there was no liver damage. I'd been lucky.

My sister Jane was at my bedside, along with my mother, Dad and Peter.

'You do realise you need help?' one nurse said.

'Yes,' I replied, while looking intently into Jane's eyes, 'but my sister can sort it out.'

Tellingly, it did not occur to me that I should turn to Peter for help. Jane had been my pillar of strength for so long and I trusted her implicitly, so it was to her that I automatically turned. Jane immediately gave her word that I would get help and said she'd already called my psychotherapist, Suzanna Rose, who arrived a little later that morning. You see, without this assurance I'd have been forced to see an NHS psychiatrist and would not have been allowed to leave the hospital. However, it seemed I was beyond Suzanna's remit as I never saw her again, although I think she helped Jane research into some clinics I might consider.

I felt so sorry for my sister as 1 January is her birthday and I'd completely and utterly ruined it for her.

While the onward psychiatric arrangements were being sorted out, Mother, Dad and Peter faded into the background; I think their nerves were completely shredded and they knew that the ever-efficient Jane could deal with everything.

The very next day Jane drove me around to visit various rehabilitation clinics to work out where I wanted to go; the Cardinal Clinic was the first, set in pleasant wooded surroundings not far from Windsor. It didn't look like a clinic, being a two-storey, Tudor-style building complete with white walls and black wooden beams. The rooms were more like those you'd find in a small country hotel – light, airy and not a hospital bed in sight. In contrast, we next visited the Priory in Woking, which had the feel of a cold, Spartan hospital complete with institutional beds. It was far too clinical for my liking and I shrank away. Not quite the plush celeb-filled place its sister establishment in London is, that's for sure!

We returned to the Cardinal Clinic where I saw the lead psychiatrist, Dr Atkins, and was offered a room that very night. Had I declined the offer, I am pretty sure that my family would have had me committed as they were so worried about me and my rash actions. There was a little plus to being at the Cardinal Clinic: it was located right next door to my physiotherapy clinic so I could just trot across the lawn for my continued hand and finger bending sessions.

It was termed an 'attempted suicide'. And, yes, in a way I

suppose it was. I certainly wanted things to stop and wanted to close my eyes, go to sleep and not have to wake up to the hurt, pain and constant anxiety again. I wanted an end to the nightmares and flashbacks. Taking eight pills wasn't something I did in a conscious way; I believe it was a foolish accident. Albeit also a subconscious cry for help.

For the next six weeks I retreated from the world to have my mental wounds attended to. My first-floor room was spacious, bright and airy, beautifully decorated with comfortable facilities and a large double bed, plus an en-suite bathroom. For the first time in ages, I felt safe and cosseted. As it was in the corner of the building I had the benefit of large windows, giving me views across a wide expanse of lawn sweeping down to a wood on one side, and overlooking the cedar-flanked gravel driveway from the road on the other. It was certainly both a beautiful and peaceful place.

During my first two weeks I didn't venture from the room confines apart from seeing Dr Atkins for my sessions each day. I shied away from eye contact with any of my fellow patients: I didn't feel up to mixing with people, let alone trying to have a conversation. It was hard enough answering Dr Atkins's questions and my thought processes seemed to slow down to a snail's pace, as if my brain was drowning in aspic.

'What you need is sleep,' Maurice Atkins said. 'You need to sleep, relax and do nothing. Forget about the Survivors' Group. Forget about home. Forget about everything apart from getting yourself back on your feet.'

I remember those words so vividly; it was as though someone had given me permission to let go and stop fighting. And sleep. Oh, how I slept! It was absolute bliss.

Every day began with a nurse bustling into my room at about 6.30 a.m., rousing me brusquely but kindly to ensure I was up and dressed in time for breakfast an hour later. That was probably the only time I was actually made to conform to procedures, to be honest. The food was good and I was allowed to eat in my room because of my mask – it wasn't comfortable eating with it on, but neither was I yet able to allow anyone but doctors or very close friends and family see me without it. Though I now didn't have to wear it twenty-three hours a day and could remove it for periods and sleep without it on, the mask had given me a form of confidence which I feared I'd lose without it. I was not yet entirely comfortable with looking at my own face sans mask, let alone allowing other people to peer or stare at me.

After breakfast a nurse would arrive with a small plastic cup of tablets. I didn't really know what they were, aside from the fact that one of them was an antidepressant. When queried which one sent me into a zombielike state, the nurse just smiled. After about ten days, and through a process of elimination, I figured out it was the little blue one in the bunch and so I started palming it each day and flushing it down the loo. I felt hugely better for losing it but did wonder if there might be some seriously zonked-out rats in the clinic sewerage system.

Dr Maurice Atkins was a very dapper little man; he must have been well into his sixties, with white hair and a white handlebar moustache, which he sometimes stroked while we spoke. He was always well turned out in one of his pinstripe suits, which I swear all had a Savile Row look about them, complete with waistcoat, gold watch chain and a perfectly folded handkerchief peeping out of his jacket breast pocket. Immaculate is the word I would use to describe him. He continued as my psychiatrist throughout my stay and had a gentle yet insistent way of talking to me which began to penetrate the defences I'd erected around my true internal feelings. My previous psychotherapist, Dr Rose, had been seeing me for about eight or nine months but to be honest I had found myself telling her what she wanted to hear; although I was having nightmares, I always told her I felt fine and had no problems at night. I felt easier with Maurice Atkins and a little better able to bare my soul, though I was still guarded in how much I told him. We had two sessions a day every day for the first two weeks, and I began to trust him. He recommended I also talk to the in-house psychologist, Stephen Keene, so that they could work in tandem on my treatment.

Stephen was charged with talking to me, or rather trying to get me to talk about myself to discover the root problems of my mental issues in order to then exorcise them. Stephen was a good listener and continually managed to get me to talk about the crash; he was trying to help me release my anger about it, and was prepared to shoulder any directed at him. However, one assumption he – and others made – was that I *was* angry. In fact, I felt no anger. Quite simply, the crash had happened, so what was the point in getting angry? Frustration, pain, bewilderment, self-pity and several other emotions, yes, I felt them, but anger, no. I continued seeing Stephen for almost three years, although it wasn't until after the first year that my self-imposed mental wall crumbled enough for him to breach it. In fact, in the end Stephen became the only person I could really talk to without feeling guilty, and without feeling that I was burdening him with my problems as I do when I speak to others.

Being shut away in the clinic afforded me a buffer from the goings-on of the world outside, although Peter came to visit every couple of days and brought me little luxuries like chocolate, magazines and books, and he would keep me up to date. He told me that Tony and Jan had stepped into my shoes in the PSG so I didn't have to worry – I have to admit I wasn't particularly worried as I was enjoying my seclusion too much.

Then out of the blue Peter did something that I couldn't

forgive. He shared the news of my recent breakdown with a man from a local news agency. Peter later told me that he'd been coerced into it, which I found hard to believe as I had never seen anyone coerce Peter into doing anything he didn't want to do. I was furious and felt hurt and betrayed that the press should be reporting on what was a private and emotionally charged matter. I was at a vulnerable stage in my mental recovery and media embellishments about my suicide attempt had a negative effect.

The clinic duly started receiving telephone calls from journalists and one of the male orderlies even had to chase a photographer off the grounds. I felt threatened, and worse still I felt I'd lost my trust in the one man who was supposed to be the closest person to me.

Unsure what to do, I called Martin Minns. He suggested I take control of the situation by telling my story myself, and knowing I was about to protest, he reminded me, 'Give them five minutes of your time, then they'll leave you alone.' As it happened he'd already been approached by a journalist from the *Daily Telegraph*, and suggested she should be the one I speak to; Sandra Laville arrived the next day to interview me. She was very kind, gentle and promised to report things just as I said them.

The subsequent article, 'Nightmare goes on for survivor of the Paddington crash', told the story, my story, largely as it happened: how I had overworked myself, how I'd become dispirited after Hatfield, how Gerald Corbett leaving Railtrack had been a major setback for the PSG and how I had made a cry for help by taking an overdose on New Year's Eve. It was neither comfortable nor pretty reading but it was more accurate than the lurid stories the local news agency had been circulating.

I suppose the seeds of my suspicion as to Peter's attitude towards my recovery had already been planted when Mum and Jane had been against him being in charge of my care after I left hospital. What he was doing now caused those seeds to start sprouting. My trust in him was shattered and I felt betrayed and angry with him. However, I could not stop the situation he had set in motion so there was no point in venting my anger at him but, in hindsight, I think this was definitely the beginning of the end of our relationship.

I asked Peter not to visit me in the clinic anymore and gave the staff instructions not to put his phone calls through either. I had to come to terms with what he had done before I could see or talk to him again. Funnily enough, he didn't seem too put out.

Meanwhile, life in the clinic continued. There were numerous activities such as yoga, massages, music classes, writing classes and an art class where you could paint how you felt. The thought of taking part in any group activity or therapy filled me with horror but fortunately Maurice Atkins excused me from them, although not without a little friction from the powers that be, who felt 'every patient should involve him or herself in these therapies'. Yes, well, every patient is different and not all want to – as Maurice thankfully recognised. I did, however, rediscover the really relaxing pleasure of back massages during my stay.

After a couple of weeks I was feeling a little more robust and confident enough to explore my surroundings and meet some fellow inmates – as I rather uncharitably thought of us – though on my terms and not in an enforced activity. I certainly discovered how the Cardinal Clinic was home to a wide variety of people for whom life had just got too much in one way or another. Importantly, it made me realise I wasn't alone in having problems. I had now been formally diagnosed with post-traumatic stress disorder (PTSD) brought about by the train crash and one of the symptoms of PTSD is depression…

Smoking wasn't allowed in the clinic, but there was a hut – a bit like a thatched garden gazebo – set aside in the grounds for all of us nicotine addicts to puff away in, nicknamed 'the coffin'. I'd resumed my unfortunate habit, which while helping perk me up, I knew wasn't good for my poor lungs, which had obviously been severely damaged during the crash. In hospital, smoking had never crossed my mind – except when Peter had come to visit and I could smell the odour of cigarettes when he walked into the room, which sickened me rather than made me think about what I was missing. But as I physically improved at home and Peter continued to smoke in front of me, quite a lot, I eventually took one of his proffered cigarettes and smoked it. Such a shame, as I was instantly hooked again. Considering the damage done to my lungs from the fireball and the scarring that is left in my throat, this is probably one of the most stupid things I could have done and I kick myself to this day that I did not remain off the cigarettes permanently.

Anyhow, I found myself gelling with a number of inmates in 'the coffin': there was a man who had been self-harming, though I never felt it diplomatic to ask why, and another suffering from depression as a result of what he described as 'an obsession with women … particularly the married variety'. In the central courtyard, around which the clinic was built, I got to know a young girl in her early twenties who was withdrawing from drug dependency. Then there was another lady, in her forties I guessed, who was a recovering alcoholic; she was absolutely charming and a delight to talk with, and to me seemed very balanced. Though after I left the clinic I was told that her illness had sadly got the better of her and she had died, leaving two small children behind. That really shook me.

Initially my new friendships were limited to the courtyard or hut, and people were polite enough not to ask about the mask, though they probably knew all about it in any case as there was certainly a great appetite for gossip there. As time passed we struck up more regular conversations and even knocked on each other's doors to say one of us was watching a video and would anyone else like to see it? As I was fairly quiet and would listen to whoever wanted to talk to me I was quickly dubbed 'Auntie Pam' by some of the other patients and I got to hear the backstories to their problems, which more often than not I found both fascinating and heartbreaking. I forget the number of times I quietly cried as they poured their hearts out to me. I only wished my giving them a comforting hug could wipe away all their problems.

The communal television was in a large oak-panelled room on the ground floor, with spacious armchairs and a couple of huge sofas that people would snuggle up on in the evenings in pyjamas and dressing gowns. One such evening I was happily sitting there watching a film – *Sleepy Hollow* with Johnny Depp – when I heard someone shout, 'Oh my god!' and the next thing I knew a huge blanket was thrown right over me. It transpired the guy who owned the video suddenly realised there was a scene with a fireball coming up. Everyone laughed as I tried to struggle out from under it! I was touched by their concern, though.

With these friends I formed, if not a very close personal relationship, at least a bond of necessity and mutually shared experiences that I guess must be familiar to prison inmates or hostages! Just to prove we still had our sense of humour we sometimes rebelled against the system, by doing something like hiding all the paintbrushes before the art class, creeping into the kitchen to make a midnight snack, or sneaking out to have a few hours in Windsor. The nurses turned a blind eye to our antics, taking the view that it was OK as long as the more stable and balanced inmates were responsible for organising these forays.

Martin Minns drove over to see me several times and we'd slip off for a long lunch so he could keep me up to date on developments with the PSG and the many media requests that were still coming in – lots asking about me and how I was getting on in the clinic – which I avoided getting involved with directly, letting Martin and my other fellow PSG members deal with them instead.

After about six weeks, during one of our sessions I told Maurice Atkins I felt it was time for me to reconnect with the outside world. Maurice was a great believer in the patient knowing when they were ready for something, so he readily agreed, providing I continued coming in as an outpatient once a week to see both him and Stephen Keene and continue with the medication he prescribed, one being an antidepressant called Seroxat. It was a long time before I was made aware of Seroxat's implications, which I will discuss in the upcoming chapters.

Just before leaving on my final day at the clinic I thought I would visit the infamous art class – not to paint how I felt, but to see the others I had come to know for the last time. The young girl I had grown close to asked if she could paint my mask, which I agreed to. As I left that day, I knew things were going to be different. It was time to face the world again without my mask, both metaphorically and physically.

CHAPTER 14

THE MASK COMES OFF:
DESCENT INTO THE ABYSS

I knew this chapter was coming and I've not been looking forward to tackling it. You see, it marks the beginning of one of the most shameful times of my life and one I would rather forget about.

With the official OK to leave the Cardinal Clinic, I of course had to contact Peter again. He arrived to collect me and my copious amounts of Seroxat, which had helped, or so I thought, to level out most of my emotions. But that was in the clinic – a calm, ordered and ultimately fake environment within which to use it. But once I had left the safe surrounds of the Cardinal, I had to face real life situations and Seroxat, far from helping me, became my worst enemy. The drug has since been proven to have very serious side effects for some patients such as behavioural changes, paranoia, even suicide, and accordingly this has led to many lawsuits in America against the drug manufacturers. In my case, the side effects far outweighed the potential benefits, but I trusted the advice of doctors that it would help me. I am in no way trying to mitigate my behaviour on discharge. However, I do believe Seroxat played a big part in my being hugely irritable, rude and snappy towards people.

As mentioned, Peter came to collect me from the clinic. He offered a clumsy hug on meeting and, to be honest, my body language reflected that I was still pissed off with him about leaking the news of my suicide attempt. On the 45-minute drive home, rather than asking about me or my treatment, he started to offload his own feelings of being unhappy and his business problems. I sat mute, letting him talk.

'Why don't you find a therapist or psychologist to talk to?' I suggested. 'Someone who can help you cope?'

'Certainly not!' was his reply. 'It's not as if I'm nuts!'

Well, that's charming! I thought but changed the subject and talked about the future. I said that I did not feel I could live in our house any more as there were too many memories of the past, before the train crash, which constantly reminded me of what I had lost.

'Perhaps we should consider moving and starting afresh?' I asked.

It was something we had touched upon during one of his visits to the clinic before I 'banned' him but I now thought it was time to get serious.

Perhaps it will be a fresh start for him and me too, I thought to myself. We agreed to start looking for a new home, little realising running away from the past does not guarantee a shiny bright new future.

My own world was about to stop turning for a while as the security and safety, together with the health benefits, my mask had afforded me were about to be taken away with its removal. Logically, I knew my own little healing greenhouse had largely done its job by now but it had become part of my 'normal' life, however far from normal it really was. The prospect of losing it filled me with fear and apprehension; the mask had been a window through which I gazed at the world – and through which the world gawped at me. It had become my protective barrier, my shield against everyone on the outside as well as a veil hiding the real me from them. Without it I was going to be forced to face people, be judged by them and deal with them on a more intimate basis, with no plastic to separate us.

Over the preceding twelve months I had lost count of the number of times journalists enquired when the mask might be coming off, and whether their newspaper or television programme could gain some sort of exclusive report on the story. It seemed that it would be quite a big event in media terms, but the very thought of TV cameras jostling with newspaper reporters as I confronted them bare-faced and perhaps holding the mask was something I shuddered to contemplate. I thought about keeping it quiet, but of course the first time I then appeared in public without the mask might induce some sort of media frenzy. It was a no-win scenario. Again, Martin's words of *give them five minutes of your time and they will leave you alone* came back to haunt me.

I had been the public face of the PSG in the mask, so I guess I couldn't really dodge the moment of being the very public face of the PSG without my mask. Plus, I had courted the media for our campaign, so I suppose it was only fair they should court me now…

After a long chat with Martin Minns, I decided the most appropriate – and most sensitive – approaches had been from ITV's *Tonight* programme and the *Daily Mail*. I therefore agreed to meet Trevor McDonald to film a report in the days leading up to my mask being removed, while giving an exclusive print interview to the *Mail*. I hoped this would placate the media interest and they would leave me alone afterwards. I wasn't campaigning this time but, stupidly, it never occurred to me to ask for a fee!

A filming schedule for late February into early March was agreed upon, during which time the crew from Granada followed, filmed and interviewed me as I went about my daily life, went horse-riding, took a walk along the river with Peter, prepared lunch, met with my plastic surgeon and so forth. It was a veritable 'fly on the wall' documentary, getting to know who (or who they thought) Pam Warren was, how she had reached this point and what the next stages in her life might hold.

On 13 March 2001, I attended what was to be my last public

function with the mask on, with the TV crew right behind me. It was for a speech I was giving to Barnet College in north London as part of a conference they were staging called 'Turning Points'. One of the other speakers was athlete Roger Black; he'd been one of my heroes and I remember watching him and his teammates winning gold in the 4x400m at the World Athletic Championships in Athens back in 1997. Unfortunately, I didn't get a chance to speak with him as he left pretty quickly after he had given his speech – well, he always was quick off his mark. As I stood up on the podium three hundred teenagers listened politely and intently as I struggled to deliver a speech. Perhaps it was the large colour photograph of carriage H that Martin Minns had arranged as a backdrop behind me, or because I was disconcerted by the thought of the major turning point that lay just ahead of me … Either way, I had to deliver my speech through tears, sobs and a fluctuating voice that I feared might give way. I managed to get through it, though, and hope I offered a little inspiration and food for thought to some of the students too. As soon as I'd finished one of the TV crew came up to me and told me that you could have heard a pin drop as I spoke, and that some of the students had actually ended up crying themselves.

I have to say, I hated every minute of the filming process. I felt so exposed, as though any pretence of privacy had been ripped from me, and I also knew how disparaging some people would be about my participation in the programme. I'd heard rumours claiming I was enjoying media exposure a little too much, from people who didn't have the first clue about me. Having said that, the TV crew themselves were lovely, genuinely caring and thoughtful people who kindly allowed me to look through the viewfinder, seeing how they framed shots, and also told me about the technical side of shooting, with lights, lenses and cutaways, which was something I found fascinating.

Two weeks later, on 27 March, the mask was removed, and on 29 March Trevor McDonald's programme aired, on the same day that the *Daily Mail* published the story. All of the other newspapers carried a photograph, submitted by Martin Minns, of me holding a plastic mask against a black background.

The *Tonight* crew started off filming me with the mask still on, but when it was time to take it off I banished them from the room. It was with a fair degree of trepidation that I removed the mask for the last time. I'd previously contacted a friend of mine, Lisa, who was a trained make-up artist and asked her to help. I was so nervous about looking at myself in the mirror I could feel my stomach flip-flopping, I started to sweat and I could feel the beginnings of a flashback clawing at my consciousness. I knew I still had to carry on with more filming and did not want to let anyone down, so I didn't look in the mirror as I removed the mask – I was scared that the face I would see would be one I didn't recognise. Since looking at my scars that first time I had managed to avoid even catching a glimpse of myself. I knew my eyebrows would have grown and that, despite all the good work the mask had done, some scarring would still be visible. Dear Lisa, who'd taken a day off work, set about ensuring I wasn't unveiled before the cameras looking like Denis Healey. Swinging into action, she plucked, smoothed, moisturised, covered and made up my face to camouflage some of the scarring. I looked in the mirror: I was happy; I looked passably normal. I only allowed my mind to acknowledge there was nothing so horrendous people would be appalled. All other thoughts and feelings I deliberately shoved to the back of my mind. *I'll think about it properly later, when I'm alone*, I told myself. This was not the time if I was going to get upset: I had a job to do, to get the filming finished so they could go home and leave me to myself and my privacy.

When it was time to call action and walk into the kitchen, greeted and hugged by Peter, I at least looked fairly respectable. Later on the crew wanted to film me having drinks with friends in the local pub for some variety. As we walked the short distance down the road it started to rain and I jumped six feet in the air! It had been what seemed a lifetime since I had felt any wind or rain directly on my face – funny the sensations you forget in such a short space of time.

The final scene of the film showed me preparing to put the mask away for the last time. 'Stupid thing is,' I said through choked tears, 'I'm going to miss it.' And I truly meant it.

I was soon to find out just how much had been hidden behind the mask.

Although I tended never to look at any programmes or news that I was featured in, I unusually watched *Tonight*. In one sequence, I sat with Peter on a bench in front of the River Thames near our home.

'We've got each other, which is the important thing,' I said to the camera while turning and looking at Peter. 'We've always enjoyed each other's company and this has definitely made us stronger.'

I felt sick as I watched and listened to those words, knowing them to be untrue. We were not in a good place. I had still not forgiven him for betraying my trust, and I was beginning to resent his efforts to care for me when he usually turned things around so he could moan about his problems. I'd stopped him driving me to and from my therapies, relying on the good nature of friends instead – anything to spend less time with him. It was simple: I did not trust him anymore and without trust, one of the most important underpinnings of a relationship, we were ultimately doomed. I'd not listened to Mum and Jane when they expressed their worries about my relationship with Peter when I was first discharged from hospital, and had even defended him to the point of saying, 'He is my husband ... you have a choice ... either accept him and continue to see me or don't and I am gone.'

After I had been discharged from hospital, while Jane stayed with me at home for much of that first year, Mum had taken a much-needed sabbatical from everyday contact to rest and recuperate herself. I was aware she had taken a dislike to Peter and that she preferred to have as little to do with him as possible. Despite this she stayed in contact and visited whenever she could.

After my suicide attempt and stay in the clinic I tended to turn to Mum for help but became confused as to why she only seemed to visit intermittently. She has since told me that she knew I would need and want her more but when she would phone and speak to Peter to find out when it was best to visit he put her off, assuring her that I was getting much better. But I wasn't. As the PTSD intensified, the bouts of depression began to get worse. A black cloud would descend over me, leaving me feeling physically heavy and exhausted and completely unable to get out of bed. The only thoughts running through my head were ones of despair and hopelessness, and I felt there was no point in even trying to function. This meant I turned away from all human contact and would stop speaking or interacting with anyone. And these episodes would normally last a week to ten days.

Peter would not tell Mum or Jane whenever the depression hit me, leaving me unfed, unwashed and without water. Eventually, the depression would lift enough for me to ask him for water and to call my family, which he would then do. Mum would drop everything and rush over, taking over my care for a while, ensuring I was clean, fed and watered and cooking and cleaning the house. She was not happy with how things were and was worried as to why Peter was not getting more help for my mental state but she felt powerless to intervene not knowing my own wishes and not wanting to come between husband and wife. I am just thankful that she hung on in there with me during these difficult times until I was ready to ask for her advice and help in taking positive steps out of the hell I found myself living in.

However, at the point of the *Tonight* programme, I was beginning to wonder if they might have been right: did Peter still have my best interests at heart? Had I been stronger, I would have tackled him about 'us' but I was a coward and did not feel I had the strength to deal with the fallout. We were becoming two people coexisting without very much else to hold us together.

Two weeks after the *Tonight* programme the Paddington Survivors' Group gathered at a hotel in Stroud to mark our first anniversary, on what was a beautiful warm day with bright blue skies. We had a lovely meal, together with some of our families, and felt as though we had something to celebrate – we'd achieved a lot in a year and rail safety was now at the top of the government's agenda; we were all alive and well and some were moving on with their futures. One of my fondest memories of that day is pausing outside the door that led to the large dining room and hearing the cheerful chatter and laughter inside. It made my heart swell with pride for all of us.

Our lunch went on throughout the afternoon and into the evening. I was staying at the hotel, as were a few others, so thought nothing of having a few extra glasses than usual. But it ended up being more than a few as evening soon became night which then became morning; we drank all night, and I could have probably gone on longer. Looking back, that was the start of my drinking problem.

In May, Peter and I completed on the purchase of a new house a few villages away and moved our stuff, lock, stock and barrel. My family were marvellous helping with the move as my hands were still not up to much, so I stood back and directed everyone as to where things were to go. Strangely, I was never to feel at home in this new house. Yes, it was a new start and had no memories of the past but it took me some time to realise that it was quite an impersonal house, a typical suburban building without much character, and it had two people living in it who were fairly impersonal too.

Though I say my hands were not up to much, they had improved to the point where my physiotherapy sessions had been cut down to once a week. Movement was getting better and, although it will never be perfect, I was able to do more and more for myself. One of the tasks Kate set me was to pick up a bundle of buttons that she would spill onto the table one by one and put them back into their box. I can't tell you how frustrating this was! Although I could see the buttons, my hands had no sensory feeling in them, so I was never really sure whether I had hold of a button or not. It was galling and the words I used to express my annoyance were quite choice!

One day, around the time of our house move, I was talking on the phone while I held and stroked one of my new kittens on my lap. All of a sudden I became aware of how soft her fur was ... I mean, I could actually *feel* it, its softness, its texture, everything. I dropped the phone in shock and couldn't stop stroking the poor cat! Even though it was the weekend I phoned the Hand Clinic and excitedly left a message for Kate. 'The feeling in my left hand has come back! Woohoo!!' I then rushed around the house stroking things – even the wallpaper! It was such a breakthrough that I must have been smiling for days. Sadly, the feeling only returned patchily to my right hand and even then not very much. The nerve endings must have been too damaged but, hey, at least I got one back!

But that positive aside, as I entered the second part of 2001 two major problems were about to emerge: my marriage started to fall apart, and I began drinking far too much.

It was soon after the PSG anniversary gathering that I realised I had a problem with alcohol. When I was on morphine I avoided booze on doctor's orders, aside from the odd sip of champagne, yet nine months after I had stopped taking morphine I found myself replacing its soothing qualities with booze. I was becoming a binge drinker with a serious problem.

I began to use alcohol as a way to try to forget the past and to blot out the nightmares. Being totally drunk meant I would eventually pass out in bed and wouldn't remember or dream. I would wake in the morning feeling absolutely dreadful and sick, but I passed a night without the awful sounds and scenes that had bothered me in the past. I would suffer with a hangover, dehydrated, feeling dreadful all day, until the evening when I'd pour myself another drink. If I opened a bottle of wine at home, I'd finish it and then maybe open another one and start on that. Quite often I'd drink a litre of wine, or perhaps it would be vodka and tonic, but it wouldn't just be one, it would be five or six … or seven or eight … I just couldn't control it.

Medication, post-traumatic stress disorder and now booze … my behaviour suffered and I became a horrible person. Whenever I'd been drinking I'd wildly pick up on any little thing Peter or a member of my family said and irrationally turn it into a big argument. I would rant and shout, then dissolve into tears, before drying my eyes simply to start ranting and shouting again. Sarcasm by the bucketload came into my tirades and I could see in the other person's eyes just how hurtful I was being. But it made me want to do it again. I was horrified at what was coming out of my mouth, and what I was doing, but I seemed powerless to prevent myself. I would eventually stop and go to bed, only to wake in the morning feeling remorseful and being extremely apologetic. I couldn't put the 'why' into words or explain what was happening as I didn't understand it myself, and I kept it all hidden from my psychologist.

The combination of my three demons brought on a depression which confined me to bed for a week. Everything seemed dark, I was wrapped in misery and life just appeared futile. People have since asked me to describe my feelings, doctors included, and I can only really compare depression to being at the bottom of a long, deep, dark well; you can see daylight at the top of the shaft and you can hear the world and people up there, but you can't quite make it up the walls to join them. It is a horrible feeling that can't really be fought against once it hits. I didn't want to eat but would drink gallons of water in an effort to flush out the after-effects of the alcohol and, once the depression had passed, a period of sobriety and contrition would follow for a few weeks before the cycle started all over again.

I know I've been pretty negative about Peter, and it wasn't easy for him to be the target of my tirades or to put up with my drunken behaviour – in private or public. When I was drunk he would argue and shout back, which was pointless, and then in frustration leave me to my own devices, often then finding me passed out on the sofa or the bed when he returned home. Even when I was sober he didn't seem to know how to support me, and when I was depressed he would leave me alone in my room, completely alone, only popping his head around the door in the morning and evening to check up on me.

Why had I fallen down so badly? What was behind it? Did the Seroxat exacerbate things? Or was I just being a self-pitying, selfish diva? Perhaps a bit of all of the above, but I think the root cause was my deep unhappiness with my life – the loss of the business and my career, the loss of my looks, the fatigue of continually fighting against pain, the fear I felt about my future and my crumbling relationship with Peter.

So I continued to seek solace in the bottle.

Back in January of 2001 I had been due to meet Falklands veteran and burns survivor Simon Weston, but my stay at the Cardinal Clinic had put paid to those plans. However, now, a few months later, I was invited again to meet Simon, at his home in Cardiff. John Hart, chief executive of the Healing Foundation (a charity that both Simon and I were ambassadors for), had arranged the meeting and kindly drove me. I am forever grateful that this was during one of my more lucid periods. After the friendly but formal introductions and inconsequential chatter, John – ever the diplomat – left Simon and me to talk on our own. I felt more and more at ease as Simon and I chatted, to the point where I blurted out, 'Look, Simon, one of the problems I have is that I can't stop drinking. I keep doing it, then turning nasty with my friends and family, and afterwards I feel awful about what I have done.'

Far from being critical, Simon treated my admission quite lightly, smiled and said in his lovely Welsh lilt, 'For God's sake, I've been there several times. Don't beat yourself up over it, but you do have to make a decision. You have to decide if you want to go down the route of becoming a complete alcoholic, or do you want to go back to being sensible about having a few drinks now and again with friends, being in control and not ending up consumed by it?'

I didn't even have to think about how to reply, and that was undoubtedly a turning point for me. Like a large oil tanker, it took a little time to change course – but change course I would eventually and that was the day I began.

On 7 June 2001 Tony Blair secured a second term in Parliament for the Labour Party. It wasn't necessarily an important milestone for me, but the publication of Lord Cullen's report into the crash twelve days later certainly was.

Lord Cullen's recommendations were numerous. They tackled the main points of the cavalier attitude towards safety within the rail industry at the time and the unacceptable shortcuts being taken in the name of profit, and his report laid out stringent changes that should be undertaken to bring all safety matters up to an acceptable standard. We at the PSG were overjoyed as all the areas we had been campaigning for were covered in his findings. We never really doubted that Lord Cullen would recommend many, if not all, of the things we had requested in our campaign as we had researched everything stringently and most were common sense. Our concern, however, was that the government and rail companies would fail to implement them in full and in a short enough time frame; this had been the case following earlier inquiry reports, such as those of Clapham and Southall. The PSG swung into action with the next phase of our campaign and by early August 2001, we had agreed a strategy solely aimed at ensuring Cullen's report was implemented in full.

It was really at this point that the PSG stopped being a support group to concentrate on pushing forward with the campaign. Since our anniversary lunch many members had faded into the background, still keeping in touch but no longer attending meetings; it was a good sign as it meant people were returning to their own lives and moving on to their future, and they knew we were still there if they needed us. I had said when the PSG first formed that 'the success of this group will be apparent when it is no longer needed' and I truly believed this. Happily, it was beginning to happen. But those of us who were left continued to exert pressure on the government.

Our ambitious plan was really quite simple: we would first list, in date order, the recommendations and when they were due to be completed as detailed in Cullen's report. Next, we'd bring together the politicians, rail company executives, trade union leaders, health and safety executives, and anyone else who would have a hand in realising Cullen's recommendations, and ask them to sign a public declaration that they would each commit, in full and without reservation, to implementing every point. Only with this type of industry contract did we believe real change could be achieved. To add further momentum to our plan, we organised a series of meetings with each group we were inviting to sign, plus political figures from all major parties, getting them all on side. This would really be a highpoint in the history of the PSG as it would mean that we would be able to positively influence the future of rail safety and help ensure that future train passengers would never have to experience what we had.

However, on a personal level, I was at my lowest ebb. I descended into deeper drunken despair – despair about my marriage, despair about the looming second anniversary of the crash, despair about my future and despair about everything else in my life.

There was one small upbeat moment in all of this: I was deemed fit to drive again. My hands had enough grip in them to be able to manage the steering wheel, though they could not change gears so it was just as well my car was an automatic. I started off just making small journeys to build my confidence. I even took a few advanced driving lessons and, though still nervous, I was soon zipping myself around, which gave me such a sense of freedom after over a year and a half of being reliant on others. I hasten to add that I only drove during my sober periods, being very well aware myself of my drinking problem and how that impaired me even a day or two after I had come out of one of my binges.

On the morning of 11 September 2001 I checked into the Novotel hotel, just off Lambeth Bridge, in central London. It was still very early when I joined Martin Minns and Janette Orr to begin a round of meetings, but the previous evening had been an alcohol-fuelled one for me so I was dreadfully hungover. I thought I would be able to cope and behave professionally.

First we were due to meet with Gwyneth Dunwoody MP, the chair of the Transport Select Committee. That encounter passed in a complete haze. I later learnt that Martin had told Mrs Dunwoody I wasn't feeling too well and was suffering from the side effects of my medication. She said she quite understood, but I'm sure she knew the truth – she was a very canny woman.

Our next meeting was at midday on the House of Commons riverside terrace with Charles Kennedy, leader of the Liberal Democrats. He was totally charming, and happily seemed as keen as I was by then to have a drink. 'Hair of the dog' can seem an attractive idea when you are hungover but it hardly ever is. By one o'clock, and two vodka tonics later, our meeting was complete and Martin, Janette and I retired to an Italian restaurant on Victoria Street for a vodka tonic aperitif, and a bottle or two of wine with our lunch.

As we left the restaurant I stumbled and badly banged my knee as I crumpled forward to the ground; I then felt a stab of pain in my hands as my delicate skin splayed on impact with the pavement. As Martin helped me up and bundled me into a cab, he said I was mumbling about catching my heel in a gap in the pavement. I slumped back into a semi-drunken daze in the black cab, but remember the driver continually turning to talk to us; it made me feel quite dizzy actually and confused me hugely as to where I was, until I tuned in to what he was actually saying: 'Have you heard? Have you heard? Someone's flown a plane into the Twin Towers in New York. They're both down ... thousands dead ... and another hit the Pentagon. They don't know how many planes are up there. It could be us next. You know, don't you? You know?'

Our last meetings of the day were with the trade unions ASLEF and the RMT. Both were set against a background of TV pictures beaming in from New York, and total shock as to what was happening.

Martin came back to the Novotel for an early evening drink before heading home to Wimbledon, whereas I didn't have to go anywhere so carried on drinking. Janette became increasingly concerned at the state I was getting myself in and by 7 p.m. I was telling all the hotel staff that the press were after me and they were not to tell anybody I was there.

An hour or two later I called Martin saying I needed to see him; I said it was urgent and he had to come at once. After a little initial reluctance he agreed to drive back. I can't recall what it was exactly amongst my ramblings that ignited Martin's full force of anger but that is hardly the point – I deserved it. I'd never seen him lose his temper before, but that night he exploded at me.

'You don't get it, do you, Pam? You've got to get a grip. You've got to sort yourself out! You were like a zombie in those meetings today.'

That stopped me in my tracks. I sat bolt upright.

Janette added that she didn't want to be part of the campaign if it was going to be like this, meaning if *I* was going to be like this. I realised I'd upset them both deeply; I in return was immensely ashamed and sorry. Moreover, I discovered 11 September was Martin's birthday and he'd left his wife – who had prepared a special meal – to drive back to see me, and hear the drunken 'gospel according to Pam'. The memory of this whole day continues to make me squirm with embarrassment every time I think about it and my cheeks still burn with shame.

The next morning we all met in the lobby, and aside from exchanging superficial pleasantries, nothing was said. I had managed to sober up overnight so, though not looking my best, was thinking clearly again. I was so ashamed about the previous evening that I didn't know quite what to say to Martin and Janette and was uncharacteristically quiet.

We went outside to hail a taxi for our next meeting, which was with Stephen Byers MP, Secretary of State for Transport. His eleven-storey glass office complex was a short ride across the Thames to Victoria Street and we met other members of the PSG outside. I wasn't sure what to expect of Mr Byers; at best I thought he might be cagey and would make all the right noises, but stop just short of fully committing the government to what we were asking.

I actually found him to be a very relaxed, friendly man who – along with his private secretary David Hill – smiled and laughed, leaning back in his chair with his knee nonchalantly propped up against his desk. At one point we began discussing Railtrack and I said we felt concerned by the nature of the commercial company, whose first priority seemed to be to deliver a profit to its shareholders, which didn't really provide the correct atmosphere for safety to be a prime concern.

Stephen Byers leaned further back in his chair, turning to momentarily smile at David Hill before saying, 'Well, you can watch out for an announcement around the eighth of October that you might find pleasing or at least of interest.'

After leaving what we all considered to be a very positive meeting, we walked the hundred yards or so from the Department for Transport to a little bar we'd noticed earlier – not to get drunk, as I was on best behaviour after the previous night – but rather to discuss excitedly what Byers had meant by his intriguing comment. One thing was for sure, whatever it was it wouldn't be good news for Railtrack.

Three weeks after my London meetings, the TV channels and newspapers were again reporting the anniversary of Ladbroke Grove. I took myself off to a hotel in Beaconsfield without telling anyone where I had gone and stayed in my room alone for two days, where I just drank from the moment I woke up until I fell unconscious in the evening. I drank anything too: vodka, wine from room service and the entire contents of the minibar. It's only lucky they didn't supply mouthwash in the bathroom as I'd have likely downed that too.

As I emerged from my weekend binge, I discovered a plethora of missed calls and messages from Martin Minns, asking that I call him right away. He informed me that Stephen Byers had announced that Railtrack would be put into administration following his refusal to grant it additional government funding. So that was what he had alluded to at our last meeting. The press release was dated 7 October.

It was great news as far as the PSG were concerned and a huge milestone.

A week later I had the very pleasant task of attending the Savoy Hotel to collect a Women of the Year award. I was presented with the Frink Award for my work with the PSG, and other awards that day were picked up by yachtswoman Ellen MacArthur and journalist Marie Colvin. Little were the Women of the Year organisers to know how incongruous them giving me this award was bearing in mind the state I was in – something I was desperately trying to keep hidden. I used my speech, which I nervously delivered to the hundreds of women gathered for the lunch, to formally announce that the PSG would hold a rail summit in early December at which our declaration on rail safety would be launched. My hands were shaking so much from nerves that I found myself unable to turn the pages of my speech; fortunately newsreader Moira Stuart, who was acting as host, leaned over and kindly turned the pages while smiling encouragement.

It was actually 11 December when I met with other members of the PSG at the Institute of Directors on Pall Mall for the signing of our Declaration of Intent on Rail Safety. It was the culmination of our whole campaign.

A few days prior Stephen Byers's office had called the PSG to say that he could no longer attend the signing. Luckily, I had had the temerity to say, 'OK, that's fine. I will simply announce to all the others attending and all of the media assembled that you have backed out.' As I walked up through Waterloo Place I saw the many broadcast trucks, radio cars and reporters and journalists all preparing to record the event. A short while later I smiled to myself as Stephen Byers's office called to say he'd changed his mind again and was attending after all.

So there he was, Stephen Byers MP, together with Theresa May MP (who was at the time the shadow transport spokesperson), Charles Kennedy, and representatives of the trade unions, Railtrack and the Association of Train Operating Companies. Meanwhile, Prime Minister Tony Blair had sent us a letter of good wishes, as had William Hague, the leader of the Conservative Party.

At 11 a.m. the assembled all put their names to a document which stated:

We the undersigned publicly declare that we will strive to fully implement, assist with the implementation of and encourage the implementation of all recommendations set out in the [Cullen] reports, within the timescale set down in the reports (or as from time to time amended by the Health and Safety Commission, the Secretary of State or Parliament), as set out in the summary below...

This was what the PSG had been striving so hard for, for so long, and we all went home that day feeling a deep sense of pride in knowing that, no matter what, we had done everything in our power to make a difference and to prevent the tragedy we'd experienced from ever happening again.

Janette and Martin were not the only friends who had tried to put me straight on my drinking. Just before Christmas I went to Gloucester to see another survivor friend, Helen Mitchell, whom I had always regarded as a kind, caring and understanding friend. Yet I tested her understanding to the limit when, in a drunken state, and for no apparent reason, I argued with her over something trivial – so trivial, in fact, that I can't even recall what it was. She lost her patience and snapped.

'Pam! I will go to the ends of the earth for you if I know I am helping my friend who's trying to cope with being in a rail crash, but I will not help you when it's just the drink that's causing the problem. I will not help a drunk! At least not until you realise you've got a problem.'

I burst into tears. I knew yet again I had upset and been rude to someone who had become a dear friend. Helen went to bed and I stayed downstairs chewing over what she had said, drinking water and trying to sober up again. Eventually, I decided it would be better if I left so I picked up my bag and, at 5 a.m., drove home. That was the only time I can remember having driven while still under the influence and I was in no fit state to drive. Thank whatever God there is that I didn't harm anyone on that journey.

With Martin, Janette and Helen's words ringing in my ears, and remembering Simon Weston's warning too, I knew I had to stop drinking. It was, as Simon had forecast, consuming me. Deep down I wanted to stop and without doubt the jolt I'd had from Helen had made me realise that if I didn't I would end up a very lonely person, and a person destined for an early grave. I got home, grabbed every single bottle of booze in the house and poured it all down the sink. For the next twelve months I didn't touch a single drop of alcohol.

CHAPTER 15

'THAT BLOODY WOMAN'

Having chucked all of the alcohol out of the house, I gradually came to appreciate some of the things I had done as my sober period kicked in. One of my first tasks of the New Year was to sit down and write letters of apology to people like Janette and Martin, and to talk to Peter and my family, telling them how genuinely sorry I was and that I hoped they could forgive my behaviour. These kind people, to a man, agreed to forgive and forget, and with their acts of compassion I tried to make amends and to start the work of forgiving myself.

On 11 December 2001, at the declaration on rail safety meeting, I believed that the PSG had achieved something quite momentous: we'd brought together all of the political and management figures responsible for rail safety, and witnessed them agree publicly to implement the recommendations of the Cullen Inquiry. We held this valuable document within our group and intended to use it if any of the signatories tried to backtrack on their agreement − a powerful document indeed. Added to this, at the Ladbroke Grove trackside John Prescott, the Deputy Prime Minister, had earlier reassured us 'money would be no object' and a year later Lord MacDonald, sitting beside Prescott at the Department for Transport when we all met, had reiterated that Lord Cullen's recommendations would be 'funded and fully implemented'.

It was early in 2002 that I made a huge tactical campaign mistake. There had been one signature missing from the declaration: that of Mick Rix from ASLEF, as he had been otherwise engaged on the day of signing. *Not to worry,* I thought, *we'll courier it to him for signature and return.* Knowing how powerful this document was and that it might prove a burden to government and the rail industry, I should have been more careful about how I tried to get Mick's signature. Off went the document with a motorbike courier marked private and confidential for Mick. It was duly signed for at the ASLEF headquarters ... and that was the last we ever saw of it. When I discovered its loss I tried to track down the person who had signed for it but, of course, the signature was so squiggled that it was impossible to make out the name.

Of course, we had a copy of the declaration but not with all the signatures on it. In due course I did try asking Stephen Byers's replacement, Alistair Darling, if he would sign a new copy but was turned down flat by the Department for Transport. Without the government minister's signature on it the document was as good as useless so there seemed little point in asking any of the other signatories. You have to remember that the government, via their representative Stephen Byers, had not wanted to sign the declaration in the first place. They had tried to wriggle out of it and I had to effectively blackmail them into signing by threatening to make their non-cooperation public. With the document's 'loss' somewhere within ASLEF I had now presented them with the perfect opportunity to refuse re-signing and they could ignore anything that the declaration held them accountable to or for. I am still suspicious to this day as to where that document disappeared to but of course this would only be my own conjecture.

We had lost our weapon with which to hit the government and the rail industry if they began to renege on their promises. Without it all we could do was fall back on our previous tactics of harrying and trying to persuade them using the media's influences where we could.

From a campaign point of view our two-year journey had ended on a huge high, which was rapidly followed by a low when we realised that our declaration document had gone and with it our ability to hold people accountable. I felt responsible for letting the others in the PSG down when they had trusted me to look after it. I was tired and jaded and for a while at least did not want to think about trains, rails, red signals, rail companies or politicians. Nor did I want to front any more interviews. The PSG had had a natural break point forced upon it as far as I could see, and I thought it was time to start concentrating on my own personal life; I asked for someone else to take over from me and Simon Benham took up the chairman position.

No sooner had I retreated, though, than our campaign began running into sand. Just one month after he had signed the declaration, Stephen Byers announced to the House of Commons that there would be no extra government money to help pay for the ten-year plan for the railways, as commissioned and drawn up by the Strategic Rail Authority. Furthermore, he said, there would be no funding for the higher levels of track maintenance work introduced after the Hatfield crash, nor for the fitting of the ATP (automatic train protection) safety devices, recommended by Cullen for introduction by 2010. It didn't take a genius to work out that if the government reneged on these two basic commitments, then the other Cullen recommendations would be extremely vulnerable.

At the time of our crash there was an AWS (automatic warning system) in place on UK trains which was simply a horn that sounded in the train driver's cab if the train crossed a red signal, and this could be overridden and ignored. This is what was fitted to the Thames Turbo, and what Michael Hodder overrode and ignored.

A newer system called TPWS (Train Protection and Warning System, for trains running at less than 70mph) and TPWS+ (for trains running over 70mph) was being introduced, but we wanted to also push for ATP, which, with its system of two boxes – one on the tracks at the base of the signals and one in the driver's cab – did more than just sound warnings. This would physically stop a train if it crossed a red light. The system had been available in 1999, but had not been fitted across the network as it was considered too expensive by the rail industry.

We knew of a new system, ETMS (European Train Management System), which was similar to TPWS+ but it linked signals, tracks and trains, providing a highly comprehensive level of safety which would make things even safer. We were also pushing for this as soon as possible, but of course this was even more expensive than TPWS+ so there was government and industry resistance to commit to it.

Weeks later, in April 2002, it was reported that Rail Safety Ltd – an independent subsidiary of Railtrack – had delivered a report to Stephen Byers stating that ATP would not be fitted for another eighteen years, a full ten years behind schedule. Far from finding it unacceptable, Byers more or less shrugged his shoulders as though there was nothing he could do, and thereby publicly refused to adhere to the dates set by Cullen for fitting ATP. The delay was putting lives at risk unnecessarily.

A month later, on 10 May 2002, a train travelling from London's King's Cross to King's Lynn in Norfolk was derailed as it approached Potters Bar station in Hertfordshire. The engine slewed sideways and toppled to one side before mounting a platform and coming to a halt wedged between the platform and station canopy. Seven people were killed and seventy-six were injured. I felt a sickening tightening of my stomach again, coupled with a nausea that seemed to sap the strength from my entire body, leaving me weak-legged and tired. Why, oh why had I been so stupid and caused us to lose the one document we could have been beating the government over the head with? I

just couldn't believe it. I broke down and cried, all the time thinking how it was all so avoidable.

'Another rail tragedy,' stated many of the next day's newspapers.

I felt incandescent anger at the government and was so dispirited that all we had worked for now risked being unravelled. More
and more people would die or be injured, but no one seemed to
care, or be interested in improving things. Were we all just totally
dispensable as far as the powers that be were concerned and all
in the name of profit? It was so bloody frustrating but we were
impotent.

My anger was further fuelled when, a week later, I watched
Byers in a news report standing at the despatch box telling the
House of Commons that he had never planned to put Railtrack
into administration, and had only made the decision to do so on 5
October 2001 after witnessing the 'parlous' state of the company's
finances, making a formal announcement on 7 October 2001.
He was obviously under pressure after the Potters Bar crash to
account for why rail safety had not been improved.

Wait a minute, I thought, *he said 5 October was the date he decided
to put Railtrack into administration…*

I furiously scrambled for my diary and flicked back through
the pages. Yes, yes, as I thought: I met Byers with Martin, Simon,
Janette and the others on 12 September 2001.

At that meeting I raised concerns that a company such as
Railtrack ought to be replaced by a company whose first priority
was not to shareholders. In direct answer to this he said there
would be an announcement on or around 7 October which we
would find 'interesting' or to our 'liking'. It was pointedly obvious
that Byers had fully intended to put Railtrack into administration
long before his now suggested 5 October date. As I watched, the
anger continued to well up inside me, but now that anger had a
direction in which to be aimed. I realised Byers had no intention

of sticking to any agreement, or even of telling the truth. How dare he? He was a minister, elected by the people and a servant of the people, yet here he was flying in the face of all that I had been brought up to believe was his constitutional duty. If he could be this dissembling to his peers, we could kiss goodbye to him carrying out his signed pledge on our declaration on rail safety, which had disappeared into the ether.

In the past I would have immediately called Martin Minns for his advice, but since I had stepped back from the PSG, he too had felt it was time to move on and his contract had ended. The last I'd heard of him was that he was in the Bahamas working on an election campaign. I knew I had to do something, but what? Who could I call?

I looked through my contact book and decided to phone Ray Massey, the transport correspondent at the *Daily Mail*. Ray had tirelessly covered our campaign and I had always found him very supportive of everything we tried to do. I guess any journalist receiving a call saying, in effect, *I have just heard a cabinet minister lying in the House of Commons and can prove it* would regard it as manna from heaven. I explained everything to Ray about our meeting with Byers, and was quite clear about the dates as I had been careful to keep dated notes. He recorded our chat and said he needed to check a few facts and would call me back.

Having given vent to my anger, I then gave way to nervousness. I'd vowed to step back from the media, and here I was now starting it all up for myself again. But this time I was taking on a government minister, which really raised the stakes.

It transpired that Martin Minns had returned from the Bahamas and was on holiday with his family in Cornwall, so Ray managed to reach him on his mobile and explained about my phone call, asking Martin to confirm who else was at the meeting on 12 September. Martin said he'd call back and immediately phoned me, asking why I'd called Ray and what the heck it was all about. He hadn't yet seen Byers on the news. Martin, in turn, called Ray back and confirmed the details of our meeting with Byers and said that yes, he had intimated something big was going to happen to Railtrack that would please us. The very next day, 22 May, the *Daily Mail* ran the story under the headline '"I know Byers lied to MPs," says Paddington survivor'.

To be honest, I was a little disappointed that the piece was relegated to page twenty-eight of the newspaper as I thought a minister lying to Parliament should deserve higher public scrutiny, but Martin Minns assured me not to worry.

'Pam, you've just gone public about a government minister lying in the House of Commons. There are a lot of things you can get away with in there but lying is not one of them. The other papers will pick up on it. Believe me, shit and fan are about to come together on this one.'

Martin was right. On 23 May all the major newspapers ran with the story. Stupidly, I had not thought through the full consequences of what I had initiated; I assumed that I would only have to tell the *Daily Mail* and then other people would take it over and investigate Stephen Byers. A naive error that, after my experiences with the PSG, I should have known would not be the case. TV and radio stations were queuing up with requests to interview me; the frenzy started all over again. Oh, what had I done?

Byers had been interviewed by the BBC's political editor, Andrew Marr, about the story, and had said that he and I were 'in agreement over what had been discussed' at the meeting on 12 September and that he had not specified putting Railtrack into administration. He reiterated that the decision to do so was 'not made until 5 October'. He continued, 'I think when people see what Pam Warren has said and what I said to the House of Commons, there is no conflict.'

Ray Massey called me for my response to what Byers had said. Still furious, I snapped. 'It's nonsense, Ray. He's twisting the truth and using semantics. There is a clear conflict. He's not bothered about the travelling public and rail safety. He's only bothered about saving his own skin. He intimated something big was going to happen to Railtrack on or about 8 October. He couldn't have been any clearer, and then made the announcement on 7 October. I have witnesses to everything he said and they are willing to stand up in court to that effect.'

Before I had a chance to scan the morning's newspapers, Andrew Marr called from the BBC and asked if he could meet me. I agreed, with the proviso that Simon Benham, chairman of the PSG, who had also been at the meeting, was with me.

Andrew Marr was as charming and disarming as he appears on television. We discussed the PSG campaign, my accusations against Byers, and his response. It became apparent through speaking to Andrew that I had ruffled an awful lot of feathers in Whitehall, even up to the Prime Minister, who apparently referred to me as 'that bloody woman'. It wasn't until a little later that I discovered the total extent of quite how irritated government officials had become!

Meanwhile, the next day's – Friday's – headline in the *Daily Mail*, this time front-page news, stated 'Byers lying again over winding up Railtrack'. The pressure was certainly on. I dare say Byers thought long and hard over the weekend and carefully considered his position, which was growing ever more difficult. On the following Monday his decision to resign from office was communicated to the Prime Minister.

Understandably, my accusations against Stephen Byers sent paroxysms through the Department for Transport. On 23 May Dan Corry, a special adviser to Byers, sent an email to the Labour Party headquarters in an effort to find out whether those involved with the PSG had a political agenda. As with so many government emails before and since, Dan Corry's 'confidential' correspondence did not remain confidential for long. It was actually *The Independent* which broke the story on 6 June, two weeks after the now infamous email was sent.

'Department for Transport's secret email to dig the dirt on victim of Paddington' was their front-page headline.

The report stated, 'Senior figures in the DfT sent a secret email to uncover information on Paddington rail crash survivor Pam Warren in what has been seen as an attempt to discredit her.'

My God, I thought. *They've certainly got the knives out for me.* However, I was not unduly concerned as I had no particular political views or affiliations and, unlike some others, I was not lying. I believed in the power of the truth and that it would out in the end. I was more shocked that they would even think to stoop so low just because someone had annoyed them, let alone attempt it. It belied my beliefs in our country's democracy and freedom of speech.

The Independent went to press without the full text of the email, but their report forced the Department for Transport to release it in full. As it turned out, I wasn't the main target after all. Corry's email said: 'Can you get some sort of check done on the people who are making a big fuss on the Paddington Survivors' group attacking SB please (i.e. the ones taking over from Pam Warren) … Basically, are they Tories?'

The response came back, 'Checked excel [Excalibur, the Labour party's database] and there is no record of them as Tories.'

Dan Corry persisted: 'I'm told their spokesman Martin Minns (?) works for a PR company. Can we find more on this please?'

'This is all I can find – I'm not sure about Benham,' was the response.

'Any more on Minns' company? (and is he still there?),' asked Corry.

The Times reported that the Labour Party had sent electronic press cuttings on Martin Minns and Simon Benham to the transport ministry but these were not released for 'reasons of personal confidentiality'.

The Independent's front page on 7 June was, in its way, one of the most remarkable headlines I have ever seen: 'A sorry, sorry, sorry affair.'

It was positioned directly above photographs of Alistair Darling, who had taken over as the new Transport Minister, Stephen Byers and Tony Blair, and the text of their apologies.

Alistair Darling: 12.16 p.m. – 'The Department for Transport wishes to apologise unreservedly for any distress caused to Pam Warren, the Paddington survivors or their relatives.'

Stephen Byers: 12.33 p.m. – 'I want to apologise to Pam Warren … This email should never have been sent. Indeed, had I been aware of it, I would have stopped it.'

Tony Blair: 1.27 p.m. – 'The Prime Minister shares [the] view that this should not have happened. It is wrong that it did happen and he shares in the regret that it happened.'

For good measure Dan Corry, the transport ministry special adviser, who was in Japan for the football World Cup, also issued a statement apologising 'unreservedly'.

It had been a bruising encounter for me, Simon and Martin. My own naive assumptions of politics, politicians and their assurances were all swept away by the realities of the past few weeks. A politician's promise was rather an aspiration or a target, I discovered: apologies are issued by those who have been caught; and prime ministers do not apologise, they 'share regret'. It also left a nasty taste in my mouth: if a member of the public sticks their head over the parapet, standing up for truth or honesty, they are most likely going to have it shot off by the government. I know this to be a truism as it has happened to many others.

I do feel that this whole sorry episode did eventually turn around and the truth did win in the end as a few years later I was stood in my kitchen and Stephen Byers was talking on a news channel I happened to have on. I had my back to the TV but remember clearly hearing Byers mentioning me by name and admitting that he had lied at the time. I turned around slowly and hit the replay button – yes, he had definitely said it. I jumped around the kitchen pumping my fists in the air and shouting, 'Yes, oh yes! At last!' I felt completely vindicated and right in what I had done.

Mr Blair may have 'shared' many regrets during his time in office, the Corry affair being a relatively minor one in comparison to some others, but at least it put the pressing importance of rail safety at the top of the agenda again, for a while at least.

CHAPTER 16

SEPARATION, DIVORCE AND COMPENSATION

Apart from the spat with Byers in 2002 I was pretty much now able to concentrate mainly on myself again. Being clear of the booze, I was also better able to consider where I was in life. The side effects of the Seroxat continued to bring on depression cycles with monthly regularity but I assumed this was just part and parcel of the PTSD and would have to be interwoven into daily life.

With the medication and protein drinks I'd been consuming for over two years I had put a lot of weight on. From being a seven-and-a-half-stone woman before the crash I had ballooned to almost eleven stone; being of diminutive height, the extra weight did not sit well on me and because I avoided mirrors, I ignored it for a while. But then my two cousins came over to visit me one day with Jane and we had our picture taken in the garden; Dad took it and then presented me with a framed copy of it. I was absolutely horrified! I looked like a little round ball with arms and legs sticking out of it. Even with the scarring to my face I looked at least twenty years older than I actually was and my clothes were straining at the midriff. Oh no, this was something I was no longer going to accept.

I took up yoga to help with the arthritis in my joints; from the research I'd done on the internet, I found that Hatha yoga would help loosen joints and encourage the synovial fluid within them to flow. I was still touchy about my scarring and concerned about my immune system being quite weak, so mixing with new people was a constant worry. Thankfully, I struck lucky with a teacher called Karen who was happy to hold sessions at my home and I've kept it up even to this day. Karen has come to be a dear friend, although we tend to chat and laugh more than actually do yoga! Anyway, during one of her exercises I had to sit on the floor with my legs spread wide open (nice image, huh?) and then bend from my waist, towards the floor, in between my legs. Well, I couldn't even bend two inches – mainly because my stomach was in the way! – and the floor seemed an awful long way away as I huffed and puffed trying to bend further.

Having made up my mind that I had to do something about my weight, I hunted for a personal trainer in my locality. This is how I met Mandy, a lovely lass hailing from York. I instantly took a liking to her and she was very good at taking on board my physical and medical constraints. We began a weekly session with her pushing me to my limits but making me smile and laugh at the same time. It took a long time to shift the weight – almost two years – but shift it I eventually did and I began to feel healthier than I had in a long time. Ever since the crash and all the medication I had to take I have continued to battle with my weight. Mandy moved back to York to be closer to her family, and today a male physical trainer, James, who is ex-army and knows all about how to push you, keeps me at it.

What with trying to get physically fit, doing yoga, relaxing tense muscles with massages, still attending psychologist sessions, managing my PTSD symptoms by resting when tired, still having my fingers waggled (despite having got these sessions down to once a week) and trying to reconnect with pre-crash family commitments my daytimes were pretty full. It was at this time that I told Nick Percival that I had had enough of operations.

'There are still some aesthetic things we can do to improve your scarring and new techniques are developing all the time,' he said.

'No,' I replied, 'I really have had enough and am prepared to leave things as they are.'

Nick acquiesced and I think that was the last time I saw him as a patient. Not long after this I stopped my sessions at the Hand Clinic too. I really wanted to leave the past behind and if things weren't perfect with my looks or my hands, well, hey, nothing in life is perfect.

One thing that certainly wasn't perfect was my marriage. I realised how bad things had got when I was exchanging emails with a mutual friend and she pointed out that I never once mentioned Peter in my missives anymore. *How true*, I thought afterwards. *But then he doesn't really feature that much in my life anymore*. We were just two people living in the same house, nothing more.

I suppose that Peter had done what he felt was his best to be supportive but in my eyes he had fallen short of how a loving husband should have been. He definitely did provide a shoulder to lean on, both figuratively and literally, when I appeared at the Cullen Inquiry or attended the early press conferences. I would not, and could not, have got through those things without him; being mobbed by the media was at first shocking and worrying in equal measure. I soon learnt to cope with it but I was never comfortable with the disconcerting melee that accompanied my appearances at PSG events or the Cullen Inquiry. I did what I had to do, and then scuttled off home. Peter on the other hand rose to the occasion and was not fazed by the media's attention.

He was not uncaring, but his lack of forethought often bordered on the insensitive. If only it had been as easy as he believed it was. I tried to overlook these things, thinking, *Oh well, I suppose I might have acted that way myself if I didn't know.* Deep down, though, I don't think I believed this was true, particularly when my sister Jane questioned his actions; she was the opposite of him and always tried to put herself in my position, thinking what was right or wrong for me. Peter couldn't.

After Peter released the news of me being in the Cardinal Clinic, I realised I was not happy being around him and don't believe I ever forgave him. Even after operations I always flew up to Aberdeen, where Mum had moved during the year Jane looked after me, to recover at her house rather than staying at home. That probably said it all.

I did try to discuss our growing apart with him but he seemed to believe it was all down to me and it would somehow get sorted out by my counselling sessions.

It was actually my mother who helped me make up my mind to confront it head on. It wasn't that I discussed it with her – well, at least not until I was sure it was over – but she gave me the strength to decide to face Peter, and told me that for my own sanity I needed to end it. This coincided with my psychologist telling me that I couldn't make any further progress in my mental recovery until I sorted out my personal life. It was still a hugely difficult subject to confront Peter with. After all, I kept telling myself, he had stuck with me through the bad times since the crash, so I had a huge guilt trip about telling him it was over. Then something happened that shocked me so much I began to look at him with far less sympathetic eyes...

Since 2000 Bernard Clarke, my solicitor, had been pushing on with a claim for compensation from Railtrack's insurers as they'd already admitted liability for the train crash. While it rumbled on in the background, Bernard kept me informed. Sometime in 2002 he had to appoint a barrister to argue my case; I met two or three before I settled on a chap I felt comfortable with. Peter came with me to these meetings as my medication still affected my memory badly, and my concentration was so poor that I felt it prudent to have my husband to support me. At one particular meeting in Lincoln's Inn, Peter and I had popped outside for some fresh air after the barrister had spoken about possible figures for the amount of compensation I might expect, although it was all conjecture. Outside, Peter was excited.

'Do you realise that this might be an absolute fortune?' he said. I hadn't but then I wasn't the type to start counting my chickens just yet. He rubbed his hands together and I hadn't seen him so animated in ages.

'If it's as much as I think it might be, we could put some into a trust for my kids' – he had three – 'some of it into my property business...' He continued on in this vein and none of what he was saying seemed to include me. I was aghast.

'Hang on, this is supposed to be money to pay for my medical expenses. I have to live off this for the rest of my life and I don't know what other problems may crop up as I get older. And anyway, nothing is guaranteed at the moment.'

He then dropped the subject.

Anger welled up inside. Was that the reason he was still with me? It was clear to me from our lack of any intimacy that he no longer found me physically attractive. I also sensed he no longer cared whether I was happy or unhappy, so was he only interested in the money?

Before seriously beginning negotiations with my barrister Railtrack's insurers had been waiting for me to become 'medically stable', i.e. for my physical injuries to become static, and 2002 turned out to be the year they were deemed to be so. Railtrack's insurers wanted their own medical experts to examine and test me and they seemed to have a separate specialist for every single part of the body; over a number of weeks I was poked and prodded by a variety of doctors and surgeons and felt like a prize heifer at a cattle market. To prove if I had feeling in my hands or not they even went so far as to cover my eyes and stick sharp needles all over my hands. As I did have some feeling in my left hand it bloomin' hurt and I yelped a fair amount during that session. I lost count of the doctors and the number of medical instruments that were shoved at, on and into me. Suffice to say, I was very glad when it was all over and they appeared satisfied that I was not exaggerating the level and extent of my injuries.

In 2003 my mother moved from Aberdeen to a rented house in Devon as she wanted to be a little closer to me, and was worried about my marriage. For a few months I spent two or three days a week at the marital home, primarily to attend therapy sessions, before going to Devon to stay with my mother. She was a total tower of strength. Eventually on one trip I admitted to her that I couldn't see a future with Peter. 'I hate seeing my beautiful daughter like this. You will never get better if you stay with him.'

Her opinion confirmed what I felt deep down but I was still too fainthearted to face a confrontation with him. I sat down and wrote a letter to Peter detailing all the reasons for my unhappiness with our marriage as I wanted to be rational in my approach to him and not lose any conversation in a mishmash of emotional rhetoric. I wanted to be clear that I had reached the end of the line with trying to make things better between us. Mum agreed that she and her husband Dan would drive me home the next day to finish things with Peter and then take me back to Devon with them.

As I reached my house I felt physically sick and my face tightened as I became rigid with nerves – something I always encountered when feeling stress, ever since I started wearing the mask. Mum and Dan made themselves scarce in another part of the house so they would be close by if things got out of hand.

Peter and I sat on high bar stools in the kitchen, which seemed to be our meeting place whenever there was something serious to discuss, and the only place in the house that we allowed ourselves

to smoke. Before saying a word, I reached for a cigarette, physically shaking as I tried to light it, and handed Peter my letter. It
took a couple of attempts before the end ignited and I inhaled
more deeply than ever. I told Peter we couldn't carry on, that it
had gone beyond anything we could repair. I said that I had tried
to tell him time and time again that it wasn't working, but now it
was too late. I wanted to end it and I wanted a divorce.

I held my breath as I waited for Peter's reaction.

Peter appeared quite calm at first and said that he'd always
believed he could never make me love him if I didn't want to,
and asked why now I felt it had to be so final. I reiterated some
of my letter and explained, giving all my reasons about how we'd
grown apart, how I felt him to have become uncaring, how I
didn't trust him to have my interests at heart … the whole lot.
The more I spoke, the angrier he became. He then blamed me
and my drinking. While I knew the drinking hadn't helped and,
for a while, had placed an inordinate amount of pressure on our
relationship, the truth was I drank because I was unhappy. To me
it was a symptom and not the cause. By this point I had been
sober for over a year, but things between us had got worse, not
better, so I asked myself how was the drinking still to blame?
Our relationship had always been built on unsure foundations
and, in my view, the train crash and its aftermath had tested it
beyond breaking point.

Peter became more and more angry. I found myself switch-
ing off from what he was saying, already afraid of his reaction.
Suddenly he stopped. He looked at me icily and with an eerie
calmness, told me that if I gave him what he wanted he would
walk away. So there it was.

His bald demand left me shaken and in shock. This is what our
marriage had boiled down to.

I didn't answer him straight away – my nerves were too frayed, plus he was confirming my suspicions that money was why he had stayed with me and I needed to come to terms with that. I offered to move out of our marital home and stay with Mum; I felt it a fair offer to make, thinking he should suffer as little inconvenience as possible. However, and this might be me being too harsh in my judgement of Peter, I was puzzled as to why he felt it was OK for me to move out and put up with long transits back and forth to Reading to attend my medical therapies when he knew that I was still very unwell. On reflection, I probably expected him to say 'Of course, I'll move' but he didn't and accepted my offer. So I packed a few things before Mum and Dan drove me back to Devon.

I had hoped, as had been the case with Scott, that we might have settled things amicably. I discussed the mechanics of divorce from Peter with a specialist solicitor and did say that if and when any compensation came through I wanted Peter to be 'well looked after'. It had never been a case of me walking away from Peter and hanging him out to dry so I suggested that he and I sit down and talk about it. As my hands still couldn't write easily, I asked Mum's husband Dan to sit in with us and take notes for me. Peter greatly resented his presence, but Dan had unwittingly been dragged into this already and knew what was happening, so who else should I get to do it, I asked? We both knew Dan and agreed he was a fair-minded person who would not want to take sides, and I didn't want to bring strangers into our mess. Truth be told, I will also admit that I knew Peter had a knack of talking, talking, talking until he wore the other person down and they agreed to whatever he was asking, a talent I had seen him use to great effect in the past. I thought Dan's presence would help me stay strong and only agree to what was reasonable and not be browbeaten into submission. I also didn't trust that if it was just us two anything that was said might not be twisted out of context in the future, especially as my memory was still adversely affected by medication; I wanted a witness to our discussions.

From that point on, our various meetings became increasingly difficult and acrimonious. Every time we reached an agreement on something, be it the house, the business, the other assets, the possible compensation etc., Peter would go away, alter his demands and then return with a fresh set at the next meeting. It was like heading back to square one each time. From my point of view, it was so frustrating. I would leave after each encounter thinking *Good, that all seems fair, maybe we can move on to the next step*, before being sadly disabused at the next meeting and having to consider Peter's new set of demands, which seemed to increase each time.

'Is it just me?' I asked of Dan on one of our drives back to Devon after such a meeting.

'No,' Dan said, 'he keeps moving the goal posts each and every time.'

Try as I did to be amicable, after three months we couldn't seem to settle on the letter of agreement that would form the basis of our divorce.

All of a sudden, Peter said he was moving out of the house and going to stay with his accountant and friend Len Shore in Basingstoke. I couldn't understand why he had changed his mind so abruptly but I was not complaining as it meant I could move back home and not have to endure the tiring travelling back and forth from Devon.

At what was to turn out to be our final meeting – at Len's house – Peter moved the goal posts yet again, only this time his demands were huge. He obviously felt being at Len's would give him the psychological upper hand, and, boy, was it a hand he played with great nastiness. It all culminated with him literally spitting out: 'If I hadn't given you a chance, you wouldn't have been what you became.'

Something finally snapped. I began to shake with rage. 'That's it!' I shouted and stormed out of the room with Dan in my wake.

As I walked out of the door, I heard Peter's now almost plaintive voice call out, 'But what about this agreement letter?'

'Fuck the bloody letter!' I shouted back. 'I don't care if you sign it or don't fucking sign it.' I don't like swearing but it seemed very appropriate at this particular moment. I called my solicitor and told her I'd had enough and didn't want to see or talk to Peter again, and that she should take over from now on through the courts.

In July 2003 I received a call from Simon Benham at the PSG about an inquiry; it wasn't a press or media request, but rather from the playwright David Hare. Apparently he was working on a play about rail privatisation and asked if Simon and I would consider meeting him to talk about our experiences after Ladbroke Grove. We duly met on a warm summer evening at Simon's house in Slough, and chatted for over three hours. I liked David Hare immensely and he wasn't anything like I'd pictured – he was tall, slightly shambling and totally interested in everything we said. I hope I was of some help with his research.

His play, *The Permanent Way*, included a character in a plastic mask and opened in York before touring the country from Newcastle to Oxford, and then moving on to London at the National. It was greeted enthusiastically. I never got round to seeing it but only heard positive things from friends who did.

The play itself begins at breakneck speed as a group of dissatisfied commuters, brandishing newspapers, launch into everyone's favourite topic of conversation: what's wrong with the railways? This is followed by a series of interweaving monologues by three senior Whitehall, Treasury and City figures who narrate, from the inside, the privatisation of British Rail. The scene is set, and the play's principal subject matter comes to the fore: the disasters of Southall, Ladbroke Grove, Hatfield and Potters Bar. Testimonies from victims, the bereaved, an investigating police officer and a campaigning lawyer express the anger felt by those who were caught up in these tragedies. The inadequacies of the court cases and public inquiries which ensued are challenged. The less sympathetic face of this story is given a hearing also: the managing director of Railtrack, for example, is allowed to defend himself against those who painted him as a murderer, and we do sympathise – to a point.

The production won the Best Touring Production award from the Theatre Management Association, and the radio version, with the original director and cast members, was made by Catherine Bailey Productions and broadcast on BBC Radio 4 on 14 March 2004. It was runner-up in that year's Sony Radio Academy Award for drama.

One review, in *The Guardian*, summed up the play as 'a great production and you leave the theatre aroused and angry, though also desperately impotent'.

That was exactly how I felt after many of our PSG meetings. I was fired up and enthusiastic, but ultimately when broken promises and lies prevailed, I did feel totally impotent…

By September 2003 I was living back in the old marital home. My mother and her husband had moved from Devon to my village soon after the break-up with Peter to make sure I was not completely alone and to help me where they could, assisting with my ongoing medical and therapy needs as I still could not drive very long distances. They were also there for me to turn to whenever the depression started creeping in, which it often did, though the periods in between were beginning to get a bit longer. I still found my mood swings difficult to control and, quite often, couldn't think straight enough to even feed myself. Mum took all the stress of this away from me, cooking and fussing over me. 'You just concentrate on getting yourself better,' she would cluck, just like a mother hen.

Nearly four years after the crash, I had still not reached a settlement with St Paul International Insurance, the rail insurers. On 14 September 2003 St Paul announced they had run out of money and passed on my claim, along with those of other survivors, to a different insurer, AIG, who in turn appointed solicitors to deal with us. Suddenly our efforts to achieve compensation were turning into huge legal battles, which threatened to go on for years, or at best many, many months. Bernard, my solicitor, called me with the news of AIG taking over and said he feared their solicitors might want to start the whole process over again. My heart sank. I had already endured being poked and prodded by St Paul's medical experts as they tried to disprove the extent of my injuries so they could reduce the amount of compensation they would have to pay, which they had never achieved. Now it was likely that AIG would want me to go through it all again. Combative as ever, Bernard suggested we should go public and fight the insurers through the media as well as through the legal process, and effectively embarrass them into paying up. I was stuck between the devil and the deep blue sea. Either put up with what was beginning to happen and continue living in limbo for, possibly, years more litigation or deliberately invite the press to help me. This time I chose the media route and crossed my fingers (figuratively speaking, that is, as I can't cross my fingers!) that they might be able to bring some pressure to bear. Bernard called Martin Minns, and with his help, we were about to witness the true power of the press!

On Tuesday 16 September, two days after St Paul made their announcement, at Martin's instigation I arrived at the St

Stephen's Club at Queen Anne's Gate in Westminster shortly before 9 a.m. I was about to hold a press conference with Bernard and fellow survivors from the PSG and Martin had lined up virtually every TV and radio news programme you can imagine, along with many journalists and photographers.

Bernard chaired the meeting and introduced me to read my short prepared statement about 'tactics of delay' by the rail insurers, before he went into the detail of what had happened and where we were in regard to the insurance companies. I then retreated into a side room to rest and gather my thoughts. I felt totally deflated by the whole thing, particularly the prospect of many more months of battling – I simply could not see a clear future. This was one of the few times I genuinely felt that I had no energy to keep on fighting them. I began to weep quietly but deeply. Martin came in and asked me to meet two of the TV news crews outside on the steps, and maybe answer a few questions for them. I really didn't have the energy or motivation so I said no, but Martin cajoled and coaxed me to do 'one last session'. A few minutes later, with Martin at my side still whispering words of encouragement, I walked through the inner double doors of the club to the steps outside, and could again feel the tears welling up from deep inside me. Not really hearing the first question, I just sobbed and said exactly how I felt: 'I have reached the stage where I do not believe what I am being told anymore. I do not believe it will ever be resolved, to be honest. I know this might sound melodramatic but all I want to do is go to sleep and not wake up. In a way, I really now wish I had not survived that bloody train crash.' It was all I could manage.

Martin raised his hand to the press, put his arm around my shoulder and led me back inside.

Martin later confided in me that he asked me to do 'one final session' with the press because the lighting inside the conference room wasn't brilliant and he'd had complaints from the film crews; also he didn't feel the press conference had really ignited. He had felt that one final push from me – also knowing I was emotionally charged – outdoors might be just what was needed. He hadn't expected me to say what I did, but as far as he was concerned that was a huge bonus to the PR campaign.

By 1 p.m. the *Evening Standard*'s front-page headline read, 'I Wish I Hadn't Survived Paddington – Crash victim's despair as insurance claim is delayed.' It was followed up that evening as a top story on the London television news.

The next day's papers continued with the story. The *Daily Mail* headlined, 'I wish I had never survived that bloody train crash,' and the *Daily Express* wrote, 'I wish I had died.' The headline in the *Daily Telegraph* meanwhile read, '"I can't take much more," says rail victim.'

What tends to happen with a story is that the national press run it and then move on to the next. However, the *Evening Standard* had other ideas after identifying a news item which they felt could run and run. The next day's edition carried the head-line 'Heartless', devoting two full pages to the story and naming Martin Ballinger as the 'multi-millionaire chief executive' of Go-Ahead Group, the parent company of the 'lead rail company in the case', and Martin Hudson, the chief executive of St Paul, as the main culprits for the delay in settling compensation.

The *Standard* continued their campaign into a third day with a double-page interview with Janette Orr, and a 'How you can help the victims' column giving the telephone numbers and email addresses of Thames Trains and St Paul International for readers to contact.

To my amazement, the newspaper then delivered 100,000 leaflets to the capital's twelve mainline stations calling on commuters to complain to Thames Trains and St Paul.

On the fourth day, Friday, the *Standard* maintained their attack by running a story on the Secretary of State for Transport, Alistair Darling, saying he had 'ordered rail bosses to take urgent action'. They also profiled Martin Ballinger and attacked his company's £34.5 million dividend payments to shareholders over the four years since the crash.

The following Monday, day five, the newspaper reprinted the numbers and emails for readers to contact, but by then Bernard Clarke had received a phone call from the insurers asking for a meeting to resolve 'this crisis'. Within a few days the insurers raised the white flag.

I really cannot thank the media enough with regard to this episode. They had all been supportive in the main to our campaigning for rail safety in the past but this went above and beyond what I would have expected from them. Without their help I truly believe that I and many, many others would have had no option but to bow to the shenanigans of the rail insurance companies and wait for many more years before being able to settle and then turn our thoughts towards our futures.

Mandy, my gym instructor, watched me sitting on a weightlifting contraption. I had stopped moving, I wasn't talking – nor could I – and though conscious I showed no response to her insistent and repeated questioning of 'Pam, are you OK?'

It was February 2004 and I had suffered a mental shutdown. It had happened once or twice since the crash; it seemed that when everything became a bit too much for me to handle and compute, my body and brain just switched off. It starts with me feeling low, and then moves on to me losing all interest in what I'm doing and where I am before I disappear totally into myself. Fortunately, Mandy had my mother's number and called her to come at once. By the time I was bundled into her car and driven home the 'shutdown' was total. My mother called Maurice Atkins at the Cardinal Clinic and explained I was not responding in any way.

'Is she suicidal?' he asked.

'I don't know. I can't get her to talk.'

'I can't leave right now. You'll have to bring her here to me,' he said. 'However, I'm so busy at the clinic that I won't be able to see her for some time.'

My mother's husband Dan decided time was of the essence and went online to search for help. He found a Dr Cantopher who was based in Guildford, a specialist in post-traumatic stress disorder, and arranged for me to see him immediately. I was again bundled into the car and driven over straight away.

Dr Cantopher took a good look through my medical records and said, 'These drugs are not doing you any good. I can't take you off the sleeping tablets as you're addicted to them. You've been on them too long, and you shouldn't have taken them for any longer than six months and certainly not for three years – we'll have to wean you off them slowly. I don't like Seroxat as an antidepressant as it has some nasty side effects which can't be helping so I can alter your depression tablets to start with and you'll find that'll help you feel much better in two to three weeks.'

He was right. Two weeks later I returned to see him, much more like the old Pam that I used to be before the crash. As the Seroxat gradually left my system I began to feel more and more human. I noticed that my sense of taste began to come back, which meant I started to enjoy my food again – before I had eaten just because I knew I had to. I found myself back in Waterstones, and perusing my shelf of biographies and autobiographies at home – Henry VIII, Elizabeth I, Eleanor of Aquitaine, Katharine Hepburn, Kate Adie. My desire to listen to music also returned: The Who, the Stones … The fog that always seemed to cloud my brain and thinking processes lifted and with the return of clarity my rationality returned.

As the new medication began to take effect, I had the opportunity to research into Seroxat as I was intrigued as to what the 'nasty side effects' might be. Jane, back at university, helped me, and what we discovered was shocking. Seroxat had been linked with people committing suicide, suffering extreme highs and lows which led to violent mood swings, alcoholism and other extremely unpredictable behaviour. No wonder I had been struggling while I was on it and had never felt quite like myself!

When I felt much better I made a point of taking a printout of our findings to Maurice Atkins at the Cardinal. 'What the hell did you put me on?' I asked him. 'No wonder I was all over the place. Do you realise how guilty I have felt about the things that have happened when maybe it wasn't entirely my fault?'

I don't think Maurice could have realised the devastating effects of Seroxat as it was a fairly new drug on the market at the time he prescribed it, but I hope he stopped giving it to patients after I left him with my findings. I didn't go back to see Maurice or to the Cardinal Clinic again. It was time to try a new approach. I wanted to get better and changing the drugs seemed to have helped start this process.

I asked Dr Cantopher to recommend a psychologist to take over from Stephen as I felt he had a clearer idea of who I was and what I needed than anyone else had up to that point. Without hesitation he suggested Anton, a South African psychologist who was based in Woking. The minute I met Anton I liked him; he encouraged me to look towards the future rather than rehash what had happened to me in the past – much more my type of attitude and one that appealed to me. He helped me set goals and set out how I was going to achieve them. He used cognitive behavioural therapy (CBT) to help me with my panic and anxiety attacks and to head off the depression episodes. Though not entirely successful with the depression I did find the CBT of enormous help with the other PTSD symptoms and for years had a flowchart of all the techniques I learnt stuck up on my kitchen wall so I could keep referring to them.

I think Anton worked out quite quickly that I pushed myself hard so at each of our sessions he insisted on seeing my diary of upcoming events and would tut with disapproval as he surveyed the crammed pages.

'You do realise you keep overdoing it?' he said. 'That's why the depression hits. It's your body and mind's way of saying enough is enough.'

I protested that I hated being bored or inactive, but I had to agree that he was right.

'Think of each day in thirds,' he continued. 'For every third that you are busy you need two thirds to rest.'

'OK, but how long do I have to do this for?' I asked.

'Pam, it may be forever. You have to appreciate your physical and mental health has been altered forever. You have to learn to listen to your body and to let it rest when it needs to.'

I listened carefully and took on board what he was saying but, I am sorry to say, never managed to meet the one third work, two thirds rest balance. Life is just too damn short! I do let my body rest more than I did before but I can't help continually pushing my boundaries and seeing how my body copes. Anton tutted over my diary for all the time I saw him, but often with a wry smile on his face as I sheepishly shrugged my shoulders at him. All in all, Anton's technique with me worked brilliantly in helping with my mental recovery, a rare gift to be able to give to someone in my opinion.

I honestly believe that Dr Cantopher and Anton helped to pull me back from my mental precipice, and gave me a future. I will always be grateful to both of them.

It was just as well I was in a better place psychologically because, as the old saying goes, the two most traumatic things in life are moving home and getting divorced – I was right in the middle of one and was about to find myself faced with the other. Moving was easy in comparison to divorce, though, I feel. The speed at which my compensation was agreed was like lightning; literally three telephone calls after my meeting with St Paul and it was sorted, and while bringing to an end an awful ordeal it also caused much bitterness between me and Peter.

In the event, the amount I settled with the insurers for was far, far less than had been hoped for in the past. I also had to sign an agreement never to divulge or discuss the compensation with anyone else and I still cannot go into it even now, and that exacerbated the lack of trust between us.

Due to the traumatic battles with the insurers and now with Peter, I was not looking forward to Christmas 2003.

What is there to celebrate? I thought.

I asked Mum and Dan to help me avoid anything to do with Christmas as the village I was living in always went completely over the top with the Christmas lights on their buildings, and one of my close neighbours insisted on playing Christmas music outside in their garden from the beginning of November to the end of January! There are only so many times you can hear 'Rudolph the Red-Nosed Reindeer', or 'Merry Xmas Everybody' over three months without beginning to lose your marbles and start dreaming of murder.

Dan was a star and took us all off to a rented house in Weymouth and he made sure any sights or sounds of Christmas were banned. This was the only year ever that I did not send any cards to other friends or relatives and I was the epitome of bah humbug. We even went so far as to take a portable barbecue set with us and we cooked and ate barbecued prawns on Weymouth beach (wrapped up like little Eskimos) for Christmas lunch. We did laugh, though, when two Father Christmases shot across our horizon on their jet skis gaily shouting 'Merry Christmas!'

Upon our return home I hit a run of bad luck with my health for a few months: firstly I contracted oesophagitis, which caused a burning session in my chest whenever I swallowed or tried to eat or drink – not pleasant and I seemed to take forever to get over it. And then I managed to fall off a chair while stupidly standing on it to reach for something, and I dislocated my shoulder. However, when I returned to hospital two weeks later because of the pain, it was discovered that I had broken my arm in two places too. I had to endure another operation, which involved inserting metal pins into my shoulder, and another couple of months of physiotherapy to get it working properly again. In between times, with my immune system still depleted, I caught cold after cold, and the arthritic pain in my joints almost drove me insane. 2003 really was turning into a right old 'annus horribilis'.

Meanwhile, increasingly angry and bitter, Peter started calling me almost every day, and day by day the calls became more and more aggressive. He complained that I had changed the locks on the house – he'd obviously arrived unannounced at some point and tried to get in, but luckily I must have been out at the time. He threatened, 'Changed locks wouldn't keep me out if I really wanted to get in.'

This frightened me. I immediately called a friend of mine, who happened to be a solicitor, for her advice. She drove over to me and found me in an agitated state. Without hesitation she phoned the police and the upshot was they called on Peter and warned him how seriously they now took domestic violence or the threat of it and not to bother me again. All further contact was through solicitors.

I didn't feel at ease in the house anymore and it really was too big for one person to rattle around in. I knew moving there to 'start again' had been a big mistake in any case.

CHAPTER 17

FIVE YEARS ON AND A CHAPTER CLOSES

Mum, Dan and I discussed my needing to stand on my own two feet and regain some independence. I also wanted to release them from their role of carers so that they could enjoy their own lives again. However, when I tackled everyday tasks to prove I was OK, I soon discovered many household cleaning products would cause the grafts on my hands to bubble up and crack when I tried to do the washing or clean the bathtub, and ironing was out of the question as I just kept on burning my hands because of the lack of sensation I had in them. These and other simple tasks which I used to take for granted were going to prove problematic so, in order that I might move forward, I suggested I get some help around the house. I certainly didn't want to go down the path of having professional carers popping in three times a day, as Peter had once arranged, never knowing if I'd see the same person twice. I needed some stability and someone I could get on with, and to not feel that I was just waiting for them to arrive and do the jobs I couldn't – which wouldn't do my self-esteem any favours at all.

Mum and I started to conduct interviews with various agencies and carers in the area and, as I tend to do when I first meet people, I trusted my gut instinct. Eventually, we found a lovely woman called Debbie, who was similar in age to me and had what I thought was a very healthy attitude to caring for people, believing she was there as a support and that she should treat the client with respect and allow them to try things for themselves. Her approach was all about encouragement, which was exactly what I wanted to hear. Debbie had a kind personality and was a hard worker. We found we shared a similar sense of humour, too, and I quickly hired her before she was snapped up by someone else. Debbie and I worked out ways around obstacles or 'how to skin the cat' as we called it; whenever I found I couldn't quite do something, we'd both sit down and brainstorm a way around the problem, be it trying to open a jar, chopping vegetables or opening a new toothbrush packet (which I defy anyone to do at the best of times). My home rapidly began to fill with gadgets and gizmos, each of which solved a particular problem, and my independence continued to grow. It's a wonderfully fulfilling feeling when you achieve something you once couldn't do. I also think I developed the ability to think outside the box for the first time, which has proven very valuable since.

Debbie was very clever in getting me to sit and rest without me realising. I'd always protest, so she'd find an excuse such as needing to vacuum and ask if I could sit on the sofa with my legs up … knowing I'd then drop off into a restful snooze. Debbie stayed with me for the next couple of years and became a good friend.

My next pressing task was to find a house I wanted to move to. I was keen to go back to my old village but I realised it was important to take my time to make sure I found a home where I would feel comfortable living alone. As luck would have it, one day driving through my old village to get to Mandy's gym for my weekly exercise sessions, I saw a house which was being renovated and had a 'for sale' sign outside. The front had been finished and as it was set up on a slight hillock it seemed to look proudly out over the street. It was as cute as a button, so on my way back after gym I popped in to have a closer look. The builder emerged as I pulled up – he was someone I knew – and as I stepped into the unfinished body of the house, which was stacked with materials and workmen showing off their bum cleavages, it just felt right. It felt safe. It felt like home.

I was able to do a deal with my builder friend and he let me choose a lot of the finishes to the house such as tiles, cupboards and wall colours so it reflected my taste from the start. I thought I'd be canny and keep the old house to rent out, providing a monthly income. What I didn't bank on was that dealing with tenants and their constant demands on even the most trivial matters would turn out to be a nightmare. I hired a property management company to take it over, but they only caused me more grief so after a year I put the house on the market, sold it and consigned all memories of it to the past.

Mum, being Mum, took over my move into the new house and brought in a specialist removal company, who she oversaw from start to finish while packing me off to her house out of the way. Both Mum and Dan were brilliant and knew that the key to my wellbeing was for me to feel settled and comfortable as quickly as possible. I moved in and soon felt as though I had been there for years.

Meanwhile, my divorce was still rumbling on, and the correspondence was flying backwards and forwards between solicitors – and achieving nothing. Peter was as belligerent as ever, but I stood my ground. However, it was still far from over and it took until December 2004 before the divorce was eventually finalised.

Fresh in my new home, I felt like sharing my newfound happiness so threw a big house-warming party! Having finally got my weight under control, I was determined to dress up and feel like an attractive woman again too, and this was the perfect occasion.

A huge marquee was set up in the back garden and I invited friends, relatives, neighbours, survivors and other acquaintances who had stood by me and supported me in the past. We had a wonderful night catching up with each other in a fun, enjoyable atmosphere ... and how we laughed! I couldn't remember having laughed so much for a very, very long time. The party became the talk of the village for quite a few weeks afterwards so I assume the others enjoyed it as much as I did.

Jonathan Duckworth had now taken over as chairman of the PSG from Simon, and he remained determined for us to try to complete our campaign aims. With the mysterious 'loss' of the signed rail declaration document I was unconvinced we had enough clout to push the government further into implementing all the rail safety improvements Cullen had recommended, and on his timetable. However, everyone in the PSG had worked so hard, and had supported me so much in the past, that I told Jonathan I would do whatever I could, and that I was there to lend him 'my face'.

In early September 2004, at Jonathan's request, we met Martin Minns in Stroud to discuss how we might ensure rail safety was still on the political agenda. In fact, all of Cullen's recommendations should have been implemented by the end of that month, but we knew that would not be the case. We decided to look at what had been done, what had been introduced and what had not, in order to produce our own report, the publication of which would coincide with the third anniversary of our signing of the missing declaration on rail safety.

Martin and Jonathan drafted the report and of course also took responsibility for coordinating a short PR campaign for the fifth anniversary of Ladbroke Grove. I agreed to fund Martin's work and also said I would stand by Jonathan's side in an attempt to raise the profile of the PSG once again. My nagging doubt, which Jonathan and Martin both shared, was that five years on nobody would be interested in what we had to say.

I travelled to the site of the now erected memorial to the train crash to meet up with Jonathan and Martin on 5 October 2004. The morning sky was totally unlike the one I remembered on the same day in 1999; it was now low, leaden and sombre, reflecting our feelings. Just after 8 a.m. at Ladbroke Grove, together with some relatives of the bereaved, survivors and friends, we stood silent, watching the tracks below us through the railings. Others faced the memorial stone that was erected on the embankment above the crash site.

The simple, dignified stone lists the names of all those who died, and reads:

Dedicated to the memory of the 31 people who lost their lives as a result of the Ladbroke Grove rail disaster that occurred at eleven minutes past eight on the morning of Tuesday 5 October 1999.

The memorial was erected and unveiled on 5 October 2001 and was paid for from a fund members of the public had sent donations to at the British Transport Police. I had not attended the unveiling as feelings had been running high between some of the bereaved and the PSG at that time and I felt it diplomatic to stay away. However, I now hoped any enmity had dissipated as I truly wanted to pay my respects to those who had not been so fortunate without feeling I was upsetting anyone.

All of us were lost in our own thoughts and in tears; some hugged, others buried their faces. The silence continued for a long time, almost as though no one dared to break it or turn away from the place which meant so much to each of us in different ways.

A policeman, who arrived on a motorcycle, stood with us. I assumed he was there in some official capacity, but as we gradually shuffled away, quietly greeting each other, he too left, followed by some of the journalists who were there. As he mounted his motorcycle I could see he had tears streaming down his face and he waved the journalists away with a sweep of his hand and a brief shake of his head. It turned out he had been the first police officer to reach the crash site on the fateful day. So many people had been affected, not just the ones inside the carriages.

Our concern about lack of press interest was ill founded. Radio cars and television vans lined the road beside the memorial, and Martin Minns began once again – as he had so many times before – to usher us from one waiting camera, microphone or journalist with pen in hand to the next. I was much more reticent than I had been before and tried to stay in the background, hanging back while others took the lead, although I was not entirely successful. We then hopped into a taxi to the Hilton London Paddington hotel to hold a press briefing chaired by Jonathan, at which he announced the PSG's plan to publish a report into progress made in implementing Cullen's recommendations. The press turned out en masse, with transport correspondents from all the major newspapers huddled on chairs and sofas in the foyer of the hotel listening to Jonathan's briefing.

At first I didn't realise that it was not just the anniversary the newspapers were interested in, until a female journalist came sidling up to me asking if it was true I was in the middle of a divorce from Peter. I was totally taken aback. I have my suspicions about who told them, but I was not willing to discuss my private life; it was no one else's business apart from Peter's and mine as far as I was concerned. However, she stood in front of me intently, waiting for me to answer. I merely acknowledged we were divorcing, and walked away.

The next day all the major newspapers carried details of Jonathan's briefing, along with the frightening statistics he'd given them showing an increase in SPADs (signals passed at danger), which simply should not be happening at all.

Some papers also carried news of my impending divorce, though it was a fleeting mention, thank goodness, as I'd have hated to think my personal life overshadowed a hugely important story. Thankfully – and of greater significance to the PSG – many of the television and radio companies called Martin and asked to be kept fully up to date with the publication of our report.

I'm not sure whether it was the press mentioning our divorce, his bitterness at my perceived trickery, or just the offer of a few thousand pounds from a newspaper that made Peter attack me with a two-page interview in the *Mail on Sunday*, with the head-line: 'I gave everything to help my wife Pam recover from terrible injuries she suffered in the Paddington rail crash ... but as she was about to get millions in compensation she handed me a typed letter saying she wanted a divorce.'

In the article Peter claimed I had (1) left him virtually penni-less, (2) reneged on an agreement with him after I received the compensation payment and (3) closed our joint account. Peter's version of events was self-serving and nasty and largely untrue. I was incandescent with fury at what he had done and said. Had he been in front of me after I had read his version of the so-called truth, I think I would have strangled the very life out him.

I suppose Peter had every right to put his side of the story over, assuming he honestly felt he was the hard-done-by husband. But, really, the article made him sound like the most saintly and doting husband a woman could ever have. To my mind, this only high-lighted his inability to accept any responsibility for his actions (or should that be inaction?) within our marriage or accept that he had contributed to any part of the breakdown. Some minor parts, I will admit, were true. However, he completely exaggerated the majority, and was libellous in the extreme.

Once I had calmed down and talked it over with a friend, I decided I was not going to join battle with Peter in the press. It would have been easy for me to pick up the phone to a tabloid and give them my side of the story but that would make me a hypocrite. Legal action was also an option but I didn't want another battle by suing him and the *Mail*. Instead I made my thoughts known directly to the newspaper and pointed out the areas I could, if I so wished, refute with evidence and witnesses. It obviously stirred things up as I swiftly received a letter of apology from the managing editor of the *Mail on Sunday* for the 'hurtful' comments expressed in their article.

That was that as far as I was concerned, but for Peter the gloves were well and truly off. What could and should have been an amicable separation had descended into an extremely bitter and protracted divorce which got worse towards its conclusion. It drained me of all my newfound energy and sapped my health but I was not prepared to capitulate to him whatever the cost to my wellbeing. I was determined to let the courts decide who was in the right and who was in the wrong.

On Wednesday 8 December 2004, I joined Jonathan Duckworth at 9 a.m. in the St Stephen's Club, Westminster, to formally launch the PSG's 'Progress Report'.

It listed twenty-two specific recommendations that had still not been implemented out of 240 in the original Cullen report. Although few in number, these unfulfilled recommendations were in fact the most important and major ones, including fitting ATP (automatic train protection), ending the problem of SPADs (signals passed at danger) and introducing licences for train drivers. If anything, there had been a rising trend in trains passing signals at danger, with 395 incidents in the previous year, of which 40 per cent were rated as 'serious'. Anti-collision systems had yet to be installed, and there were still poor radio links between signallers and drivers. The report said, 'How is it that we can call someone in Africa or South America on a mobile phone but a signal operator in Slough cannot contact a driver of a train approaching Paddington? It takes only one train to pass one red light for there to be a disaster...'

Jonathan Duckworth chaired the press conference and I made a statement in his support. Once again, the cameras rolled and the snappers snapped, and once again we achieved an amazing level of coverage in the media.

But I knew I sounded very flat, and I didn't feel I was particularly convincing either – perhaps it was just one press conference too many? Or maybe the divorce was simply draining me? Jonathan on the other hand spoke with passion, energy and enthusiasm, which is what carried the day with the media. It made me realise that as much as I wanted to help, it was definitely time to for me to stand back from the group and drop out of sight again. I spoke to Martin afterwards and said I couldn't get involved with any more press conferences; this would be my last as far as the PSG went.

I did actually have an excuse for seeming so disengaged, as the day before, and even on the day itself, I was trading faxes and phone calls with my divorce lawyer, as was she with Peter's legal representative. Finally, we were able to draw a line under our marriage; everything was done and dusted by the end of 2004 and I was at last free to move on.

In a matter of hours I had put both Peter and the PSG behind me. I knew this chapter in my life was over, and I hoped that a new exciting one could begin to unfold as I moved on.

CHAPTER 18

SURVIVING

So, the question heading into 2005 was: 'What now?' The past five years had been such a whirlwind of experiences that it was time for me to take stock and figure out what I had learnt from them.

Anton had asked me, 'What do you do for fun?' I stared blankly back at him. 'When was the last time you threw your head back and laughed?' he asked. I had to admit I couldn't remember. The five years following the crash had been the most difficult, trying and challenging of my life, and I sometimes wondered how on earth I kept going when so many massive curve balls had been thrown at me. Perhaps it was a testimony to my genetic make-up and upbringing that I kept moving forward so doggedly. I like to think it was. But fun … I had no idea, and had completely forgotten the very concept.

I had become accustomed to the generally held medical opinion that post-traumatic stress disorder would be with me for the rest of my life (depression, flashbacks, nightmares, insomnia, occasional erratic behaviour) and had coping mechanisms and medication for when I needed them, but, as time progressed, the periods in between these bouts of PTSD began to increase. They now seem to manifest themselves roughly every six months and last for about a week. Though my mother and sister still worry when the 'fugs' happen, I have pointed out that if it is only two weeks out of the fifty-two in a year then that still leaves me with fifty weeks of being well and able to enjoy myself and get on with life.

Physically, I am scarred. However, my main problem seems to be a compromised immune system that has never recovered and arthritis in every single damaged joint; weirdly, I also get it in the bony part of my nose. Thus painkillers will always be part of my life too and the UK's weather is probably not the best I can think of for arthritis.

However, I was now determined to be more positive. I wanted to stop feeling as though I had been a victim, and to start channelling my energy away from the thoughts of anger, frustration and hurt that could so easily have consumed me. I was not a victim, I decided, but a survivor. Anton's comments made me realise that I had never factored the concept of relaxation or enjoying myself into my life. I also realised life does not have to be a continual uphill struggle and a balance is fundamental to a healthy and happy human being. Coming close to death brings many things into sharp focus; I had reached a good plateau in the recovery of my health and it was important to now decide upon the person I wanted to be for the future. I began to think about what was most important to me and I realised that family was at the top of my list.

From the age of four I had called Richard Simms 'Dad' and he was, and is, as far as I'm concerned the only man who was and continues to be a constant and positive force in my life. He had a profound influence in shaping many of my strengths, perhaps more than anyone else; he was at my bedside in hospital, holding me down when I was unconscious and thrashing about, risking pulling the tubes from my mouth and arms, and he took his turn helping spoon-feed me after I regained consciousness. It is Richard I love deeply as my dad and even though he is now divorced from my mother nothing has changed between us; we still holiday together, and spend a lot of quality time together. I have joked with him, though, that I am going to get a T-shirt made with 'I'm his daughter' on for when we travel as so many of the people we have met assume he and I are husband and wife.

That might be doing his kudos some good but what on earth does it say about me that I look old enough to be married to him!

There are not enough words to express the depths of my love for my mum and sister Jane, nor for my admiration and devotion to them. My sister fought so long and hard for me, sacrificing so much of her life along the way, and is still always in my corner whenever the chips are down. I was very pleased, once the compensation had finally come through, to buy her a brand new Mini as my small way of saying thank you for everything she had done for me. It was a small gesture, I know, given everything, but the pleasure in her eyes when I handed her the keys was priceless and gave me genuine joy. My mother similarly dropped everything in her own life for me and has been a constant source of strength, love and inspiration to me. I am pleased to say that I now have a loving and very close relationship with them both and they are the two people I know I get total and unconditional love from. I love them very, very much in return. Since the crash we sometimes refer to ourselves as 'the three musketeers' and if anyone new enters our lives, they have to contend with the three of us rather than just one. They are the two people I would lay my life down for. I suppose I count myself privileged to have found such love after so many wasted years.

It would be unfair not to also mention Dan, my mum's husband. We don't have the same background to our relationship, but he has been a constant source of strength and help, which I know stems from love.

And then there is my biological father ... He may not have had any direct involvement with my life but it's not possible for me to ignore the blood that courses through my veins. In 1998, the year prior to the crash, I had told Mum and Dad that I wanted to find my father and had hired a detective agency to investigate his whereabouts. They supported me, though I am not sure they were very happy with my decision; I am not sure they fully understood the 'hole' I sometimes felt in not knowing my father. However, they helped me where they could.

I'm not sure I was prepared for what I would have done if the detectives had found him, or if I'd ever have gone through with meeting him face to face – or even if *he* would have been willing to meet me, come to that. A hundred things had raced through my mind as to what I might say if I did meet him, but alas it was never to be. The detective agency tracked him down all too late – he had died. Apparently he had passed away penniless as a down-and-out in Fiji, and had been buried in a pauper's grave. I have since promised myself I'll one day go to Fiji and try to get him interred properly so that I can have the comfort of knowing that he was remembered by someone. No one should die alone and be forgotten.

The detectives gave me a photograph and a small file of information they'd assembled, which is really the sum total of what I know about my biological father. He had remarried and apparently had two other children. I have no need to delve any further, though, and try to contact them; it is enough for me that I had at least tried to find him. More importantly, I would never want to intrude in other people's lives – they may not even know about me, and anyway, what good would it do?

I also value true friends ... when I find them. I have numerous friends and a handful I would call very close friends, many of whom have been through some of my trials and tribulations with me; they are very precious to me and I hope I treat them as such. I feel extremely blessed.

I try to take people at face value when I first meet them and assume they want to be genuine. I can be cruelly disappointed with this attitude but I try to now shrug my shoulders and say, *well, it takes all sorts to make the world go round.* There have been a few friends, though, who have taken advantage of my generous nature (and my compensation) in what I can only describe as the most avaricious and cynical manner. Needless to say, they are friends no longer. I can only cling to my belief that everything comes around and they will get their comeuppance in the end.

More than anything, I have learnt to make time for the things and people important to me; before the crash I had always been 'too busy' or, perhaps more truthfully, too selfish.

For the first time in my life I was able to take a chill pill. That is not to say that life doesn't get stressful, but I take the stance of *well, nobody's hurt or have died, have they?* which is a great personal leveller. I still hate arguing so strive to be assertive rather than combative, though I do fall down on this goal every now and then.

I have come to appreciate that material possessions are not the be all and end all either, but pre-crash I had craved so much. Admittedly I achieved a lot by working hard, but I was never satisfied and always wanted more. I have no problem with anyone wanting to better themselves in life, but I took it to extremes: if I had a BMW, I wouldn't be happy until I had the latest Mercedes; if I had a three-bedroom house, I'd want four bedrooms, and so on. Now I am grateful for what I have.

However, one little splurge that I simply couldn't resist stemmed from when I was a kid and I had loved the James Bond movies and thought 007 was the coolest guy in the universe (Sean Connery was my favourite). The Aston Martin was *the* car as far as I was concerned when I was growing up, so as my one naughty extravagance I took myself off to the local Aston dealer and bought a second-hand DB7. Oh boy, what a car! It was sex on wheels, in all its gleaming charcoal-coloured coating, carbon-fibre bodywork and graphite-adorned interior. I loved that car! However, like all realised dreams it was not quite as good as it first appeared: it was a hard car to drive, physically, and was not that comfortable over long distances. There was many a time I would climb out of it stiff-limbed! Then when someone dinked it in a car park (without leaving their details, of course) I had to get the driver's wing repaired, and when I saw the bill ... well, my jaw hit the floor. It was astronomical! That was it – the car had to go. The cost of its upkeep was simply too much for me to countenance, but I can still look back and know I achieved one of my dreams, and I got to race it around the Millbrook race track at ridiculous speeds while taking my hands off the steering wheel, which made me scream with laughter. That was me happy.

OK, I had reassessed myself as a person, so now what?

Well, my health eventually reached a stage where I was able to say goodbye to my carer, Debbie. I took on a new level of independence, and with it I wanted to explore. There is a huge world out there and I wanted to experience and embrace its different cultures, like I had a little before the crash. The problem was I had only ever travelled with someone else, be it a husband, family or friends. I was now a singleton and a woman proposing to travel alone. *Isn't that dangerous?* I wondered. However, nothing ventured, nothing gained!

I started looking at travel brochures but was not keen on the idea of package holidays and the 'touristy' things on offer. I've never been much of a beach person; I prefer finding out about and experiencing the history of wherever I go, I love meeting local people and enjoy savouring the local food and customs. Perchance, in a waiting room at one of my therapy sessions, I flicked through a local magazine and spied an advert for a travel company based not far from where I lived. They offered bespoke holidays so I took the opportunity to visit them and find out more. I met a keen and pleasant agent who seemed genuinely interested in what I wanted to achieve from a holiday. Andrew, unbeknownst to me at the time, was to become a dear (if occasionally exasperating) friend and still remains so.

'Where would you like to go?' he asked. There are just so many countries to choose from! I then thought of my favourite artist, Paul Gauguin, who had painted wonderful canvases of Tahiti. 'OK, let's start there,' I said. So, I booked and set off for what turned out to be paradise.

It was so beautiful and I absolutely adored everything about the country and the people. I only have a smattering of French but we all managed to communicate so easily and the people seemed to take me to their hearts, leaving me with hugely fond memories. I stayed on a little island near Bora Bora, called Le Taha'a, and to celebrate my birthday I took a glass helicopter ride to Bora Bora and flew around its volcano, and at the end was dropped off on a beach to be met by a guy with a horse. One of my dreams had always been to ride a horse through the surf on a beach and here I was doing it. It was all very Hollywood!

One of the most fantastic meals I've ever eaten was on a tiny neighbouring island to mine that same evening, in a small restaurant run by a large, very jovial Tahitian lady, Mama J. She served me with a dish of crab curry and as I had mentioned that it was my birthday and I'd done these fantastic things earlier on, she called me over at the end of the meal and dropped two natural pearls in my hand.

'These are for you, as you are such a lovely soul,' she said.

I was completely overcome with emotion and could hardly speak. I brought them home and had them made into a necklace, and sent Mama J a photograph to show her just how beautiful they looked. Every time I wear those pearls I smile. In fact, I smile whenever I think about my three weeks there, island-hopping, with pods of dolphins leaping around the boat. I could quite happily have run off into the jungle and never come home. It really did help me return home with renewed vigour and vitality.

The travel bug had definitely bitten me, and I promised myself then that I would see as many countries as it is physically possible to do before I have to meet my maker! I have a large map of the world hanging in my office and I stick coloured pins in every country I've visited, and it's looking pretty colourful with Russia, Egypt, Turkey, Malaysia, Tunisia, South Africa and Italy to name just a few all brandishing pins. I find travelling hugely liberating too; no one knows about my past and if they ever comment on my scars I just say 'I got burnt', and no more is ever said.

The other passion travelling reignited in me was cooking (and eating). I always used to enjoy cooking pre-crash, and found it a relaxing pastime. Post-crash, I'd stopped enjoying cooking, and thought of it as a chore rather than a pleasure. But the different dishes I experience on my overseas adventures tend to lead me to buying a cookbook to try dishes out back at home – Chinese, Indian, Greek, Italian, Mexican, French, British … it doesn't matter what it is. If it tastes nice, I'll give it a go and, on the whole, my efforts have been pretty good. The only cuisine I avoid, because of pretty dire experiences, is Russian – it's just too stodgy and has no flavour, with the exception of borscht, which is delicious.

I'm often found wielding sharp knives and chopping away enthusiastically in my kitchen, much to the apprehension of my friends. 'Pam,' they say, 'you've no feeling in one hand, and not much in the other and you stand there chatting away while chopping … we daren't look!' Mind you, it doesn't stop them eating whatever I produce! 'Well, don't watch then,' I say, though I have to admit that a lot of the time my hands resemble those of a bare-knuckle boxer with their cuts, bruises and abrasions.

As I've consistently said, I'm not a woman who can sit back

doing nothing and the idea of spending my life just lunching and shopping sends shivers down my spine, as does daytime TV. So I offered to help a local charity fostering homeless cats. It started off OK and I was given an enclosure in my garden that could house two cats at a time. However, the second cat turned out to be pregnant and within a couple of weeks of rescuing her she gave birth to a litter of eight. So much for easing myself into the job! There was the constant worry that they might inadvertently scratch my grafts, and after heeding my doctors' advice about potential problems it might cause, I had to call it quits.

I am still involved with the Healing Foundation, which I'd joined as an ambassador in 2000. It only really involves them calling on me when they want me to talk or help out in the area of my particular interest – the psychological side of disfigurement – but it is a role I continue to enjoy.

I am also still involved behind the scenes on a one-to-one basis with people who have suffered facial disfigurement and are confronted with having to wear a mask. It's usually their family who search me out, looking for some reassurance that it does work. If I can help in any way, then I do. Initially, we always meet face to face, rather than just talk on the phone, be it in Manchester, Edinburgh or London ... It's so much easier to talk in person and every single one of the people I have met over the years has said they couldn't believe I had ever had injuries on my face. My camouflage make-up is very good, granted, but the mask did its job in minimising scarring. That's when they become convinced that it will help them too.

In 2007 the faint rumblings of possible financial crisis in the world were starting. I had what was left of my compensation invested in stocks and shares but I knew it would not last me forever and if markets did tumble I might very well be wiped out; I had to find a way to earn a wage again. Around this time a friend of mine (now one of the ex-friends) who was an event manager was running a party for me. I watched him rushing around doing one hundred and one things and, with the best will in the world, he didn't seem very organised with suppliers, and his paperwork was a bit of a mess. *That looks interesting*, I thought, *I might be able to help*.

The nice thing about events is that you work like stink in the build-up, and then afterwards there's usually a gap before the next one looms on the horizon. It was a fairly flexible occupation in that respect, which suited me and my health just fine. So, after the party, I casually asked him if he had ever thought of taking on a partner to help shoulder the burden of running events. To cut a long story short, we joined forces and started running events together.

The vast majority were corporate occasions and, boy, was it a steep learning curve. It all looks easy but in the weeks running up to each event it can be chaotic in the extreme.

My financial advisory background proved very useful in planning for deadlines and liaising with companies, individuals and suppliers. Events often involved a 6 a.m. start and a 2 or 3 a.m. finish; I was one of the first to arrive and one of the last to leave, having tidied up and turned off the lights.

I enjoyed the challenges, the problem-solving and the smiling faces, although on the downside I found myself often having to clear up an appalling mess, repair damaged items and facilities and generally handle drunken, rowdy clients. I guess there is only so much vomit you can handle. In 2009 it really all came to a head when at one event, at 1 a.m., we were not so much dealing with clients as a bunch of drunks. I had a company managing director who was absolutely sozzled, and quite a big chap, peppering me with spittle as he shouted in my face about something trivial. He then grabbed me by my arms and began to shake me. I thought, *Pam, what on earth are you doing here?*

After the crash I promised myself my life would be worth something, and now here I was throwing parties for rude drunks. That particular night was the final straw. I wanted out and closed our joint venture down in January 2010.

To avoid having to watch daytime TV, I started filling up my life with hobbies: I tried the bass guitar, though my hands were simply not dextrous enough to pluck the strings; I attempted to learn French but my painkillers are so strong my concentration and memory couldn't function well enough to remember things from week to week; I then tried t'ai chi…

Hang on a second, Pam, I thought, *this is achieving nothing*.

But what to do?

I went to see a friend, Jo, and ended up bemoaning the huge gap that would now be in my CV and my lack of skills, and stating that I was useless professionally. Her eyebrows shot up into her hairline and there was much tutting as she reached for a sheaf of paper, pens and pencils and ordered me to sit down.

'Think back and tell me everything you have done since the crash.'

As I spoke she wrote, highlighting the new skills I'd developed and mind-mapping them for me. When I had finished she then made me look at the map and I was very pleasantly surprised. What I hadn't really thought about was my work with the PSG – the public speaking, the media work, liaising with everyone from MPs to chief executives of large corporations … it was all valid. We then considered what I wanted out of a job.

'It needs to be paid work, although it doesn't have to pay huge amounts,' I said, 'and I have to consider my health so I can't take on a permanent 9-to-5, 365-days-a-year job. I prefer varied work to keep my interest engaged and if ultimately it helps other people, then that would be perfect.'

The two areas that came out top were radio work – no cameras! – and charity work, but on a paid basis.

Jo advised me to also take advantage of friendships and acquaintances I had forged over the years and call them up to say, 'I'm job-hunting – can I pick your brains?'

She said, 'You'll probably find out just how willing people are to help you, Pam.'

She was absolutely right.

To cover as many bases as I could I did try a few of my local recruitment agencies but it appears, as one nice lady put it, I am just too 'unusual' for them and they wouldn't know what to do with me. A charity employment agency initially thanked me for sending my details, but said I wasn't the sort of person they'd be able to take on. I replied, 'You haven't even met me yet,' to which they kindly suggested if I was ever up in London I should feel free to drop in on them. So I did. I arrived for what was to be 'no more than thirty minutes of advice' … and after a ninety-minute chat they ended up signing me onto their books. It just goes to show that it is not all about the CV, it is the person too.

I next met Dame Kelly Holmes through my friendship with Reading-based entrepreneur and philanthropist Sir John Madejski. She is a lovely, down-to-earth woman and such an inspiration; I was quite tongue-tied when I met her, though she soon put me at ease with her sparkling personality and she has charisma in bucketloads. She explained about her sixteen-week 'Get on Track' course, which targets local disadvantaged youngsters aged sixteen to twenty-one. The course combines team-building, communication, presentation and reflection skills for the NEETs (not in education, employment or training) and aims to get the youngsters' lives on track through the support of athlete mentors. The Dame Kelly Holmes Legacy Trust let me follow and observe the first course, which concluded with a 'graduation' dinner.

The rush of adrenalin I got seeing these youngsters turning their lives around was absolutely amazing and I felt tears welling up in my eyes as I listened to them talk about their journeys from hoodie-wearing, disengaged, grunting teenagers who never made eye contact into smart, erudite young men and women facing their future with a bit more optimism. I felt I had to get more involved.

I kept hassling the trust's CEO, Julie, to meet up for a chat because I was so passionate about wanting to play a part in the programme and happily I was subsequently appointed as one of their advocate representatives in the Berkshire area.

Next up I went to see the station editor at BBC Radio Berkshire, again just 'for a chat' and hopefully to gain some advice. As we talked his interest seemed to increase in me as a person and he said, 'It's a pity you don't have your CV with you as I'd like to check it out...' Well, it just so happened I did have a copy in my handbag! He read it and excused himself for a few minutes and when he returned he asked me, 'Why not come here and work with us as a casual reporter on special one-off projects?' I was gobsmacked and over the moon. He didn't have to ask me twice! I jumped at the chance and have since developed and helped to produce a few aired programmes.

The programme I am most proud of was called *Fight or Flight* where I interviewed other survivors who were involved in some of the biggest national disasters or wars. I was exploring why we had all survived so well and whether this was down to our natures or our past experiences. I was lucky enough to talk to Simon Weston (a Falklands hero), John Peters (a pilot shot down and tortured during the Gulf War), Tim Coulson (a survivor of the 7/7 Underground bombings) and Janette Orr (my survivor friend from the PSG who also got caught up in the Boxing Day tsunami!).

Aside from my occasional radio work, the media still regularly sought me out for comment, but I had begun to find it increasingly difficult to find a link between my story and the news item I was supposed to be discussing, such as when they wanted to interview me around the time of the 7/7 attacks. It was quite different from being a train crash of course; this was a terrorist attack with bombs. The press, though, as I have come to learn, immediately start looking for 'experts' to comment. I'm very careful about what I comment on and so when the calls came through to Jonathan Duckworth, at the PSG, requesting I be interviewed about 'the trains' I refused as I knew they'd want to talk about how I thought people would be feeling, and what emotions they were going through. It was simply not appropriate, and I told them so. I've no wish to be a media commentator on people suffering injuries and losing their lives. Similarly, when the Chilean miners became trapped underground in 2010, *Newsnight* wanted to discuss what I felt the trapped miners were thinking. It really was a bizarre request and I find it puzzling how the press think whipping up social comment from someone with such a tenuous link is news.

I tend to shy away from the rest of the media, though I know they still sometimes set out looking for me. The only time I can see myself becoming publicly vocal again would be if there ever was, God forbid, a train crash and I discovered rail safety was to blame. I would go back in there like a shot and cause an almighty noise then. Though I pray that day never comes.

In 2011, in my quest for diversity, I signed up to the Prince2 project management course and took exams to formally prove what I know I am capable of doing. Well, it doesn't do any harm to formalise one's knowledge into a qualification.

From having started 2010 thinking that I was on the scrapheap career-wise I was slowly reinventing my career path in a more varied, flexible structure that appealed to my sense of interest in the world. I still do a bit of public speaking, I keep myself open to considering anything that crosses my path and am continually evolving as time passes. Basically, if it gets my juices going and sparks my interest then I'll give it a go, providing I am happy I can do a good job. Just don't ask me to conform to what's 'usual'.

CHAPTER 19

LOOKING TO THE FUTURE

Even before the crash, I never considered myself to be attractive, and even less so since. While my camouflage make-up does a pretty good job of covering the scars on my face, there are still the ones to my hands and body. I'm not saying looks are the be all and end all – relationships should be deeper than that. However, I am tremendously conscious about intimacy and bearing my scars to scrutiny and so the thought of ever 'finding love' seems as remote as my winning the lottery.

In the few years since my divorce I had had a few dates and brief dalliances but that was pretty much it. They were perfectly pleasant but never progressed very far – I was just too wary, I guess. I missed the romance, the companionship, the affection, the being close to someone, but I had survived for so many years without it, even while I was married to Peter, that I think I had begun to doubt I would ever find someone to share my life with.

But in late 2007 I did, for a while, think I had.

I was with some friends in my local country pub one evening and got chatting with a handsome guy, Ed, who was funny, charming and seemed to be very much on a similar wavelength to me. After a few months of pub encounters as friends, he asked if we could start seeing each other. He didn't seem aware of my past and never mentioned my scars.

'Before I answer, there are a few things you need to know about me...' I said, and proceeded to tell him about the crash, my health problems, my PTSD and the depression and ended by saying, 'As you can see, I'm very high maintenance.' He laughed and said he still wanted to date me.

We started seeing each other and before I knew it I had fallen head over heels in love with Ed. I hadn't felt love like it before – it made me feel happy, excited and bubbly, like I had an effervescent tablet fizzing away in my bloodstream the whole time. I couldn't wait to see him and whenever I did I lit up like a beacon. For the first time in what seemed like a hundred years I felt womanly, sexy and attractive.

In our first year together we seemed to have loads in common and he was terrific in every way, from allowing me space when I needed it to giving me reassuring cuddles, being romantic and passionate, and being a great companion and listener. I thought I was the luckiest woman in the world and had finally met the right man for me.

Sadly, it was not to last.

In the second year I asked him to move in with me. I knew some of the intensity of our first year would die down and things would become a bit more settled, but in fact it was like a light switch being turned off. Gone was the romance, the consideration, the intimacy. Living with someone who appeared to prefer spending time in the pub or on the golf course rather than spending quality time with me was simply not going to work.

Having said all that, I am sure I could be very trying sometimes and I know PTSD must be a real burden for those close to the sufferer. I tried to talk about our problems with Ed, and then tried to ignore them; I even made us both go to couple counselling for a while, but nothing seemed to help.

As with any normal relationship we argued, but in the second and third year things got worse. Eventually, with me growing increasingly unhappy, I had a light-bulb moment: why was I hoping to change him and why was he expecting me to change? I should be happy, he should be happy and if we couldn't do that for each other, there was no point in postponing the inevitable. I decided I could not let it drag on. I sat him down and told him a big, fat lie – 'I don't love you anymore.' I did still love him but felt I had no choice but to end it as decisively and quickly as I could. He moved out within a couple of months and I gritted my teeth against the pain of our split.

As an aside, Ed was of Celtic origin too, a fact not missed by my family or close girlfriends. I have had to promise that, in the future, I will not succumb to my obvious preference for Celts, as history has proven they have not been good for me. I have even been threatened that my girlfriends will hold an interview panel for any potential candidates that I might want to date more than once so they can vet and approve them beforehand!

And so I marched back into singleton status again. I have since come to realise that I know exactly what I am looking for in a partner, or should I say what I am *not* looking for in a partner. The dates I have been on since have, so far, fallen into the 'not' category. What is it with men of my age? There seems to be very little understanding of what a modern, self-sufficient, independent woman might want in a man and complete ignorance as to how to nurture and look after a romance to achieve long-term happiness. My views on love have changed because of my past experiences and I now consider 'love' as a collective noun – it is a sum of many, many parts – and I want someone who loves and lives this way as well. Some sensitivity and finesse would make a lovely change too – one can but dream.

In the summer of 2009, and totally out of the blue, Trevor McDonald's production staff contacted Lesley Pollinger, my book agent at the time. It was about three months before the tenth anniversary of the crash and they were interested in making a programme about how rail safety had improved in the nine years since I had last featured on the *Tonight* programme.

When Lesley told me I vacillated, completely unsure what to do.

'You have to think about it,' she said, 'there will be others looking for you – it is the tenth anniversary after all.'

Again Martin Minns's words drifted back to me from the past: *Give them five minutes of your time and they'll leave you alone.*

In the past I have sometimes thought to myself *I wonder what happened to so and so* after I've seen a TV documentary or news programme about people with interesting stories. Also, having avoided trains or train travel for a decade I thought the premise they were proposing, of me coming back to talk to the rail executives about the improvements made since Paddington, would be an interesting one on a personal level too. The programme I had been in nine years earlier was quite negative and critical of the rail authorities; whether the crash and our campaign had had a positive impact would be the question now.

It was all very loose to begin with, and I had a few meetings with the team where things started taking shape and we all felt happy with the progress. Then they dropped a bombshell: 'Would you take the train and complete the journey you started ten years ago?'

Wow. I never saw that coming, though it's a pretty bloody obvious idea when you think about it. They added that Trevor McDonald wanted to travel with me and interview me en route to London.

After much soul-searching, I agreed to try but gave no guarantee I would or could board a train, and reserved the right to walk away at any time. They agreed and were hugely supportive of me. This would really step everything up emotionally for me but perhaps it would also give me the opportunity to put my one last demon to bed.

I went to see my psychiatrist to talk it through. He thought it was definitely worth trying and put me back on some medication to calm my anxiety. As I left his office he gave me an extra box of pills, and wrote on the box, 'In a crisis, take one of these.'

I also went back to see my psychologist, Anton, and agreed to visit him every week beforehand in the coming couple of months and every day in the last week before the programme filmed. He offered me lots of good advice, the best being to put myself 'in a protective bubble'. I suppose it might have helped that my views on dying had also changed dramatically with the travelling I had been doing. You do become far more fatalistic about things, especially if you have had to catch an internal flight in Russia via Aeroflot! To be honest, though, if something did happen in a plane then I would be dead. There would be no surviving, no living with the consequences or aftermath of injury; it would simply be over, and I am fine with that. The alternative of not travelling or experiencing the wonders of the world is not acceptable to me, so I take my chances.

I arrived at Slough station on the day of filming. First Great Western, Rail Safety Ltd and all the staff at the station had obviously been told and knew what was going on, and, crikey, I now think I might know how the Queen feels when she arrives for an official visit. The platform yellow lines and signage had all been painted; every door and window had been polished clean. The place was gleaming and all I could smell was fresh paint.

All the station staff came out to greet me, and all said they were really rooting for me and asked if I was OK. It took me aback as to how nice, warm and welcoming they were. It was very touching. Well, I was as OK as I would ever be under the circumstances; Dr Cantopher's drugs were working (I felt comfortably numb) and Anton was by my side giving me pep talks all the time.

First Great Western sealed off a carriage exclusively for us. I say 'us' as it was not just Sir Trevor and me; there was a whole film crew behind and my (then) boyfriend Ed, my book agent Lesley, my psychologist Anton and a lot of the staff from First Great Western.

Walking onto the platform was difficult; stepping onto the train was like experiencing a roller-coaster of emotions packed into a punch. I gritted my teeth, braced myself and put one foot in front of the other. Things had certainly changed in ten years, I remember thinking: the carriage was quite swish, with nice seats, power points for laptops, electric sliding doors between compartments and clean floors!

I sat down opposite Sir Trevor and concentrated on his face all the way. Behind him, and the cameras, were the people I had brought along and other friendly faces all smiling with encouragement.

The twenty-minute non-stop journey (they ensured it was the non-stop one so I couldn't get off!) seemed like an eternity. I remember feeling the sensation of the carriage pulling away from the station and my stomach flip-flopping while I felt the sweat of fear break out all over me. Then we passed familiar landmarks, such as bridges, graffiti-filled walls and the Eurostar siding – nothing had changed there. A train rushed past in the opposite direction and I jumped out of my skin. But looking up at my friends' faces reassured me everything was OK. As we passed through Ladbroke Grove and the scene of the crash I very, very deliberately refused to look out of the window or acknowledge in any way that that was where we were. Finally, the train pulled into Paddington. We were greeted like royalty and my relief was immense. I wanted to kiss the ground as I stepped out of the carriage. I felt so proud of myself. It was a huge emotional victory (partly achieved as a result of my 'crisis' pill). The sense of closure, of finally finishing a journey I had started so many years before, was fantastic.

I've since taken the train again, quite a few times, as it is easier and often quicker than driving into London. I don't enjoy doing so but needs must and I always take my friend Giles with me, who knows to keep (incessantly) talking to me and diverting my attention. I have had horrible flashbacks while on the train, which worried my friend and completely freaked out the other passengers, to whom I do extend my apologies. I also think the interviews I had been able to conduct with the new rail safety board helped me face train travel again as I had probed quite deeply into the new safety culture and attitudes and was happy that, while not being 100 per cent safe, UK train travel was as safe as reality allows.

To this day I keep in touch with the rail regulator, authorities and safety board, constantly quizzing them as to improvements, changes and effects of cutbacks. The ETMS has now been superseded by ERTMS (European Rail Traffic Management System) levels 1 and 2 – an even better integrated system than the original ETMS and run commonly on all European train infrastructures. This is gradually being fitted to UK railways and trains as I write, though again implementation is linked to costs and budgets so is not happening across the entire network.

In recent times I have been asking questions about the ongoing Reading station redevelopment project's safety cases. Because of our train crash I tend to keep an eye on issues related to signals, the safety systems on trains and the track as well as the communication between the driver and signal boxes. I have visited the new Didcot signalling centre and been shown the systems now in place and watched some simulated events and what the signallers can now do to prevent a crash. I have even investigated into the safety of the proposed HS2 project as that may be part of our future. To be fair, the rail industry always respond positively to my questions and go out of their way to try to satisfy them. I am probably given access to information that not many members of the public can get to and for that I am grateful. Don't get me wrong, I am not a rail expert and don't wish to be one but as I say to everyone, including the industry, if I am catching a train, I do not want my life put in unnecessary danger again.

I am hoping this continued observance might give me a heads-up if things begin to get dangerous again. Let's put it this way: if I stop catching the train again, you should all be worried.

A simple train journey I started in 1999 ended up changing my life, and that journey was not really complete for ten long years.

With the passing of the decade anniversary I felt a huge weight had lifted from my shoulders, almost as if I could shed the years like a second skin. I had been urged to complete a book about my experiences long before but had really not felt ready or engaged enough to tackle it, or to be truthful about having found my way out the other side. That has now changed and I can say hand on heart that I have learnt so much from my experiences, and I hope they might in turn help someone else face their future in the sure and certain knowledge that things do get better.

In the years since the crash I think I have become a more rounded person, more comfortable with myself and who I am, and I certainly value life with everything it has to offer. In the past couple of years I have become far more 'spiritual' – I don't mean that in terms of religion or any other form of structured belief system; it is more a feeling of wellbeing that makes my life much more enjoyable and exciting than ever before.

I believe that all of us have a soul. I remember reading some-where about an experiment where a person was weighed as they neared death and as they died their body became lighter on the scales. What is it that left their body to cause this? There are also so many unexplained things that continue to happen in my life that have nothing to do with tangible events. Could it be down to positive thinking, some form of energy, a force? What is it that has come to my rescue so many times – is it my inner soul? It is really difficult to explain and most of me just wants to accept and enjoy whatever it is. However, I keep my mind open to possibilities and my curiosity leads me into all sorts of new, intriguing investigations, experiences and reading, though I don't always agree with the accepted truths or doctrine in these various areas. If I find it helps me in a beneficial way, I take it on board; if not, I discard it.

I am no longer afraid or worried about death. Having faced it before, I know it is not scary and I don't believe it would even be painful in the normal course of events. All I want when I face the actual time of my death is to be able to say to myself *Boy, oh boy, now that was FUN!* I've even got my funeral sorted out: a cremation (might as well finish the job off) with 'Knocking on Heaven's Door' by Bob Dylan as I get taken in and 'Smoke Gets in your Eyes' sung by Bryan Ferry as I disappear behind the curtain. There is going to be champagne flowing and a New Orleans-style band playing, with my guests having an absolute ball and partying to send me off.

The only concern that does occasionally nibble away at my conscious mind is about getting old and infirm. Not having had children – not that it seems to count for much these days even if you do – there is no one to take care of me. The idea of an old people's home, losing my marbles or being unable to look after myself fills me with dread and I hope euthanasia will have been made legal by that time should it come. I have mooted the idea to my girlfriends of, when we are old, clubbing together and building a veranda on the front of my house overlooking the high street so we can sit in our rocking chairs, rigged up to pub optics behind us with our favourite tipple being intravenously pumped into us, being cared for by young, hot Australian male nurses in very short shorts as we shout abuse at anyone passing by. Believe me, I already have a huge waiting list!

I am certainly not perfect – very far from it – and I remind myself of this fact each and every day and with every decision I make. I am just doing the best I can with what I have at my disposal and trying not to cause harm along the way.

Before Ladbroke Grove I was just an ordinary person, a financial adviser trying to make a living. I worked hard and played hard but life then was pretty black and white: do your best and make money. Without Ladbroke Grove I would now almost certainly be an older version of what I was on 5 October 1999.

I will never be able to forget the crash – I still have the physical injuries to contend with, the emotional ups and downs, and the therapies and medication. But that all said, I feel I am a better person for the crash, and here's the rub, which you might find hard to believe: as difficult as life has been at times since, and in no way negating all the pain and suffering it caused, in all honesty, I have to say the train crash is probably the best thing to ever happen to me.

INDEX